Group Action: The Dynamics of Groups in
Therapeutic, Educational and Corporate Settings

Group Action: The Dynamics of Groups in Therapeutic, Educational and Corporate Settings

T. Martin Ringer

Jessica Kingsley Publishers
London and Philadelphia

First published in the United Kingdom in 2002
by Jessica Kingsley Publishers
116 Pentonville Road
London N1 9JB, UK
and
400 Market Street, Suite 400
Philadelphia, PA 19106, USA

www.jkp.com

Copyright © T. Martin Ringer 2002

Printed digitally since 2004

Library of Congress Cataloging in Publication Data
A CIP catalog record for this book is available from the Library of Congress

British Library Cataloguing in Publication Data
A CIP catalogue record for this book is available from the British Library

ISBN 1 84310 028 2

Contents

Part 2

To Françoise

Acknowledgements and locating
the book in a social context

The writing and publishing of a book is a social phenomenon rather than a purely personal one. The following acknowledgements are intended to serve two functions: first to recognize those who have contributed to the finalproduct and secondly to place the book in the social and intellectual context from which it was conceived, grown and made public. For me there were two origins of this manuscript. One was the development of my capacity to write about groups and the second was the origin of the specific project that resulted in the book. The two stories are interwoven.

At the age of four and a half years I was allowed to attend the tiny rural school where my father was the sole teacher. For the next seven and a half years I belonged to what I now understand to have been an active experiential learning group that was facilitated by 'Mr Ringer' the teacher and included pupils ranging from five to thirteen years old. For these years I experienced being a member of what was primarily a successful learning group. That was a powerful building of the capacity to work with groups and has cemented into my psyche an unshakable faith that groups can be generative and positive places to be. It is more than twelve years since Bob Ringer died but it is my pleasure to acknowledge that I am building on what he started. Then from the age of fifteen I started a long association with adventure activities and experienced the building of personal confidence and further positive group experiences during more than twenty years of adventure recreation in New Zealand. Hence, there are many leaders of adventure groups to whom I owe my thanks.

Then, in 1990, I left New Zealand as an emotional refugee – trying to escape from the pain of the impending loss of my primary relationship and the loss of my professional role as Director of Northland Wilderness Experience, an adventure therapy programme. The staff at Northland Wilderness Experience collectively created an outstanding environment for learning and growth. In particular, without the quiet confidence of Tahu Robertson I would not have sustained the demands of that role for as long as I did. Les Gray, Rosie Guild and Dr Margaret O'Brien combined warmth, understanding and professional direction for me during those challenging years. At this time too, Maraea (Pompy) Tipene and many Maori people from around Tai Tokerau showed remarkable patience with me in their coaching of me in tikanga Maori. Gary Poole's courage and trust in me was another essential part in the development of my understanding of groups, organizations and human change processes. Diana Rands, Lizzie Baker and Howard Reti also made significant contributions to the emotional container that nurtured our work together. In retrospect I now understand that my fascination with the dynamics of groups in organizations was fired up by my experience in the overall umbrella organization for Northland Wilderness Experience. I owe my thanks to that organization for both generosity and providing me with the generative disturbance that arose from being in an organization where many things did not make sense to me.

After running from New Zealand in 1990 I landed in Western Australia to attend the Wasley Centre ten-week intensive training in psychodrama, sociodrama, sociometry and role training. This key event created a temporary safe place for a cathartic re-examination of my life after leaving New Zealand. The subsequent welcome that I received as a trainer and member of staff at the Wasley Centre provided an essential backbone for my early years in Perth. Working with Trish Williams, initially at the Wasley Centre and later in an independent partnership, proved to be a challenging educative adventure that contributed to my professional development and triggered a drive to learn more about the vagaries of the human psyche.

The book itself was born from a conversation with Dr Lee Gillis and Cindy Simpson who at that time (1997) were both working for the therapeutic arm of Project Adventure in the USA. They suggested that I assemble my writings to date into a monograph that Project Adventure would publish. This was really a continuation of Lee's long supportive history with me as a co-thinker and co-author. In fact many people from the Association for Experiential Education (and in particular from the Therapeutic Adventure Professional Group) have encouraged me to write and to present. For the two years following 1997, Rufus Collinson supported the slow development of the manuscript and remained friendly and supportive even after the content of the manuscript had changed so much that it was no longer suitable for publication by Project Adventure.

The increasing depth of focus of the manuscript was in part due to the hundreds of productive conversations that I was having with Françoise Spanoghe who by this time was my partner not only in thought but also in life at home. It was in the context of this supportive, loving and stimulating relationship that the embryonic book began to find a better shape. (Françoise and I later married and she is now known as Françoise Ringer). I am constantly aware that containment is an essential element for writers just as it is for groups.

In fact, my friends and colleagues in Perth provided an outstanding degree and variety of containers. My dear friend Phil Robinson and I met regularly and created a 'thinking space' of outstanding quality and it was from this productive space that the basic concepts underpinning Chapter 12 emerged. The Change Consultants Learning Network provided a safe place for licking wounds and for thinking together about our respective dilemmas as facilitators, trainers, group leaders and management consultants. My work with Maria Harries, 'teaching' experiential group work to social work students at the University of Western Australia, was an important catalyst and testing ground for new ideas about groups. The 'Writers' Group' journeyed with me through the psychological jungle of projection, identification, anxiety and many other aspects of the group leaders' and of the writers' world. Helen Costello reliably engaged with me as a professional supervisor whose considered and astute way of being supported me in managing my professional life. Richard Hester's long history as my therapist had by this time clearly helped to build for me a more solid sense of self.

In the corporate world I have also found many allies and supporters. This may surprise some readers because those in the helping professions often regard business as fundamentally exploitive and overly rationalistic. Some of my experience has been very different to this generalization – in particular my work with Mark Warren, Jacqui Butterworth and Les Gilan. Over a period of years we collectively thought, wrote and worked together in an exciting coalition that resulted in some significant changes to organizational culture(s) and to the development of ideas about groups in business. Maarten van der Wall and Mike Konrath were other examples of people whose wish for ethical and fair process in the Government sector also provided me with important encouragement to explore the applications of group dynamics in corporate settings.

The emotional containment that was necessary for me in my role of author of a book was also quite strong in other parts of Australia. Anthony Williams has for many years been a consistently appreciative colleague and has directly assisted with some key thoughts. Robyn Mulholland too has, since 1984, played a key role in helping me to build my understanding of myself, of relationships and of groups. Tonia Gray and James Neill have consistently encouraged me to write and to present on groups. A number of other people around Australia have worked hard to organize workshops on 'unconscious processes in groups' that I have facilitated. Many workshop participants have been enthusiastic about early material from the book that I used as workshop notes. In fact hundreds of workshop participants from dozens of different countries have either stimulated my thinking about groups or directly made suggestions that have ended up in the manuscript, often without specific acknowledgement. My heartfelt thanks go to you all. Above all, the group that contributed the core plot for the 'wombat story' deserves particular thanks and it is a pity that the need to protect the anonymity of their clients means that I cannot name those skilled and courageous people.

As I look around my mental map of the world I am also reminded of many people who have either knowingly or unknowingly supported my thinking and writing about groups. Chris Loynes stands out. For years Chris has arranged visits and workshops for me and both he and Soo Redshaw have offered their home as a crucible for friendship and thinking together. In other parts of Europe I have experienced warmth and support: Reino Bragge and many others in Finland which is a special place for me; Ton Duindam in the Netherlands; Sue Couglan in Eire; Rüdiger Gilsdorf and Mario Kolblinger in Germany; Luc Peeters and Johan Hovelynck in Belgium; Jan Neumann in the Czech Republic and many others in other countries whom I have not specifically named.

My Italian colleagues also deserve special mention and, of these, Claudio Neri stands out. The quality of our conversations more than makes up for the relatively small number of years that I have known him. Claudio's thinking, his warmth and his support have been a significant addition to the containment that has made this book possible. The warmth and encouragement of Stefania Marinelli and the others in the Funzione Gamma editorial team add to the overall appreciation that I feel when Italy comes to mind.

Malcolm Pines was directly responsible for referring the manuscript of this book to Jessica Kingsley Publishers. His confidence in my work and his generous support confirm a widely held view of Malcolm not only as a highly regarded professional but also as a warm and generous person. Now, as the publishing process nears its completion, I am very appreciative of the efficient and hard work and high level of professionalism shown by Graham Sleight and Jo Gammie as they turn a manuscript very quickly into a book.

Foreword

When I began to read the manuscript of this book, I wondered what adventure group leadership could contribute to group psychotherapy and group analysis, how could they be linked? Soon, I was converted. Martin Ringer combines a sure grasp of the complexity of group dynamics with an admirably clear style of exposition. In fact, I found reading this book an exciting adventure and Martin Ringer a leader upon whom I quickly learned to rely on as my guide through the complexity of group dynamics. As he writes, 'leadership of groups is one of the most complex tasks human beings can undertake'.

Through reading this book I hope that the reader, like myself, will be persuaded of the relevance and value of action methods for the psychodynamic practitioner. Were I younger, I might commit myself to some of the experiences he describes, even to abseiling.

As group psychotherapy developed during World War II, S. H. Foulkes, together with other leaders in the field, tried out Moreno's psychodrama at Northfields. Eventually he gave it up, saying that the group-analytic group was enough of a drama and adventure in itself. There is some truth in that and I can appreciate that after returning to civilian life after World War II, he and others preferred to develop group analysis at the Maudsley and the Tavistock and in private practice. However, I think that Foulkes would have appreciated Martin Ringer's work, particularly his chapter on art and psychotherapy.

When Foulkes summed up his life experience in *My Philosophy in Psychotherapy*, he wrote:

> The true therapist has, I believe, a creative function – in a way like an artist, in a way like a scientist, in a way like an educator. If he can avoid wanting to educate people in his own image, he will be able to help them creatively to become themselves, to lead a fuller life, to make use of happiness and to avoid adding too much further suffering to their miseries. There is great satisfaction in this creative part of our function. I have sometimes compared this function to that of a poet, especially in conducting a group. By this I mean the therapist's receptiveness, his ability to see a bit better, a bit deeper, a bit sooner than others what his patients are really saying,

wanting or fearing; to help them to express this and sometimes, though rarely, to express it for them. (Foulkes 1990)

My own experiences in therapeutic community, group-analytic large groups and my own training in psychodrama have given me some acquaintance with the experiences that come from participation in adventure groups. I agree with Martin Ringer that we should do more to integrate and reconcile experiential learning and psychoanalysis, passion and reason.

Malcolm Pines

Foreword

Martin Ringer relates the world of psychoanalysis to that of experiential learning and adventure therapy, and vice versa. To reach this goal, he relies on three special skills: the ability to make complex psychological concepts almost visible; a remarkable talent for narration; and a tireless persistence in addressing many concepts, looking at it from different angles and at various levels of interpretation.

The result is brilliant. Some children's books contain pictures of people and landscapes folded up in their pages that pop up when one opens them. Likewise, when one opens Martin Ringer's book, the pages bring forth the scent of the New Zealand bush, the desert winds, small animals, kayaks gliding down rivers. The people Ringer speaks of do not sit in a closed room, but out in the open, around a fire, or in a van travelling down the highway.

Leonardo – the great Italian Renaissance artist – said, 'A painter must paint mainly two things, that is man and the concept in his mind'. Today we are becoming increasingly aware that it is also important to paint a third thing: the living Nature that man is a part of. A poet of ancient times wrote:

Curl up and drink blood,
like a child in the uterus of the heavens.

Claudio Neri

Author's Preface

The purpose of this book is to engage readers in an exploration that builds their capacity to improve their quality of group leadership. This should result in an improvement in the results achieved and an enhancement of the quality of interaction in the group.

The book is for people who want to develop their ability to create their own activities and ways of intervening in groups, rather than for those who want to be given ready-made interventions. This is because I believe that technique that is grown from understanding is much more powerful and versatile than techniques that are learned without a deep understanding of the rationale from which they were drawn.

Introduction

Imagine that you have been facilitating a group for an hour with good results. Now a person sitting in the corner interjects with a loud outburst of anger and disappointment in how the group is functioning. This seems to blow apart all of the good work that the group has done for the last hour. You are shocked, and remain quiet for a very short time, taking space to scan your knowledge of groups and review your understanding of progress in the group to date. You pay close attention to your feelings and intuition and simultaneously you recall a number of models that describe group behaviour and that could be useful in this situation. In less than five seconds you have identified an intervention. You choose your words carefully and speak for less than half a minute. Within two more minutes it is clear that the group has regained its direction and is working towards its agreed goal.

The fantasy that leading groups can be simple

This fantasy is very appealing and can be achieved by some people some of the time. However this book is based on the view that groups are often not as easily influenced by simple interventions as I described in the preceding fantasy. In the western world we tend to base many of our ideas about how teams and groups function on the principle that people act by following linear and rational influences – like billiard balls that will travel at predictable speeds and in predictable directions if we can only hit them correctly. I do not agree that these linear ways of thinking are the most useful guide to human behaviour, though rationality has its place. I think of groups as small social units that develop their own ways of communicating, creating meaning and taking action. Furthermore, each group is situated in the context of complex organizational, cultural and social milieux. So the study of groups becomes the study of small complex dynamic social systems where the leader is an integral part of that system and factors outside the immediate group are considered to be relevant. For these reasons the study of the leader – presumably yourself – is an integral part of the study of groups and the study of groups needs to be considered with reference to the context in which they occur. Thus, a great deal of value can be gained from the study of the aspects of interaction encompassing the whole leader–group system that occur beneath the awareness of all parties and the implicit patterns of understanding that exist in the context in which groups occur.

This book is intended to offer a coherent set of principles that either complement or challenge the ones you have now, and these principles are intended to be useful to you in the midst of the action with groups. It is hoped that the models, theories and perspectives that are offered here will become your mental companions who in a symbolic sense 'sit alongside you' as you work and who assist you to feel confident and competent.

I aim to do in this book what an effective leader does with his or her group, that is to provide the conditions for the participants – in this case you, the readers – to take the next step in their development. This means providing an appropriate framework or 'container', offering something new that nudges your development. It also means 'being there' with you as you read, to help you manage the anxiety, distress or excitement that results from being stimulated in the direction of growth.

Recipes are necessary but not enough

This approach of writing a book as a companion to and container for the reader's thinking is quite different from giving advice or offering prescriptions and recipes. It is not a 'how to' book that offers the illusion that running groups is simple. In contrast, I develop the theme that the leader's role is aided less by technique than by a 'presence' aided by conscious awareness of one's own subjectivity. That is the presence of the whole person in each moment of the action. Not control of the group, not dazzling groups with your knowledge and skill, but simply maintaining your self fully present with the group and providing appropriate support for the group to achieve its agreed goal. This dynamic presence calls for much higher levels of personal functioning than do the views of group leadership where the importance of techniques and methods is emphasized (Ringer 2000).

Not knowing is vital

I, along with most people I know, feel uncomfortable when I cannot find a reason or explanation for something important. 'Not knowing' is hell! I am constantly searching to find the meaning of events and patterns of events. Unfortunately, groups are too complex to allow most mortals to 'know' what is going on at any time. An implicit purpose of this book is to help the reader become more comfortable with the experience of not knowing exactly what is going on, but remaining fully present in the experience rather than finding some psychological escape from the anxiety caused by not knowing (Bion 1970). This principle of working with 'not knowing' may make parts of the book frustrating to some readers. I do not (very often) provide definitive answers to problems because I do not believe that general definitive answers exist for general problems in groups. I think that the most powerful events occur in groups where there is a space made for leaders and participants to collaborate on the task of evolving the group towards its purpose.

Developing your own style

What the book does offer is an opportunity for you to grow your own style of group leadership where you can be satisfied that you are doing your best. Growing your own style means paying close attention to the complex con-stellation of feeling, thinking, action, intuition, and memories and fantasies that is *you*. It means addressing and dealing with your own vulnerability and failings. I have found the path to competence in leading groups quite difficult. When I first started I was scared before each group began. I imagined that group members might criticize or attack me. Then I began to try to meet my needs for social contact from the groups that I facilitated in a professional setting. These groups were a wonderful source of positive feedback and ego sustenance. I started to depend on people saying things like, 'It was a bit like you worked magic with us.' 'Wow!' I would say to myself, 'What a champion!'

Now I am uncomfortable with the level of dependency that I used to have on positive feedback from my clients. I have struggled with the inappropri-ateness of the desire to impress those with whom I work. At one level I wanted to empower group participants through clearly describing what I do. At another level I still wanted them to remind me that I was a great guy. That is what I mean by group work being challenging. My need for positive feedback from groups was exaggerated beyond useful levels and so I was inappropriately using my clients for my own needs rather then just empowering them to lead better lives. Whilst I may not be entirely free from having an inappropriate dependence on client feedback, I have moved to a point where I am not *so* driven by my need to look competent in front of groups with whom I work. It is my wish that in accompanying me on a journey through this book, you will be stimulated to examine your own strengths and vulnerable aspects and to develop yourself in becoming more effective as a group leader and perhaps more passionate about your work with groups.

A note about the reader's reading of the text

There are many ways to view the activity of reading, just as there are many ways to view the activity of learning. One view of reading is that the reader simply absorbs the information that is included in the text. This being the case, the reader has no particular emotional connection with the ideas in the book and effective reading involves memorizing as much as possible of the content of the book. This view resembles the view of education as 'filling the empty vessel' and in my view is just as unhelpful.

In contrast, I find that when I am reading a book – such as this one about groups – my mind is very active doing things that do not usually include the process of deliberately memorizing content. At times when my eyes are scanning the text my mind is not consciously receiving the words that are written. Instead my mind is on a journey of association where an idea that I have just read has sparked off connections between things in my mind that have previously not been connected. These connections are as much emotional as they are cognitive. The journey of reading can be exciting and stimulating or distressing and anxiety provoking. So the text of the book that I am reading serves not only as a direct source of information but also as a source of stimulation to my own associative thinking and feeling. (Here I am struck by the similarity of this process to some of the associative processes that occur in groups.) A book or an article then, can be read many times and each time the text will trigger different associations in the mind of the reader. Books such as Ashbach and Schermer's (1987) *Object Relations, the Self and the Group* that are both 'dense' and powerful create for me a different journey each time I read them and this can be as many as five or six times if I count the dipping in that I do while I am writing.

So I invite you to read this book with a roving mind and open feeling state. Allow the associations to occur. Do not worry if pages go by without your noticing what you are reading. The pages will always be there if you choose to re-visit them. Celebrate, rather than chastising yourself, when you pick up the book and read a few pages before realizing that you have already read them once before. See this book as creating a frame within which you can think. At the same time, think of the book as a series of points from which your thinking can diverge. Allow the possibility that reading this book will be valuable because the process of reading will reorganize your existing thinking as much as it will be valuable because you will learn new ideas from it.

Intended audience

The book is intended to inform the views of group leaders, and so is mainly written from the point of view of the leader. Three main applications of group work are addressed: therapeutic, educational and corporate/organizational. The limitations of the space available in the title to this book did not allow the mention of a sub-theme of the book, namely that of the integration of theory from experiential learning with theory from psychoanalytic group work. Some readers will not be fully familiar with the basic tenets of experiential learning which is a powerful means of achieving learning outcomes in the domains of affect, values and behaviours. For this reason I have included in this introduction an introduction to experiential learning.

Other readers will be familiar with psychoanalytic and socio-systemic ways of understanding human behaviour and group behaviour and so the first chapters will provide a review of existing knowledge rather than contributing a large amount of new understanding. These first chapters provide an outline of the way in which individuals perceive, make sense of and respond to the world around them. The description is not restricted to the group setting, but is intended to provide a basis for understanding some of the group-specific characteristics of human behaviour that are described in later chapters. These early chapters focus mainly on developing a view of the 'dynamic' of human perception and interaction and consequently much attention is paid to the roles played by different levels of consciousness. Because group phenomena are so complex, I focus early in the book on illustrating the main aspects of internal and interpersonal functioning rather than moving directly to how these dynamics fit into the context of the group.

While experienced psychoanalytic practitioners may find as much familiar as they find new information in these early chapters, they will find that much of the work of translating complex psychodynamic concepts into relatively comprehensible language has been done. This can be of assistance in making a bridge between psychoanalysis, socio-analysis and the rest of the world.

In an attempt to ground the book in some form of practicality, I have included comments throughout on 'technique'. These are intended to offer some ideas about the practical implications for leaders of some of the concepts described immediately prior to the comments on technique.

Over-simplifications and omissions

The problem facing most authors is not a lack of knowledge, but knowing what to leave out. In the process of writing this book I have often had crowds of ideas clamouring for attention. My mind has been like a street demonstration with hundreds of ideas pushing forward shouting noisily for attention. 'I'm important, notice me, write me down...' Perhaps I have adopted the conceptual riot gear and fired tear gas into the crowd. Some ideas flee, never to be seen again, but others appear again in quiet times and surprise me on street corners, catching me at more receptive times (such as when I am on the edge of sleep). But the result is that a great number of good ideas remain unwritten here. Many important authors do not get a mention and some concepts have been so reduced in complexity from their original richness and subtlety that they are now mere shadows of the original forms. In most cases where the simplifications seem to be very significant I have given specific references to further reading.

Layout and themes

The main content of each chapter is presented in a sequence, so that concepts and language introduced early in the book are used without further explanation later in the book. Some more complex theories are separated into text boxes that can be read alongside the main text. Most of these ideas are used later in the book and so the content of the boxes is a part of the main narrative. Other text boxes are stories or anecdotes that are intended to illustrate the concepts being described in the main text. Longer anecdotes, and stories too, form an essential part of the book. One story that I use extensively in the first half of the book is the 'wombat' story. It is derived from a real experience that was related to me by a group of people who use adventure as a catalyst for personal growth and learning. This saga is woven throughout the duration of Part 1 of the book because it seems to capture so many aspects of group life.

An introduction to experiential learning

Experiential learning involves the combination of action and reflection to assist learning. Many of the groups that I have led have been based on experiential learning and some of the examples used in this book to illustrate group dynamics are based on experiential groups and in particular on adventure-based groups. This early introduction to the principles of experiential learning is supplemented later by a fairly thorough account of how psychodynamic principles can be applied to enhance our understanding of experiential learning. The description below is one that I have used extensively in my work to introduce the ideas of experiential learning to people who are about to participate in training and development groups that I have led or co-led.

An introduction to experiential learning as written for client groups

Below is a description of the basic elements of experiential learning and the way that these principles can be related to the process of enhancing skills, modifying attitudes and improving knowledge in the work place.

> Experiential learning can be defined as generating an action theory from your own experiences and then continually modifying it to improve your effectiveness. The purpose of experiential learning is to affect the learner in three ways:
>
> 1.   The learner's thinking is altered.
>
> 2.   The learner's attitudes are modified.
>
> 3.   The learner's repertoire of possible behaviours is expanded.
>
> These elements are interconnected and change in one part leads to changes in other parts. (Johnson and Johnson 1991, pp.40–41)

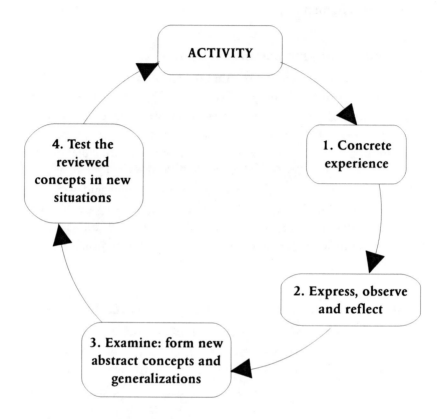

Figure 1.1 The experiential learning cycle
Source: Greenaway (1993) and Kolb (1984)

The contents of each of the boxes in Figure 1.1 are described in more detail below.

ACTIVITY AND CONCRETE EXPERIENCE

The activities that provide the concrete experience occur in two places, the work place and the learning group itself. The concrete experience that you will be reflecting on can be a 'case study' or even just a small incident from your work. It could also be some interaction in the learning group or a specific exercise or simulation that has been set up for you to do during a workshop.

EXPRESS, OBSERVE AND REFLECT

This is the aspect most neglected in traditional work places. People seldom reflect on what they did that led either to achieving a positive result or failing to achieve a positive result. Usually we make a quick (and often unconscious) decision about why something worked or did not work and then we move on to the next pressing task. Breaking this pattern is a key to enabling us to develop self-responsible ways of learning. Most of the ideas about 'learning organisations' (Senge 1992) are based on developing individuals' and organizations' ability to reflect adequately on what they do. The critical element of this stage is to describe to someone else in your own words what happened. What did you do? Describe your action, thinking and feeling. What did others do? What was the interaction between yourself and others? What happened in the wider work environment that is related to the incident that you are describing? Stay clear of interpretations and explanations at this stage.

EXAMINE: FORM NEW ABSTRACT CONCEPTS AND GENERALIZATIONS

In discussion with someone else, look 'backwards' to identify the principles you applied that led you to taking the action(s) that you did. For example, when you selected Fred, an electrical engineer for your team, what were the underlying assumptions that led to your making that choice? What was your thinking? What principles did you apply? What 'hidden agendas' were there? What was your implicit goal as compared to your stated goal?

Has this exploration to date identified any theories, models, values or beliefs that no longer serve you well? If so, this is the time of exploration to find new ways of thinking, believing or valuing. Explore new possibilities and consider how they fit with your way of being in the world. This is the place in experiential learning where theory plays a vital part. Having different theories and models to describe how people and organizations function will enable you to choose the theory or model that best suits the situation at hand. One theory cannot adequately explain all human and organizational phenomena. Each theory provides us with a different 'window' through which to view the world. Each window is useful in some ways but limits our ability to see the whole picture. This stage in the experiential learning cycle enables us to try out a number of windows and select a best fit. (For a ready-made set of 'windows' on organizations see Ringer and Robinson (1996)).

In the case of choosing Fred for your team, perhaps you realize that your main motivation was to have him in your team because he is good at resolving conflict and there are already too many aggressive people in your team. So, on reflection, you realize that you are not confident in resolving conflict yourself and you do not feel well supported by your project engineer in resolving conflict in a way that maintains good morale in your teams. Now you understand that you have made a good choice of person (i.e. Fred) for keeping your team functioning well in the short term, but you need to address a better means for resolving conflict in your teams in the longer term.

TEST THE REVIEWED CONCEPTS IN NEW SITUATIONS

Now we are back to the action component again. In this 'step' you either try out a different action because you have realized that your last action was based on premises that were not the most useful for the situation, or else you test your original choice to see if it really works. For example, you may talk to the project engineer about why you chose Fred and let the project engineer know that you want to find better ways of dealing with conflict in your teams. You might re-consider your choice of Fred and find another engineer who is more technically competent but less able to deal with people.

Your overall learning from the above experiential learning cycle could be that in the past you have tended to choose team members more for how they will get along together than how technically competent they are. You may in the future pay closer attention to balancing technical skills with interpersonal skills. Perhaps too, you have learned that you tend to try to solve problems in the short term rather than talking over long-term solutions with your project engineer. This results in more stress for you and in the same problems reappearing week after week.

Now you are back at the first element of experiential learning – action. The process never ends!

Finally, experiential learning is the most natural way of learning in the world; we do it all the time in real life. The reason that we focus on it as a 'technique' in this workshop is that we have learned at school and university to separate our learning from real life experiences. In school, learning of theory tends to be valued above personally experienced learning. I am suggesting that we redress the balance and combine theory with action in our lives in a way that we find useful and satisfying.

For further reading on experiential learning I recommend Warren (1996) and Warren, Sakofs and Hunt Jr (1995).

A brief introduction to ways of thinking about groups

This section offers a lightning tour of the history of groups from a subjective point of view. Here I take the view that it is futile to attempt a rigorous definition of the word 'group' because the term has multiple meanings. Instead I will allow the reader to build progressively his or her own understanding of what I mean by 'group' as the book unfolds. This frees me up to provide in the section that follows a deliberately selective sample of extracts relating to the evolution of thinking about groups, particularly as relevant to experiential learning groups.

When I was fifteen I attended my first 'bushcraft' course. In New Zealand bushcraft was the name given to the set of competencies that enabled bush walkers (called 'trampers' in New Zealand) to survive and even thrive as they travelled on foot through the bush. I was awed by the amazing knowledge of the instructors. I listened to every word they said and drank in the knowledge. Then as I grew older and my own knowledge grew, I started to become critical of the instructors who each year seemed to repeat the same story with minor variations. But I dared not challenge them in the presence of the others in the group. These people were the gurus of bushcraft and everyone around me acted as if they were providing a very high quality of training. How could a young upstart like myself know better? I had no idea about how groups worked and no idea that groups of people often act as if something is true even when the majority of group members know that it is not. Nobody suggested that we as a learning group could understand the way in which we were interacting. 'Leadership' was taught as though this mystical subject was a part of bushcraft but the principles taught were not actually applied to the groups that we took part in as we learned about leadership.

Now, as I work and travel in corporate settings and experiential learning groups I often get the impression that people are not conscious that most interaction in the world goes on in groups. To describe this strange phenomenon I have coined the term 'the no-group illusion' in recognition of Didier Anzieu's (1984) term 'group illusion' that we will encounter later in this book. In short, rather than engage with understanding the complexity of group life, most people prefer to act as if groups are just collections of individuals and the same principles can be applied to managing groups, teams and meetings as can be applied to managing one-to-one conversations. I am still regularly in contact with otherwise competent professionals who just do not seem to know how much more effective they could be if they were more effective group leaders.

Groups are the vehicles that take us on many different kinds of journeys. All educational institutions use groups as a basic unit of instruction. Organizations are groups nested in groups nested in groups...and so on. Workshops of all kinds are groups, whether for development, education or therapy. All experiential forms of education, development and therapy use groups as the predominant medium for working. There exists in the world a huge amount of knowledge about groups but a large percentage of this valuable knowledge does not reach those who run groups and teams in their everyday lives. Why is this?

The lack of general knowledge about groups that exists in the everyday life of educators, managers, facilitators, trainers, and so on, is in part due to the politics of knowledge (Holland 1977). Specifically, some of the most powerful knowledge about groups has been derived from the study of the dynamics of therapy groups. The people who have studied and written about therapy groups are usually psychologists and/or psychoanalysts and therefore they publish in psychological jargon in psychological journals. Therefore, specialist knowledge of group dynamics has in part become the 'private business' of psychologists. Only a relatively small amount of theory has been translated from specialist psychological language to describe the functioning of groups in everyday settings involving experiential learning or corporate life.

The adventure-based experiential field has developed a sound body of literature about experiential learning, but one that includes relatively little about the dynamics of groups. The corporate/management field has developed extensive knowledge about facilitation in corporate settings but this largely ignores the body of knowledge that exists about 'psychological' processes in groups. The field of group psychotherapy and, more recently, the field of psychoanalytic/socio-analytic organizational psychology, has produced a plethora of outstanding publications with high levels of sophistication. Unfortunately, the complexity and specialization of language in many of these publications makes them inaccessible to all but the most specialized readers and so this wealth of knowledge remains relatively inaccessible to people who spend much of their lives running groups.

Thus, much of the valuable knowledge that exists about the psychology of groups remains beyond the reach of the average group leader because it is published in places outside their usual reading range and is written in inaccessible language.

Sociology – another field of study – has also spawned a lot of knowledge and literature about group 'dynamics' and in fact the phrase 'group dynamics' is most often used as a blanket term to cover the sociological understanding of groups. Sociological views of group focus on topics such as:

- group goals
- stages of group development
- decision making
- power and influence
- leadership
- conflict.

Overall, the sociological approach to groups examines patterns of behaviour in groups. Research based on sociological principles uses qualitative studies to determine how collective behaviours change with changes of group conditions. Sociology favours understanding the collective. This sociological knowledge provides useful mental models for group leaders that help them to create optimum conditions for groups. The sociological studies also help to explain such things as power dynamics, role differentiation and acceptance/rejection dynamics. Two such books that are well written and well researched are Brown (2000) *Group Processes* and Johnson and Johnson (1991) *Joining Together: Group Theory and Group Skills.*

What then is a group from the sociological or from the psychological point of view?

In reality there is a huge diversity of theory in both sociology and in psychology and so there is no such thing as a 'sociological' point of view or a 'psychological' point of view. However, I will simplify these categories and make some broad generalizations about how groups are viewed.

Ideas about groups that are derived from sociology tend to favour the point of view of the external observer of groups and so in sociological terms a group is more than two people who share common characteristics but who may not have a subjective experience of being together or being members of the same group. In other words, the sociological point of view tends to take an external perspective and allocates people to groups on the basis of having characteristics in common. For instance thirty people who have never met each other but who share a common characteristic could be called a group.

'Group' then becomes a classification, which does not depend on the members of a group having met or even knowing about each other.

In contrast, a psychological group is more than two people who *experience themselves* as a group. In this case, the group is subjectively constructed by the members of the group themselves. Experiencing oneself as a member of a group usually requires one to have real-life interaction with the other members and this often involves spending some time together (or on internet discussions together). After a period of time the subjective experience of being a group develops and this is often accompanied by group members sharing similarities in both conscious and unconscious views of the group. In these terms, a group that has met for a period of time and has carried out activities with a shared purpose would fit both the sociological and psychological description of a group.

So there is nothing absolute that enables anyone, whether observer or participant, to define when a group exists. The distinctions that are used to define the existence of a group will be made differently by different people depending on their point of view, their theoretical background and their subjective experience. It is with this latter rather ephemeral view of 'group' that I proceed into the rest of the book.

Given the potentially overwhelming number of theories about groups, it will be useful here to narrow the topic down to group dynamics, as suggested by the title of the book. The study of group dynamics is well documented by Cartwright and Zander (1970) who in their introductory chapters give detailed accounts of the influence of early theorists and experimenters such as Sherif and Lewin. Later chapters of their edited book include original works by well-known authors such as Bales, Janis, Festinger, and Schacter. All of the work described in this book was conducted around 1950 when as a part of the social unconscious (Hopper 2001) there was a zealous search to understand human behaviour in the wish to prevent another world war. At this time, the individual was unquestionably the basic unit of society and membership of groups was considered to be a threat to individual autonomy. Therefore, in these 'early' studies, the focus was on understanding first how people became members of groups, second how people lost or retained their 'individual free will' whilst simultaneously being members of groups and third, how power and influence worked in groups. This was the period when the idea of group norms was consolidated and the fear that the group would be taken over by 'groupthink' (Janis 1982) formed a constant undercurrent to thinking. After all 'groupthink' on a large scale had supported Nazi atrocities that ended only a few years earlier.

In parallel with the work of Cartwright, Zander and their colleagues, another group also based in the USA was actively attempting to understand group dynamics, but this time from a more experiential basis, based on the work of Kurt Lewin. 1947 was an exciting year for a small group of action researchers who were developing new ways of enhancing personal understanding and interpersonal effectiveness. The National Training Laboratory (NTL) was established in Maine, USA. It was here that 'T-groups' or 'training groups' were born. Meantime, a number of institutions such as the Tavistock Institute in England and the A. K. Rice Institute in the USA were pursuing a study of groups from a psychoanalytic frame. We will look first at the National Training Laboratory approach before mentioning the work of Wilfred Bion and others at the Tavistock Institute.

The National Training Laboratory-based T-groups were built on a strong philosophical basis that sought to redress the shortfalls of the conventional educational system – particularly in the area of interpersonal effectiveness. T-groups were experiential groups where the topic of study was the members' own behaviour. Rather than being therapy groups, T-groups were intended to provide participants from a wide range of backgrounds with improved ability to live quality lives, again no doubt based on the largely unspoken wish to avoid another collapse into the savagery of world war.

The philosophical basis for the T-group was derived from a range of disciplines including psychology, sociology, anthropology, group behaviour and learning theory, engineering, psychiatry, education and social work but with the overarching principle that 'understanding and skills of participation can only be achieved by the learner taking an active part in a group experience (Bradford, Gibb and Benne 1964).

The National Training Laboratory was a cauldron of creativity for approaches to using groups for education, personal development and social change. People whose names keep reappearing in the literature about groups were involved in this venture. They included Kurt Lewin, Dorothy Stock, Bradford, Benne, Lippitt, Gibb and Leiberman. A number of these people later moved to the Tavistock Institute in the UK and further developed the work of Bion. One aspect of T-groups which resembled the 'Tavistock' approach was the relative lack of structure and the lack of overt leadership on the part of the 'expert' group leader. Being in an apparently leaderless group like this leads to high levels of anxiety on the part of group members and can even be terrifying. We will examine the relationship between tightness of group structure and the level of anxiety for participants in later chapters. Even Carl Rogers, whose group work emerged from different roots, used 'leaderlessness' as an integral – even essential – part of the learning process (Barrett-Lennard 1975). It occurs to me now that it is likely that there was present in the social unconscious a fear of leadership that emerged directly from the trauma of the Second World War.

Another key link in the chain was the resemblance between the principles of experiential learning and the principles described as central to the T-group approach. The following principles are taken from Bradford, Gibb and Benne (1964) but could equally have been taken from a more recent paper on experiential learning or indeed, from my own set of principles about effective group work. They are that the T-group experience emphasizes:

- generating of behavioural output for analysis and learning
- a climate of permissiveness and inquiry
- collaborative relationships for learning
- maps for understanding and organizing experiences
- experimentation with new behaviours
- generalizing and planning applications (pp.40–44).

Two other contemporaneous fields of group work were derived from quite different principles. Both the Tavistock-related approaches and approaches based on psychodrama emphasized the role of the leader in group work. Tavistock-related approaches put significant weight on the role of the leader in establishing boundaries for groups and for interpreting interactions in the group. These approaches are briefly introduced next.

Wilfred Bion followed a direct conceptual route from Sigmund Freud through Melanie Klein and other post-Freudians. Bion's work on groups is exceptionally well described by others, many of whom are referred to later in this book and so here I will only touch on a few essentials. Bion and groups that have subsequently developed his thinking focused strongly on unconscious processes in groups that led to 'group-as-a-whole' phenomena and that rendered the intrapsychic functioning of any one individual relatively insignificant in the overall dynamic. Here, the group and its subdivisions is/are visible and the power lies primarily in unconscious processes derived from psychological defence mechanisms. Groups become exciting, perhaps dangerous, and largely unknowable. The dynamic is understood from self-analysis of the feelings of the leader and from subtle cues in the patterns of interaction in the group. Destructiveness was always present in some form or other and anxiety was seen as a primary driver of mental processes and behaviour. This approach could perhaps best be summarized as group work that is informed by psychoanalytic principles.

In parallel with the English and American work on groups that was largely informed by psychoanalysis, Europeans who wrote in languages other than English were making some rapid progress in understanding group dynamics. Didier Anzieu, René Kaës and colleagues in France and others in Italy developed approaches with a strong psychoanalytic basis but also incorporating psychodrama. They included in their work the thinking of Bion and his colleagues, but the English appeared to pay little attention to their non-English speaking colleagues across the channel! There was also developmental work occurring in group theory in Italy, Germany and Switzerland amongst other places.

In a curious parallel, a further school of group theory and practice was emerging in England. S.H. Foulkes had escaped from persecution in Nazi Germany. In contrast to the Bion 'school' with its unashamed focus on destructive aspects of the unconscious, Foulkes developed practice and theory that emphasized generative aspects of human interaction in groups. Whilst also deriving much of his original theory from Freudian thought, Foulkes moved to integrate a more interpersonal view of groups than did Bion (Hinshelwood 1999, Dalal 1998).

Psychodrama was unambiguous in its approach; the group leader was 'director'. Psychodrama as created by J. L. Moreno was a group-centred methodology with strong action and experiential bases. The development of the family of psychodrama-based systems (psychodrama, sociodrama, sociometry and role training) led to a whole movement that soon claimed to have invented group therapy. However, psychodrama as a field of endeavour continues to surprise me with the absence of a theory of 'group' that supplements the 'role theory' of individual functioning and the theories of human change that are also present in psychodrama literature (Williams 1989, 1991).

Carl Rogers is also well known for his work in the USA with groups in education and personal growth groups that became known as 'encounter groups'. He started a huge movement based on humanistic principles where people interacted in groups with relatively little directive leadership for the purpose of growth and learning. Later, encounter groups became discredited because some of them were poorly run, with consequent psychological damage to participants and because some involved sexual freedom that was not in keeping with societal conventions. Rogers, too, was surprisingly devoid of theory about group dynamics despite his heavy reliance on groups as a vehicle for human change and learning (as was mentioned to me by G. Barrett-Lennard).

Whilst the preceding paragraphs provide only a tiny sample of the historical development of groups, they do outline a basic dilemma for those of us who wish to extend the theory. That is, what theory should we extend? How can we honour the rich and diverse knowledge and practice base in group work without becoming lost in a myriad of ideas, some of which contradict others? My choice has been to pursue the fundamental principles of psychodynamic and psychoanalytic group work, where there is significant focus on unconscious processes, but to add what I see as the essential element of conscious processes. I draw heavily from literature on group therapy because it is there that so much of the cutting-edge thinking about groups has been done. My task has been to translate some of this work from heavily jargonized language into language that is accessible to the average reader who does not have a background in psychoanalysis. To the psychodynamic material I have added a number of ideas from experiential learning, and in particular from action-based experiential learning such as adventure therapy (Gillis and Ringer 1999). Into this mix has been added a systems theory (Bateson 1972; Watzlawick, Weakland and Fisch 1974). In particular, the systemic views of socio-analysis and of the systemic thinkers about groups have been useful (Ashbach and Schermer 1987; Bain 1999). More recent authors and editors such as Farhad Dalal (1998), Harwood and Pines (1998), Claudio Neri (1998) and Mario Marrone (1998) have drawn extensively from outside the conventional area of psychoanalysis and have included material from areas such as attachment theory, neuroscience, sociology and self-psychology. These works have greatly enriched my thinking and this will become evident as the book unfolds.

Finally, my own life experience as an engineer, educator, adventure therapist, programme director, management consultant, and group work trainer has provided a great deal of stimuli for thinking and writing. Some say that the essence of creativity is similar to that of humour – the juxtaposition of the unexpected. Examples that come to mind are applying adventure therapy principles to psychodynamic group work and applying management consulting thinking to group work training for therapeutic group leaders. I hope that this unlikely mix provides a creative soup into which the reader can dip and find new things each time.

For further reading about the history of groups, I recommend the following. For a brilliant summary of Foulksian thinking see Dalal (1998). Between them, Mark Ettin (1999) in Part 2 of his book and Claudio Neri (1998) in his historical notes provide an excellent summary of the growth of group psychotherapy. Trevor Tyson (1998) provides a thorough review of the literature on groups, both current and historical, and those who can read French will find a significant history of thinking about groups contained in the works by René Kaës (1993) and Claude Pigott (1990).

The structure of this book

The book is in two parts. Part 1 progressively builds an outline of the principles underpinning the functioning of human beings as relevant to their behaviour in groups. This could be summarized as building a picture of how human beings perceive, believe, think and behave. In Part 1 the 'wombat' story is used as a means of anchoring abstract ideas in a living story. Therefore, the wombat story immediately precedes Part 1.

Part 2 consists of a series of applications of the ideas presented in Part 1 with a particular focus on providing concepts of group and group leadership that can be used to inform practice.

Part 1

The unlikely appearance and disappearance of a wombat provides a story around which Part 1 evolves. The prelude gives a rich description of a real group experience that is so powerful that it will capture the interest of the reader and provide many questions about how people function in groups. The questions asked are progressively addressed throughout Part 1. The nature of reality is a fundamental that is explored in Chapter 1. Is reality given, constructed, or both? Ideas of constructivism are outlined and teased out. Given that groups function through communication between members, the nature of communication as a means of exchanging symbols is introduced. The central dilemma then, becomes how group leaders can con-currently experience each group member's reality as being different and maintain enough sense that there is a coherent 'group' reality. Some assistance is given in Chapter 2 by the application of the concept of 'internal working models' as derived from attachment theory. These personalized mental maps of the world and self-in-relation-to-the-world form the guiding principles for each person's understanding of the world and their place in it. Understanding the way in which internal working models function provides the group leader with a strong basis for working simultaneously with individuals and with the group.

Internal working models include both conscious and unconscious elements and so the next logical step is to speculate on what is involved in unconscious functioning. This is a big job and so some classification of unconscious processes is provided and some aspects of the unconscious mind are excluded from this book because they are not altogether relevant to human change processes in the context of groups. This clears the way to study in more depth aspects of unconscious, preconscious and conscious mental functioning that are relevant to groups as described in this book. Chapter 4 provides an outline of these three levels of consciousness and, in an interlude, describes recent findings from neuroscience that shed light on memory systems in relation to human consciousness. Specific applications of thinking about the different levels of consciousness in the context of groups are addressed towards the end of the chapter. The presence of unconscious processes raises questions about where communication fits in the range between conscious and unconscious and so Chapter 5 attempts to provide some expansion on this question with a brief sojourn into semiotics, language and communication. The 'mechanics' of communication underpin group functioning and so understanding the nature of language in relation to communication gives some more cognitive power to the leader.

Nonetheless, communication through conscious use of language is only one part of the story. There are many processes that occur in groups beneath the awareness of all participants including the leader. These processes – mainly projection, identification, projective identification, transference and countertransference – are introduced and their existence is related to the life of groups. The existence of these phenomena places a great deal of responsibility on the leader to pay close attention to his or her own internal world of intuition, feelings and fantasies. These phenomena exist in all groups whether or not the group is run on psychodynamic principles or not. Of particular interest in a book about 'group action' is the application of psychodynamic principles to experiential learning groups.

By this time it is abundantly clear that I believe that the group exists as an entity that is interdependent with the members of that same group. The term 'group-as-a-whole' has been introduced earlier but finally in Chapter 7 it gets its own special place. Here I briefly explore some of the ways that exist of thinking about the group-as-a-whole in relation to group members. In terms of conceptual progression in the book there is another essential view here too – the existence of 'phantasy'[1] level functioning in groups that occurs as a fantasy that is beyond conscious awareness. It is the phantasy level functioning that provides the coherence to views of the group-as-a-whole. In my opinion the ability to work with group-as-a-whole issues differentiates the intermediate level group conductor from the advanced. Even in groups such as meetings in corporate settings, where mention is seldom made of 'unconscious processes' or 'group-as-a-whole', the consultant or facilitator gains immeasurably from having a working knowledge of collective unconscious processes in groups, teams and meetings.

Part 1 is concluded with a systematic description of the fundamental principles underpinning psychodynamic and experiential group work.

Part 2

Chapter 8 deals with some of the contradictions involved in applying principles derived from the 'talking cure' to activity-based groups and vice versa. For instance, how does one tell the difference between action and acting out? Some comparisons are made between action-based experiential learning groups and 'talking-based' psychodynamic groups, with an effort being made to lessen the divide between the ideological differences that exist at present.

An underlying theme in this second part of the book is that of combining conscious and unconscious elements in groups. After all, most people in corporate and educational settings do not openly talk (or even think) about unconscious elements in groups. Therefore, the establishment of overt principles that can be communicated to group members is a vital part of group leadership. Chapter 9 uses the metaphor of the group as an egg. There is an external container and an internal structure. If the egg is raw the internal structure will leak out when the container is broken but if the egg is cooked the shell is no longer vital for the integrity of the group. Less obvious, but equally important, is the notion of the 'affiliative attachment' that group members experience in relation to the group. This attachment provides some of the glue that makes group membership a vital part of life for the participant.

Given the presence of the group as a safe, bounded and purposeful entity as described in Chapter 9, the question of quality becomes relevant. What is it about groups that enables the presence of useful thinking and feeling? What constitutes the 'reflective space' in a group and how do leaders work with groups to co-construct that reflective space? Chapter 10 explores some of these questions and, although outlining some principles, seeks to avoid prescriptive pointers for technique. One could say that Chapter 10, in keeping with the theme of this book, avoids providing 'algorithmic' step-by-step recipes that are intended to substitute for the judgement and experience of the group leader. It is the balance between 'how to' approaches and principle-based ('emergent') approaches that is addressed in detail in Chapter 11. Six perspectives on group functioning are offered, and implications for group design and group leadership are derived from the six different perspectives. Balancing rational and conscious with a-rational and unconscious elements is also addressed in this chapter because there is a progressive movement from conscious to unconscious as one moves from the first window to the sixth.

Finally, the group leader emerges as an artist. Chapter 12 explores the notion of parallels between groups and art and the parallels between group leaders and artists. This creative view, it is hoped, both integrates previous material and introduces some interesting new notions that leave the whole practice of group leadership as interesting and unfinished as one could hope for. Rather than finishing the book with a definitive prescription of who should do what to achieve certain outcomes, the readers are left with the tension between knowing and not knowing. From here growth and development continue to be possible and attractive.

Prelude: stories and the demise of a wombat

Stories capture our attention. They also illustrate models and theories in a way that non-story text cannot. In reading a story we place ourselves in the narrative, we make mental comparisons between this story and others in our own lives and we use our imagination to fill out what is presented in the text. Theories and models probably started as real stories in real people's lives but so many stories followed the same pattern that a coherent collection of stories was replaced at first by a hypothesis (Edelson and Berg 1999). When more and more stories fitted the pattern outlined by the hypothesis all these stories were condensed into a theory. But if we lose sight of the fact that theories and models are just 'story essence' we lose sight of the richness that can be derived from such theories and models. So in this book I will use stories and anecdotes to enrich the text.

Preamble to this story

One story in particular stands out for me. I will tell a part of it now, and comment later on how it might add value to the book. I heard it from participants in a workshop. This was a professional development workshop on the topic of unconscious processes in experiential learning groups that ran for four days. Throughout the workshop we used case studies from participants as the raw material to which we linked conceptual material about unconscious processes in experiential learning groups. This 'wombat' story proved to be an endless source of rich material on unconscious processes in groups, and stands for me as the most powerful that I have heard during my involvement with experiential learning.

The story involves an adventure therapy group, led by 'Daniel', 'George' and 'Amy'. (All names are pseudonyms.) Both George and Amy were present in the workshop that I was facilitating and Daniel has provided further comments and clarification after reading my first attempt at capturing the real story. In using the story I have retained what I consider to be the essential elements of the original situation but changed many details. In particular I have changed the description of the leaders, aspects relating to their competence and some aspects of events that happened in real life. This is because I want to emphasize some aspects of group work leadership that were not apparent in the original story. All participants' names have also been changed.

The group leaders ('instructors') were: George, Daniel and Amy.

Group participants were: Vikki, Barry, Dennis, Katrina, Jack, Robert, Clive and Sean.

The story

A van travelled through gum forest, winding its way through the Australian landscape of granite outcrops and spiny vegetation under the canopy of a bright blue sky. The sun was high in the afternoon sky and shadows in the forest were black in contrast to the brilliance of the sunlight. Dense ochre dust billowed from the tyres, slowly settling in the sparse forest of gum trees beside the road as the van rattled its way towards the city. Two young men and a young woman sat at the front. Daniel was driving and George mused quietly about the group of adolescents in the back of the van. The planned five-day expedition had been difficult and had ended before it was scheduled to. George was disappointed. He was relatively new as an adventure therapy leader and the last expedition had gone so well that he had had an expectation that this one would be as good as the last. His work as an outdoor leader was still a bit erratic. He did not have a permanent job and relied on contract employment from local adventure programmes for his livelihood. He had thought that two successful trips with this employer would put him in a strong position for a permanent job.

This group – now sitting silently in the back of the van – had started well too. The pre-expedition activity day had gone smoothly ending with a sense of anticipation about the longer expedition to follow. The contrast with today was almost too much to believe. In the few days between the pre-expedition event and the start of this expedition, the group's mood had completely changed. Now, turning to look at the six adolescents sitting behind him, George saw only blank faces and what might have been sullenness, broken occasionally by desultory conversation and the odd half smile. Two others had left the expedition earlier.

Daniel, too was musing about what had not worked. He was in charge of this group because he was the only member of staff of the organization that was responsible for the expedition. He had worked with many different groups over the years and the events experienced during this expedition made less sense than any other. How come two participants had left the group on the second day? What could the group leaders have done to prevent that form of failure? Why had the remainder of the group then been so sullen, uncoopera-tive and finally, rebellious? Daniel's awareness of the long stretch of straight road ahead provided space for him to muse without the usual focus on navigating the van around slippery gravel corners. A small variation in the colour of the road sped under the van, but the vehicle remained travelling without a noticeable bump or any unusual movement. All that was visible in the rear vision mirror as Daniel glanced back was the cloud of dust following the van. Nothing seemed amiss.

The loud shout from the back of the van contradicted Daniel's 'no problem' verdict. Robert's strident yell accused, 'You've killed a wombat. Stop. Stop'. Robert got out of his seat, leaned into the front of the vehicle. Barry, sitting beside Robert, took up the cry: 'You bastard. You've killed a wombat. You ran over it and you didn't stop. Stop the van. Stop. Stop'. Then the other passengers gave voice to their concern. An angry chorus screamed at the driver to stop. Daniel was shocked and confused. He had not seen a wombat on the road. He thought that, at worst, he had driven over a pothole in the road. Nonetheless, he pulled to the side of the road and stopped the van, leaving the motor running. Before the vehicle had come to rest the passengers threw open the sliding door with a resounding crash and, with the exception of Dennis and Clive, ran back down the road in search of the dead wombat. The mix of angry voices over the crunch of feet running on gravel receded to silence. That left the leaders slightly dazed and laughing in an attempt to come to terms with the craziness of it all.

'Did you see a wombat?' Daniel quietly asked Amy and George so as not to be heard by the two remaining in the back of the van.

'No', Amy replied, 'but I wasn't really looking, I was thinking about what has been happening on this expedition and what we're going to say when we get back to the programme headquarters. It's been a bit of a failure.'

'But it's unreal', protested Daniel, 'there was no damned wombat. What are they on about?'

Then the sound of breaking glass came from the rear of the van. The stress had become too much for Clive. He had 'cracked' and smashed one of the side windows with his umbrella. The instructors' laughing stopped with the realization that emotions were dangerously aroused and that the situation could easily become one of widespread violence.

Even as they helped to clear up the broken glass and put waterproof tape over the resulting hole, the instructors continued to puzzle over the violent outburst of the group and the level of anger and aggression that seemed to come from nowhere. They were distressed and disturbed by the way in which the whole group had taken up the cry of 'You've killed a wombat' when most of them were not even sitting in positions where they could have seen a wombat on the road. Besides, wombats are nocturnal animals and although common in the area, they were unlikely to be on the road in broad daylight. They are the size of a Labrador dog and dark in colour. If there had been a wombat on the road, surely Daniel or one of the other instructors sitting in the front of the van would have seen it. It was almost as if some kind of madness overtook the group. A kind of contagion where one person's shout created a ripple effect that made others in the back of the van become mad at the same time. None of the instructors verbalized their fear, but they were very aware of how close to violence against others the group had become, and that the instructors were very much outnumbered by participants. If the participants did attack them they would be in serious trouble. But that was unthinkable! How could such thoughts be so present? These were not really bad or violent kids.

Should one of two of the leaders follow the participants and look for the wombat? They talked about driving back, but had not made a decision before they heard voices. Gradually the participants returned, climbed into the van, and sat waiting expectantly for the journey to continue.

'Well, did you find the wombat?' Daniel asked.

Barry looked at Robert, who spat a reply, 'Yes, and we buried it'. The rest of the group sat in sullen silence. There was no clear evidence of dirt on their hands and they had no digging instruments with them when they left the van.

This was the first part of the story that was presented to the workshop group. The group members in the story were all young people who had been unsuccessful in one or more aspects of life. Some had been sentenced for criminal offences and others had been referred by government agencies because of a perceived need to gain social skills, self-esteem and 'job-readiness'.

In the group work workshop in which the story was told and worked with, it was clear that both Amy and George were still distressed by this recent experience. They had spent time with their programme director debriefing the expedition, including this event, but barely two weeks had passed since the occurrence of the 'wombat incident'. I as workshop leader and the other participants were aware of the need to respect Amy and George's healing process while answering our needs to learn from their story. Not surprisingly, we found that the process of group-centred inquiry into the events provided powerful growth, healing and learning for both Amy and George.

No doubt, reading the part of the story that I have just presented evoked some thoughts, emotions and questions for you. That is the purpose of a story. So, as you imagine the wombat scene as described above, what captures your attention? What opinions did you form about the events described?

What answers do you seek? What urgency is there for you to make sense of this sequence of events? Whatever the response you had, it potentially tells you a lot about yourself. Each reader will have had a slightly different response *to the same story* and so the story creates a kind of 'Rorschach ink blot' onto which we can project our expectations and underpinning assumptions about the world.

I will expand on the details of the wombat story throughout Part 1 of the book and use the story as one of the central points around which to gather our thoughts. This and other stories can be used to think about such things as:

- the impact of pre-group events on groups and group members
- the influence of the organizational context in which the groups exists on the life of the group
- unconscious processes in groups and how they appear to leaders and to participants
- the relevance of group purpose in relation to the individual goals brought by group members
- anxiety, fear and the unexpected as relevant to groups
- the relevance of individual psychological development for group membership
- power and influence in groups – both overt and covert.

I will attempt to use the wombat story and others to bring the personal back into theorizing and model making. As we go along, stories will form a point on which to focus during the exploration of the multiple potential explanations for events in groups.

On first hearing the story I was transfixed by the question, 'Was there really a wombat?' Or, 'If not a wombat, what precipitated the outburst?' After all, I thought, would it not be scary if the group participants had lied and 'created' a wombat as an excuse for a violent outburst? Then it seemed even more scary that some group participants might have been hallucinating. They might have had a psychotic episode and so could have really got out of control.

However, as we unravelled the context for the story, the existence of the wombat became less relevant. What became apparent was that the kind of dynamic that developed in the group over five days was relatively common in many kinds of groups. What became really exciting was that as the workshop group used this story as a 'case study' the understanding of unconscious processes in groups created the potential for new perspectives and a consequent opening of possibilities for intervening in similar difficult situations.

Note

1.   'Phantasy' is an imagining or 'fantasy' that occurs completely outside the awareness of the subject. In contrast, the subject is aware of having a fantasy because it occurs at a conscious level.

Part 1

CHAPTER 1

Constructing reality in groups

This chapter outlines some of my views about the way in which human beings perceive, believe, behave and understand themselves in the context of life, and in particular, in the context of groups. These processes of understanding and relating to the world provide the basis for each individual's style of communication and hence the nature of interaction in the groups to which he or she belongs. The chapter is primarily a description of how people develop their sense of who they are and how this sense of self influences their interaction with others. At times in this chapter my writing style becomes quite personal. This is a deliberate choice because I only have direct access to one person's experience – my own. The experience of being in a group is an intensely personal one but much of the writing about theories of group is couched in the third person. However, theory needs to be digested and brought to life and it is my wish to assist in this digestion process by being the narrator of a story involving theory-in-action. It also seems fair to give you a view of the kind of biases and idiosyncrasies that have directed my choice of material for the remainder of this book.

A developmental view that incorporates learning from experience

The whole field of experiential learning is based on the premise that when people have an experience, *under the right conditions*, they will learn from it. Learning leads to changes in thinking, feeling and acting, so the accumulation of learning from experience leads to the continued development of each human being. Given that we are all having experiences all of the time, the logical question is, 'What's the fuss about experiential learning? Why don't we just let people get on with having experiences and learning from them?' The most obvious reason is that we would then have a lot of unemployed experiential educators, but I think that there are other reasons as well. In particular, the field of infant observation shows graphically how even very young infants develop means of not *experiencing* the impact of events around them because to do so would be too distressing (Briggs 2000). Avoidance of experience is most extreme in infants who are at risk, but all human beings develop early in their lives some capacity to not *experience the impact of their experience.* That is, we build the capacity to live through some events without their having a noticeable impact on us and we continue to exercise this 'skill' throughout life.

Nonetheless, adaptability in humans is remarkable. We see people coping with some incredibly difficult circumstances in life, such as wars, famines, having families and attending university. Adaptation is a kind of change process that involves some kind of learning, that is, learning to think, perceive, believe or behave differently. But we all probably know at least some people who have closed themselves to learning. Old age is the archetypal setting for rigidity. There is a common caricature of the rigid crotchety old man who complains about 'progress' and who clings desperately to what he is familiar with. But his way of being in the world is only a few steps away from the way many of us behave. We shrink from the fear of learning because of the vulnerability that learning would entail. Learning means making room for what is initially unknown, and the unknown is of potentially infinite size simply because it is unknown. This reminds me of a close friend who recently said, 'I feel now as though I spent many years living my life beside me and only now am I living inside my life'.

Now arrives the knight in shining armour – experiential learning – which seeks to re-connect the person participating in an event with the subjective experience, that is, with the impact on the person who has the experience of the event. Therefore that event becomes an experience that can be learned from. As outlined in the Introduction, the focus in experiential learning is very different from that taken in didactic (lecture-based) learning. Didactic learning rests in part on an assumption that all participants will learn much the same as each other from the lecture. After all, examinations are the same for all participants. On the other hand, experiential learning is based in part on the assumption that each participant will have a unique experience and will probably learn different things from the same event. This view is sometimes called the 'constructivist' view, in that there is an assumption that each person *constructs* a unique internal picture from the concrete or external events.

The long-term effect of each person learning differently is that each person will develop in different ways from the others; the process of human growth and development will occur differently for each participant. Perhaps then, at the core of understanding both learning and human growth and development is the need to understand ways in which human beings collaborate or interact with their environments in order to co-construct a path of learning. The experiential learning group is a specialized part of the total environment in which human learning and growth occur and so I will focus in the next part on the way in which people 'construct' their experience. Before that, it seems useful to name some of the underpinning assumptions or premises on which this chapter rests.

The first premise is that human beings develop and therefore change as they get older. Each stage of development is partly underpinned by the ones that occur before it, regardless of the particular view of human development that one subscribes to. For example, a child is unlikely to learn to read before it learns to speak because the language that is spoken needs to make sense to the child before he or she learns the additional skills required for reading. Otherwise, the symbols on the page make no sense other than to create sounds that in themselves have no meaning. There are many excellent works on human development and their content will not be replicated here. For instance, Erik Erikson used Freudian views of psychosexual development as a basis for a theory of human development through life (Tyson and Tyson 1990). My own views are strongly influenced by what I would call psychodynamic theories, and the core assumptions that I have taken from some of these developmental frameworks are the following:

- There is interdependence between physiological development, the development of cognition and language, the development of emotional maturity, and the development of the ability to interrelate with the world.

- Adequate development is stimulated and supported through interaction with a 'good enough' physical and emotional environment.

- Risk and experiential learning are inseparable; it is necessary to take the risk to feel the impact of events in order to learn from them. Having a 'good enough' environment supports risk taking.

- In normal development, depending on societal conditions, most people pass through the same types of developmental steps, albeit at different ages. However, taking too far the assumption that human development is sequential is unhelpful because of the inevitable variation that occurs between individuals and societies (Applegate and Bonovitz 1995).

- Failure to achieve a developmental step will have an effect on how well subsequent steps are achieved, although it is possible to re-visit successfully some missed steps after they would have normally been achieved.

- Everybody forms a unique view of themselves and of the world in which they live. This view changes with subsequent experience and is the major influence on how people relate to all aspects of the world.

These assumptions underpin the other frameworks outlined in this book, but are not stated explicitly again. The last assumption links with the earlier discussion on experiential learning and leads to the view that individual experience is largely subjective. This view provides an essential underpinning for working with groups and so is further explored below.

Science and certainty or subjectivity and uncertainty?

For some of the people described in the wombat story the van ran over and killed a wombat. For some others it did not. Who was 'right?' Robert 'knew' that a wombat had been killed, but the instructors were not convinced. Everyone was in the same van, but not everyone had the same view of what was real.

So different things are 'real' for different people and there is not *one* reality that exists independently of the persons who perceive any particular event. This subjectivity means that members of groups have their own different ways of interacting at any moment in the life of a group. Therefore a leader cannot predict with any certainty what any one person will experience, perceive or do in any given situation. As a result, group phenomena cannot be explained in a way that enables leaders to predict and control what happens in their groups. Rather, an understanding of group phenomena enables the leader to create tentative understanding of what is happening and to experiment with means of improving the situation. This is a 'constructivist' approach where the goal is to gain understanding rather than control. Some of the understanding is achieved in the moment as the group evolves, but some is achieved by reflecting on group events afterwards.

What is more, our understanding of any particular event will change as time elapses after the event. This is because learning from experience changes the way that we view events in our past (Freeman 1993).

If we acknowledge the amazing diversity of experience that occurs for group participants we can do little more than work alongside group members to help them to derive useful understanding from the events for themselves. To achieve this, we need to retain our own curiosity about the dynamic that is unfolding in the group. Curiosity provides the oil that lubricates the development of understanding (Cecchin 1987). Loss of curiosity or loss of the ability to reflect on the experience of self or others creates a stuckness that limits the leader's ability to update continually his or her understanding of the evolution of events in the group. As leaders we need to have ideas about what is happening in our groups but we cannot afford to become so attached to our ideas that we become closed to other possibilities. This requires a lot of emotional maturity on our part.

I like Timo Lehtonen's words that follow. Timo is a Finnish outdoor adventure leader, writer and trainer who thinks deeply about what he does.

> The instructor is not an all-knowing guru, but a secure fellow traveller who is himself searching and learning, not controlling the ability of others to assimilate his insights. The work of an instructor is not primarily that of explaining or interpreting but allowing space and enabling situations. The solutions are found within the group and its members and cannot thus be in the back pocket of the instructor, waiting for some suitable moment to be pulled out. (Lehtonen 1998, p.96)

Is subjectivity the only way to see things?

Subjectivity is a powerful approach to the moment-by-moment life of groups, but knowledge that has been scientifically validated is also useful in providing frameworks for our thinking. Knowledge in the form of models, theories, and techniques helps the leader to make sense of events and to decide on what actions to take. Whether consciously or out-of-awareness, the leader compares his or her evolving experience of the group with his or her models and theories about groups. The difference between what is seen to be happening and what is intended to happen according to the mental model creates vital information that helps the leader to make useful decisions. The art in group work is to take account of knowledge that is based on scientific research and at the same time stay curious about what is happening at each moment in the life of the group. There is a need for the leader to take into account at least three sources of information and to integrate these. First, there is what seems like 'personal knowledge', then there is knowledge that has been learned from others and finally there is the sensory data: information that is gained through seeing, hearing, smell, intuition, and so on.

When the van stopped and all but two of the group participants ran back down the road to look at what George, Daniel and Amy all believed to be an illusory wombat, the three leaders did not have adequate models and theories for understanding what was happening. How is it possible for an illusion to catch on so quickly in a group? Only one person claimed that the van had hit a wombat but almost instantly nearly every other participant acted as though it was true – based only on one person's impression.

Our conventional views of sanity, reality, illusion and madness simply did not fit this situation and so Amy, George and Daniel were left adrift with no means of making sense of this event.

Harwood (1998) offers an excellent explanation of the subjective nature of group members' experience and so how group therapists need to respond. She first describes Lewin's idea that each group member's perception could at times be seen merely as re-experiencing of old relationships. Harwood states that in Lewin's view, group members' interactions are

> based on old, genetic, historical distortions, which are contraposed against an *actual, correct* group reality with the therapist usually acting as judge and jury. That, however, differs greatly from the concept of intersubjectivity, which would accord validity to each participant's subjective point of view. Thus, every member's contribution (regardless of what it is) is accepted as important and valid because it brings out a particular subjective point of view which is organized around previous experience. This subjective organization of experience calls for understanding and analysis from the group therapist, not judgement. Therefore there is no need for the therapist to intervene with pronouncements on objective reality. The group members, of course, present a collection of individual subjective realities – not objective realities. Objective reality may only exist in mathematics. (Harwood 1998, p.34)

The scientific method – which usually seeks to find objective reality – has led to great advances in many fields. There are a great number of studies based on scientific method that have helped group work specialists to progress in the development of theory and practice. An excellent summary of some of these models appears in Tyson (1998). My difficulty with the purist scientific approach to groups is that there is an implicit assumption that whatever 'truth' is discovered from experiments, it will have validity for a number of people from different backgrounds and in different settings. Furthermore, experimental science is based on the premise that findings from one study can be applied to other situations so as to re-create the outcomes that were found in the situation that was originally studied. The development and widespread adoption of Tuckman's stages of group development – forming, norming, storming and performing – is an interesting example of how 'science' has led to the adoption of a model that may not be accurate in many situations (McCollom 1995a). Tuckman himself acknowledged that the model may not apply to many different kinds of group, but the search for explanation combined with a non-critical view of scientific method meant that these warnings were not heeded by enough people to prevent the Tuckman model from becoming a widely accepted 'truth'. Experimental science at its best provides results that are proven to be valid and that validity is reassuring to many people. We can be reassured by experimental evidence that some phenomena occur regularly with a high probability. What we cannot derive from these studies is the certainty that any particular phenomenon will occur in any particular group at any particular time.

Heli Clarke, another Finnish experiential educator whose thinking appeals to me asks some pertinent questions about how we know what to do *in each moment as it evolves* in the group.

> Where do you turn when you are standing in the middle of your group and you know that you have to make a decision – and you have to make it now? What can you rely on then: your own crystal-clear understanding of your aims as an adventure instructor? Or do you close your (mental) eyes, make a random choice and hope for the best? Or will you frantically try to think what your trainer would say in this situation? Do you choose the activity which happens to feel nicest at the moment? Or the one that has always worked before? One of the most important criteria for the professional competence of an adventure instructor is that (s)he can in the field, in the heat of adventure, choose those activities which best lead him or her and his or her group towards the set goal. (Clarke 1998, pp.59–60)

A further unspoken assumption that underlies much of the writing and research in the 'classical' physical and biological sciences is that passion detracts from reason. Researchers and writers are told to be 'objective' so that they do not become biased. This requirement is based on the belief that it is possible to observe a situation and to provide a description of that situation that could be exactly replicated by any other 'objective' observer. This supposition is derived from the view that human perception is universal and does not vary from person to person. I strongly disagree with this simplistic view that we all see, notice, remember and describe the same thing when we observe the same event. To cite an example, the radically different perception gained by the people in the van that did/did not hit the wombat flies in the face of claims that all observers perceive the same thing from witnessing the same event.

It is the variability in the way that humans perceive, place their attention, and make meaning from events that itself leads to the complexity of group life. So, the experience of being in or leading a group cannot be objective. In every moment there is a mêlée of emotions, ideas and actions that is different for each participant. This mêlée may or may not correspond to what is experienced by the group leader.

Therefore, the development of our capacity to lead groups cannot occur as an objective science – we need to integrate reason and passion rather than amputate passion. We need not to search for the illusion of objectivity, but to seek a clearer understanding of how our subjectivity affects what we notice, value and recall. Although I am not a psychoanalyst, I find many of the principles underpinning psychoanalysis to be very helpful in the study of groups. Claudio Neri describes some aspects of psychoanalysis that can be useful also to the general study of groups:

> The psychoanalytic method diverges from classical doctrine and develops a different approach to knowledge.
>
> Psychoanalysis regards passion as a form of knowledge. Consequently, it is not centred around the problem of the clash between passion and knowledge, but, rather, concentrates on the conditions which allow a passionate, participating observer to reach into knowledge.
>
> What is more, psychoanalysis does not separate knowledge from the process that the subject who knows has to face. Rather, it maintains that the person undergoes a substantial transformation during the cognitive process which he himself has started by taking part in the analytic situation. (Neri 1998, p.108)

I would like to replace the word 'psychoanalysis' with the phrase 'this approach to learning about groups' and then Neri's passage would capture more elegantly the essence of what I want to emphasize than do my own words.

In summary, group leaders can use scientific knowledge to assist in developing hypotheses about specific events as they occur, but need to remain well aware that they do not *know* with any degree of certainty what is going on at any time. I seek to model this approach as I accompany you through this book. I am more interested in accompanying others on a journey of exploration than I am interested in telling them where to go or where they are going.

Subjectivity in more detail

Life is an interpretive process where each event evokes in us the need to make sense of what has just happened or create meaning from the event. This making sense, or making meaning, involves more than just the rational activity of processing information. It calls on our deeply held patterns of interpreting events. In this 'age of information' we are often encouraged to think that human beings simply receive information in the form of energy – light, sound, heat, chemical reactions (taste and smell) – and then process that information. In this view, having duly processed, we create a form of communication to others. This mechanistic view is comforting in its simplicity but adds no sense or meaning to our experience of the world (Power and Brewin 1997). The facts of this energy/information exchange model of communication are difficult to dispute but the model does not help in our continual quest to create meaning from events around us. The information-processing model of human experience omits the biological needs and desires; it fails to address our needs for social contact; and it does not take into account the developmental nature of human lives. We need models that integrate the bodily experience, human interaction, the process of interpretation and the individuality of subjective experience.

For example, we need to have some ideas about what changes information into meaning. What enables humans to use information to make sense? What is it about the human experience that evokes the need to make meaning from the constant stream of events that make up life? Perhaps the next step in this exploration is to look at how each person's personal *history* affects his or her current ways of perceiving *current* events, that is, how for each of us our life experience creates a set of screens or filters that prevent us from noticing certain aspects of events that happen in the world around us. How is it that our personal history leads us to pay attention to some things but not to others? Putting it bluntly, the history of what we have already been exposed to, and also allowed ourselves to notice, affects what we are able to notice in the present and in the future.

'Creating our own experience': another chicken and egg situation?

The idea that human perception is subjective could lead us quickly into troubled waters. In this text box I will follow one of the difficulties:

Our experience of ourselves and our relationship to the world shapes who we are. But there is a difference between what happens to us and *our experience of what happens to us*. So the very thing that shapes us is already mediated or affected by the influence of our history in selecting only certain aspects of events to include in what we actually notice. That is, we take an active part in constructing our experience and so we take an active part in constructing *the very thing that affects our development as human beings*. (Here I need to emphasize that whilst we take an active part in constructing our experience, that is very different from taking a *deliberately* active part in the process. For most people, the activity of constructing their experience of events occurs outside their awareness.)

If all of this (i.e. our action in constructing our experience from events) occurs outside our awareness, then we could say that we are trapped in a pre-determined route to self-hood where our conscious selves are mere passengers on a train that is already set on one particular destination. That is, our history determines what we experience then each subsequent experience keeps the same filters in place and so we do not notice what we do not notice. We cannot notice the filters themselves and so we cannot do anything about them. Therefore, our personality is largely determined by the kinds of filters that we have in very early life. Once the train starts to travel in our infancy we have no longer got any choice about who we become. Not a nice thought, and if I believed this, the book would end here.

What other possibilities are there? We could argue either that (a) our history does not influence how we experience events or (b) that we are in control of the mechanisms that determine what we notice and therefore what we experience or (c) it is OK and we will just go on the ride or (d) free will can take an active role in influencing at least some of the 'templates' that we have in place for determining what we experience from events.

I like the latter idea myself.

Experience is comparative

Experience is fundamentally comparative. Each new experience is compared to others and to expectations of how events of any particular type 'should' be experienced. This process of comparison enables the person to make sense or meaning from each event. The activity of comparing depends both on the cognitive structures that the person uses to make the comparison and also on the repertoire of memories that have been accumulated about similar experiences.

The evolution of cognitive structures

An example of a cognitive structure is the ability to think symbolically. For a tiny baby there is no difference between the 'real' mother and the baby's thinking about the mother. The 'object' and the symbol for the object are not differentiated. However, as cognitive structures develop, the child becomes capable of creating a mental symbol (such as a word) for the mother and retains the knowledge that the symbol-for-mother and the 'real' mother are different. Communication is impossible without the capacity for symbolism – but that is another topic. (For more information see Ashbach and Schermer 1987; Fonagy 1999; McDougall 1993; Stapley 1996.)

The cognitive structures change over time and in this way can be called 'developmental' but development is not a linear and predictable process at all. Even when we have in place – in adulthood for example – the cognitive structures for symbolism, some stressful events temporarily prevent these cognitive structures from functioning. For example, the early unsophisticated ways that a baby has of making sense of events remain with us and we revert to using these 'primitive' processes at times in the stressful context of groups. The most prevalent of these primitive processes is a means of managing our anxiety by 'splitting'. Splitting sometimes involves separating good from bad and attributing all that is bad to a person other than oneself. All of what is seen to be good is then attributed to ourselves. This saves feeling confused and anxious when a person who is significant to us (such as the mother in early life) is potentially perceived as both good and bad at the same time. (Halton (1994) provides an excellent summary of Melanie Klein's contribution to this field of theory.)

So human development itself is a fickle path that makes our interpretation of events decidedly unpredictable. The collection of memories that provides the raw data for interpretation of current events is also somewhat fickle. What is remembered, for example? What kind of memories do we use as a basis for comparison? Do we only access for comparison the memories that we can call to conscious awareness? Do we have a set of memories that influence our interpretation of events yet remain beyond conscious recall? (See Epstein 1991; Marrone 1998; Schacter 1996.)

What are the factors that influence which memories we retain and which we lose? Marrone describes the idea that some forms of memory, such as memories of specific episodes, are less likely to remain available for conscious recall than other types of memory. He also suggests that our ability to recall is influenced by our early development. Freeman (1993) has written a whole book that explores the way in which subsequent life experiences change the way in which people recall and describe their earlier lives. So memories too are fickle rather than 'factual'. (For more on this topic, see the interlude about memory systems in Chapter 4.)

Response to words and concepts

Earlier I mentioned that I found useful many of the ideas derived from psychoanalysis. But the mere mention of psychoanalysis or of 'the unconscious' may create a difficulty. I expect that as you read these words you will have some intuitive or emotional reaction to them. What do you associate with the idea of 'unconscious'? Do you have an unconscious part of your mental functioning? If so, is this scary, exciting, neutral or something else? What do you think resides in your unconscious – dark repressed aspects of yourself that are too shameful to show in the light of day, or just 'stuff' that your conscious mind does not have time to deal with?

Whatever your answers, when you apply the word 'unconscious' to yourself I expect that you do *interpret* the meaning of the word. The potential for this interpretation existed before I asked you questions about what 'unconscious' means to you. In other words, you have ready, in the 'back of your mind' a set of codes that you call upon to interpret each event when the relevant stimulus occurs. These out-of-awareness codes for interpreting your experience are described in the next chapter as 'working models'.

But what exactly happens in our minds when we create associations like the one that you just created in response to the word 'unconscious'? What is the process that enables us to react to words and ideas? This associative process is important because it is at the heart of what occurs in groups. When a phrase, or evidence of an event, arrives via one of our senses, we compare this stimulus with our prior experience. This comparison can be thought of as an association of one thing with many others. So our history, our prior experience, provides a kind of template on which all further experiences are laid. The degree of fit or mis-fit provides us with further information. So the stimulus from outside is, on its own, not really information. What 'informs' us is the *relationship* between what data arrives and what existed before in our awareness (or in our unconscious). Of course the context in which this new event occurred is also an essential factor in this interpretive process.

The analogy of a biochemical enzyme springs to mind. An enzyme has a particular shape that will only link with chemicals that have a complementary shape. A million chemicals can be present in a fluid and a particular enzyme will not be affected. Yet as soon as the correct chemical approaches the enzyme, the two connect and a chemical reaction begins. In this simile a new event in our lives is represented by the chemical and the enzymes represent our set of preconceptions built from prior experience. When a new event occurs it creates a response only if it links with the pattern that already existed in our internal templates. Conversely, when an event does not link in any way with our prior experience it escapes us without creating an emotional response or possibly without our even becoming consciously aware of that event. It is important to avoid over-simplification through the use of this simile though. Unlike an enzyme, the templates we use have much more than just physical characteristics. They have visual, auditory, emotional, verbal and symbolic components.

These ideas suggest that not only do different people react differently to different events, but also that some events are not even noticed by some people because their pre-existing conceptual maps of the world do not have room for the existence of these events. We will see later that there may be a second reason for a person not to notice an event. This other form of not noticing occurs when acknowledgement of the event would create unbearable anxiety in the subject. Now I am saying that you do not even notice a whole lot of what goes on around you! How do you respond to that idea? Does it link closely enough with ideas that you already have, or is it so foreign that you need to reject it? Whatever way you responded to the paragraphs above, you did so based on what you *already believed*. So what you already believe sets limits on what new things you are now prepared to believe. This could be seen to be a bleak picture, as described in the earlier text box 'Creating our own experience'. We could think, 'Here am I trapped by my preconceptions in an endless loop where I reject beyond my awareness anything that could change the way I view myself'. Fortunately, our patterns of interpreting do change, and a part of this book involves an exploration of the way in which experiences in groups can change our habitual patterns of perceiving and interpreting.

The assumptions underpinning the scientific method in the modern western world have become so entrenched that they have become 'truths'. Western cultures have lost some of their capacity for symbolism. We seldom acknowledge that our perception of all events is very subjective because we tend to mistake our perception of the event for the event itself. As a result, it has become relatively difficult to maintain conscious awareness that every person's experience of every event is different from every other person's experience of the same event. The loss of this awareness has potentially disastrous consequences for group leaders and for group participants. This is because effective participation in groups depends on every participant being able to conceive that their own perception is not an absolute 'truth' but merely a subjective set of perceptions that is necessarily different from the perceptions of others. A great deal of the power of groups to create growth in participants can be harnessed by using the obvious differences in partici-pants' response to any event as information about the participants. Different views on what happened and what it meant can evoke awareness about the individuals themselves, rather than fuelling an argument about who was right and who was wrong. Rather than difference of perception becoming a source of conflict, it can become a source of information about the perceiver him or herself.

In summary of what has been covered so far: first, our histories have a substantial impact both on our noticing of events around us and on the way that we interpret these events. Second, some of our interpretation of events occurs fully within our awareness, some occurs at the edge of our awareness, and some occurs completely beyond our awareness. Third, our interpretive templates change, and experiences in groups can be powerful influences towards changing these templates. The work of John Bowlby and subsequent 'attachment' theorists provides a useful conceptual map for understanding how prior experience influences our interpretation of current events. In particular the idea that each of us is guided by 'internal working models' provides a useful window on human experience that helps to understand individual interaction in groups.

Other models for linking prior experience with interpretation of current events

Hundreds, if not thousands, of theoreticians and researchers have written about how a person's life experience influences the way in which they 'perceive, believe and act'. Although in this book I focus on Bowlby's attachment theory, this does not exclude some of these other theories. Each approach adds useful perspectives and has its strength in certain areas. For instance, neuro-linguistic programming practitioners describe the way in which 'anchors' are retained in our bodies and even physical touch to certain parts of our bodies can directly evoke memories (Bandler and Grinder 1975). Morenian role theorists (who practise psychodrama, sociodrama, role training and sociometry) describe human development in terms of the development of an integrated set of 'roles'. These roles include elements of thinking, feeling, action and context (Williams 1989). Psychosynthesis is based in part on a similar idea to Morenian role theory, but rather than roles, 'sub-personalities' are described as the organizing principle (Ferrucci 1986). Jungian psychoanalysis focuses, amongst other things, on the capacity for symbolic communication (Kast 1992), and on the development of anima and animus – the feminine and masculine aspects of each person's personality (Boyd 1991). There are many more models, theories and hypotheses about how experience and human development shape human perception. The book *Maps of the Mind* provides an outstanding overview of many of them (Hampden-Turner 1982).

I believe that no matter how much of a purist anybody claims to be in a specific model or theory, everyone is influenced by a wide range of views, models and theories. Sometimes I think that the most significant driver for most people in their choice of theories is their personal preferences in life. Rather than our stepping back in a dispassionate way and scanning the conceptual world for suitable models to inform our work, we are simply drawn by our unconscious yearnings toward certain models and we are repelled by others. This certainly seems true for me in my own choice of models and theories.

Technique

I have suggested in this chapter that each person in a group has a completely unique internal reality and that no one can predict with any certainty how any group member will respond to any event in the group. This leaves a great deal unknown! One could well ask, 'What *do* we know then, and what can we do in such an uncertain situation?' My response is that we can have access to information about what is happening for ourselves and that is very useful information indeed. We will see later in this book that, in the role of group leader in particular, our thinking, feeling and intuition provide us with vital information about what is occurring in the group. We will also see that whilst the timing, intensity and specific nature of any group member's experience cannot be predicted, there are useful ways of understanding group-level patterns of perceiving, believing and behaving.

The 'subjectivist' view of groups frees us from the illusion that leaders are in control of the group. We can see our interactions with the group in a new light: as influence rather than control. We can interact with the group in a way that is intended to evoke responses rather than force responses. We can see ourselves as conductors of music rather than shepherds, pied pipers or military commanders.

Curiosity becomes a key attribute for group leaders who work in a subjectivist fashion. We are constantly asking ourselves, 'What is really going on here?' We become social scientists who, whilst knowing a lot about groups, know very little about the *specific group* that we are currently working with. We get a hunch about something occurring in the group, we try something, pay close attention to the response and then re-develop the hunch or 'hypothesis' about what is going on. We pay close attention to the way in which our own personal history influences us to pay attention to some things and not others. We keep attempting to guess what the group looks like to each of the participants, and not just to us. We remain *curious* (Cecchin 1987).

Other reading on related topics

R. D. Laing (1971) in his book *Self and Others* provides a fascinating description of how humans experience themselves in relation to themselves and in relation to others. His discussion includes some fascinating and relatively readable descriptions of conscious and unconscious processes and the role of phantasy in interpersonal communication. This was the very first book that I read that excited me about being able to understand the nature of human experience. Julia Segal's (1985) book, *Phantasy in Everyday Life: A Psychoanalytical Approach to Understanding Ourselves* de-mystifies the idea of phantasy and other unconscious processes as they occur in normal life. It is an informative and readable book that requires only a basic psychological knowledge. Peter Senge's (1992) book *The Fifth Discipline: The Art and Practice of the*

Learning Organization has an excellent chapter on how 'mental models' – which are really working models – influence our behaviour. Chris Argyris's work on 'theories-in-use' and espoused theories is also helpful for those involved in organizational group work (Argyris 1993). *The Psychology of Interpersonal Perception* by Perry Hinton (1993) has some useful material from a sociological perspective about how individuals attribute meaning to the characteristics of others. This includes some discussion about Kelly's personal construct theory.

CHAPTER 2

Internal working models

Introduction

This chapter outlines a way of understanding how people build and maintain 'internal working models' which are durable sets of expectations and beliefs about themselves and their place in the world. The framework used is derived from a field called attachment theory (Bowlby 1991a, 1991b, 1991c) and incorporates the idea that whilst early life experiences are vital in building personality and identity, later life experiences can also have a major impact. The concept of internal working models provides an excellent understanding of the way in which subjectivity – as described in the last chapter – is built and maintained. The implications of 'internal working models' for partici-pants in and leaders of groups are also examined.

Each person in a group relates to the group through their personal map of the world, through his or her internal working model. These internal working models are personal, individualized 'maps' of the way in which each person expects significant aspects of the world to interact with him or herself. Here is an illustration from the wombat story.

> On the first day of the journey, the van left from Gwendyup with some of the participants. They drove to Bogtown to pick up the others from the Bogtown Community Centre. Then they headed for Big Bluff on the way to Keyhole Cave Reserve. They had not been travelling long after leaving Bogtown before Amy and George felt the energy in the group start to turn quite negative. Initially Daniel was focusing on driving and reviewing in his mind the preparation, packing and equipment. He hoped that nothing had been left behind.

> Sean in particular wanted to stop at the shop in Big Bluff and was vocally resentful when at first Amy and George both said that the van would not stop, and later when Daniel simply drove through Bogtown without either stopping or commenting. Somehow, Sean seemed to be charismatic

enough to effortlessly bring the rest of the group around to his way of seeing. In particular, Clive, Katrina and Jack grumbled loudly about the meanness of the leaders and how, if the whole trip was going to be like this, it would be a 'bummer'. By the time the van reached Keyhole Cave Reserve the mood amongst the group was as dark as the weather, with imminent rain threatening. Daniel, Amy and George felt themselves strongly affected and struggled to maintain a façade of good humour.

Using the terminology of internal working models, it seems that Sean has a working model about 'leaders' that they are withholding and will not provide him with what he wants. This is a part of the whole complex array of mental representations about the world around him that make up his working model about the world. It also seems that he has a corresponding mental representation about himself that he is deprived and not adequately cared for. His overall working model of himself and the world around him will consist of many such components and will have been built up from his real life experience, all mediated by the way in which he understood and remembered his experience.

Each aspect of the world is the subject of one or more working models. 'The term "working model" can be used to denote all the representations about the world and ourselves in it that we build in the course of experience, including people, places, ideas, cultural patterns, social structures and so on' (Marrone 1998, p.72). For instance, each person has a working model that includes expectations of how families should work: '...there are specialized forms of working model which can be defined as a set of conscious and unconscious notions about oneself as a person and the other as a significant figure in one's life' (Marrone 1998, p.72). These specialized working models describe to ourselves the durable expectations about how other people will relate to us. For instance, Sean's charismatic style may emerge from his need to experience his peers – who, in the original family are brothers and sisters – to be strongly aligned with him. Therefore, he acts in ways that effectively coerce those around him to 'be on his side'. I also think that we develop working models about the natural environment and what it means to us. Although Bowlby (one of the originators of attachment theory) focused primarily on interpersonal working models I think that those who work with people in the outdoors could benefit from understanding more about how our subjects develop useful working models about the natural environment (Ringer 1996a; Ringer and O'Brien 1997).

Attachment theory summary

Attachment theory provides two excellent aids to understanding groups. First, the idea of internal working models helps us to understand how people respond in groups. Internal working models are explored in the main text of this book. Second, some understanding of the way that different 'patterns of attachment' influence group member's behaviour helps us in deciding what to do as we lead groups. But let us start from the beginning…

The main tenets of attachment theory are the following.

From birth, the infant's innate need for social contact, safety and security is met initially by only a few key people in his or her life. The mother figure, the father figure and other people who are often with the infant both initiate contact with and respond to the infant. The quality of these interactions *as experienced by the infant* leads him or her to build a generalized set of expectations about 'how people interact with me in different kinds of situation'. To the infant, these expectations are not experienced as being chosen, they are experienced as being the only possibility. (That is, the infant has no concept of his or her own subjectivity.) In particular, the infant, and later, the child, builds a sense of:

- how much emotional and physical *safety and security* there is available through these 'attachment figures'

- how *sensitive* the attachment figures are to the child's needs

- how *responsive* attachment figures are to his or her needs (Main 1995).

Thus, the child builds durable patterns of expectations both about him or herself and about the nature of the human context in which he or she lives. It must be emphasized that these expectations on the part of the child are just as much based on his or her subjective experience as they are on what might be seen by an observer. It is patterns of experiencing on the part of the infant and subsequently the child that builds the attachment representation (Ringer 2000).

As a result of early life experiences, the child builds either a secure pattern of attachment or an insecure pattern and this pattern is carried into adult life, whilst being constantly modified by maturation and new life experiences. Thus, at any time in life a person can be said to have a predominant attachment style.

Secure attachment is characterized by the subject having a durable expectation that people will be responsive, that the world is primarily a safe place, and that the subject is a 'good' and likeable person.

Insecure attachment patterns have two main sub-categories with two additional strategies. The 'dismissing' pattern of attachment is characterized by subjects minimizing or turning their attention away from their feelings because they take extreme measures to avoid noticing any evidence that they themselves or the world around them might be a source of disappointment or pain. They often tend to idealize the world and other people in order to avoid potential distress. Dismissing patterns are often accompanied by the dominance of thinking over feeling (Crittenden 1995).

Conversely, subjects with 'preoccupied' patterns of attachment tend to maximize or get lost in their difficulties with their own emotional experience. Both coherence and thinking tend to be reduced and feelings are maximized. Trauma and loss often evoke in the subject another kind of insecure attachment described as 'unresolved'. In such cases the subject tends to be fearful and not particularly coherent, with regard to loss or trauma. Unresolved loss or trauma can occur in addition to dismissing or preoccupied patterns of attachment. Sometimes people use both dismissing and preoccupied patterns of attachment because they oscillate between the two strategies (Crittenden 1995).

In summary, all patterns of attachment can be seen as strategies or defence mechanisms for dealing with the difference between individuals' *need* for safety and security as well as sensitivity and responsiveness from others, and their *experience* of the world in terms of what is available.

Attachment patterns in groups

Any enactment of the pattern of insecure attachment has the function of being a defence against anxiety and pain. So in groups, when events evoke anxiety participants with patterns of insecure attachment will tend to revert to the strategies that protect them from pain. Dismissing patterns appear as over-rationalization, and dismissing of the impact of difficult events in the group. Preoccupied patterns appear as unmanageable emotional responses that almost hold the participant hostage, with a corresponding inability to think and to 'move on'. These patterns of attachment may appear in relation to different parts of the group. For some participants, other group members may evoke specific attachment-related responses. For others, the leader will be the most significant attachment figure. Additionally, many participants will have a mental representation of the group-as-a-whole that is coherent enough to fulfil the function of an attachment figure, and so these participants will enact in relation to the group their habitual patterns of attachment.

For further reading on attachment, a comprehensive book on attachment theory is Cassidy and Shaver (1999) *Handbook of Attachment: Theory, Research, and Clinical Applications*, and Françoise Ringer's PhD study on early attachment and eating disorders (2000) includes a very readable summary of attachment theory.

Each person's working models will be different from everyone else's because each person's experience of the world they lived in is different from that of the others. So each person will have built different expectations of significant relationships and what they mean. The individualized set of working models that each person builds is the mechanism by which people build and maintain their individual subjectivity, as described in Chapter 1. This very individualized building of our own 'maps' of the world is further complicated by the fact that any person can have different working models of the same thing so that their *own* different models may clash. This does not make rational sense, but the co-existence of contradictory working models occurs because these models are 'stored' in different parts of our memories. These different types of memory are described in more detail in an interlude in Chapter 4 because they influence how we learn about groups and relationships.

The importance of working models for us as we work with groups is that each person's working models affect what they notice, what they perceive, what they believe and how they relate to others. So, the working model of relationships is the template for relating and making meaning from relating. These templates provide a major influence on the individual's behaviour in any group. Attachment theorists focused primarily on how working models affected interpersonal behaviour, and many others have also suggested that our experiences in our original families provide a durable template of expectations about interaction in groups and our place in that interaction (Williams 1989). For example, a person who was raised in a family where conflict was suppressed or avoided is likely to have developed internal working models that lead them to be acutely uncomfortable when conflict occurs in any group of which they are a member. Sean, in the example above, may well have lived in a family where coercive behaviour was the norm and so his internal working model of family life (and now, group life) might be that successful interaction in a group depends on being an emotionally coercive leader.

Sean was in an 'adventure therapy' group because it had been identified by his social worker that his behaviour was destructive to himself and to others around him. If his social worker used the language of attachment theory he might have said that he would like to see 'Sean's internal working models for group interaction changed'. In other words, the processes of learning and personal change involve the change of working models. In fact there are forms of psychotherapy that primarily work with eliciting and helping the client to evolve working models (Marrone 1998). Other forms of therapy, such as narrative therapy, also affect working models although the language used by narrative therapists is not the same as that used in attachment theory.

But referring again to Sean, at the time he was introduced to the adventure therapy programme, his pre-existing internal working models created limitations to his perception of himself and the world so that he *could not see* the need to change. How then can anyone work constructively with him in order to engender change? This is a significant issue for all leaders who work with groups for personal change. That is, whilst anyone's internal working model evolves over time in response to that person's perception of events in the world, *the pre-existing working model limits what the individual perceives.* So the early evolution of a particular form of working model limits the possibilities for the direction that future working models may take. This is because the pre-existing model acts as a self-confirming filter through which events in the world are noticed, interpreted and remembered. Marrone provides a useful summary of some of these ideas:

> As Peterfreund puts it, from childhood to adulthood we understand the world through our constantly changing working models. We each interpret existing information in our own way, selecting and processing it to arrive at our particular view of the world, our individual 'reality'. It is through these interpretations that information attains meaning. Our working models enable us to rearrange the world we know, to imagine new contributions and possibilities, to imagine how things would appear in different circumstances and to predict the possible consequences of action to be taken. If this model is to be successfully used in novel situations, it must be extended imaginatively to cover potential realities as well as experienced ones. Thus from which working models provide a platform to test and evaluate.
>
> We cannot approach any situation or fact as totally unbiased observers, free from the learning of the past. If we are always biased observers, then the problem is to see whether it is possible to be biased only to an optimal degree and whether our biases can be modified by experience.

Internal working models show a strong propensity for stability and self-perpetuation. However, they are not fixed templates. They are not exact copies or 'photographs' of other people or interpersonal events. (Marrone 1998, pp.73–74)

The challenge for group leaders is then to enable participants to have experiences that lead them to re-consider their existing working models. Events in groups must provide evidence that can be perceived through existing working models that disturbs the stability of the existing dysfunctional working models held by any particular participant. Sean would need to have an experience that resulted in his experiencing his coercive behaviour not working in his own favour.

An example of internal working models as seen in a group

The impact of working models in groups can be illustrated by a hypothetical example:
This scene occurs hundreds of times each day in many countries around the world. It is the beginning of a group meeting.

A door opens into an empty room and a person enters, turns on the lights and begins to arrange chairs in a circle. A few minutes later two others arrive, greet the first person and sit down. Soon, all but two of the chairs are occupied and everyone present is sitting quietly as if waiting for something to happen.

This new micro-social system is a place in which, inevitably, individuals' existing working models are reactivated and brought into play. In this way,

Each person sitting in the room brings with them a complex set of working models about how they and the world work, or do not work, together. This group has been meeting once a week for five weeks. This is the 'follow-on' programme for an experiential programme for Vietnam veterans who have been diagnosed as suffering from post-traumatic stress disorder (PTSD). They are drawn to the group by the need for personal healing and by the need for belonging. Over the weeks that they have been meeting they have developed a new micro-social system (Marrone 1998) with a primary task of assisting its members to lead useful and satisfying lives in the wider community.

each group member presents different notions and ideas, different percep-tions and ways of understanding the world. These are manifested implicitly or explicitly. These notions, ideas, and so on, can refer to a wide range of themes, subjects, ideologies and areas of knowledge. (Marrone 1998, p.169)

Each individual reacts according to his [or her] own working models, but these may differ from those of other group members. These differences are

---

The participants in this group developed working models during their early lives and adolescence and then suddenly they left their usual world to enter the arena of war. For each of them, one or more sudden traumatic events occurred that completely shattered their core working models. Life became meaningless and their sense of self was so damaged that on return to civilian life, they became unable to relate to others on a 'normal' basis. The new working models that they developed as a consequence of the trauma and post-trauma experience no longer adequately matched the commonly held working models of those in the community in which they lived. For them now, the world is an unpredictable and dangerous place and people are a threat unless they are familiar. Now, they sit together in a room. This evening (as always), each person's patterns of gesture or silence or speech will be generated from his or her current working models.

---

what may highlight their non-shared quality and demand updating and modification through confrontation, dialogue and negotiation. (Marrone 1998, p.169)

As we saw in the previous chapter, each person sitting in this room believes that his or her perception of the group, of other participants, and of the leader is valid, real and true. It follows then, that every action or phrase generated by each person has embedded in it that belief system or 'working model'. Some illustrations are shown in Table 2.1.

Table 2.1 An imaginary scene from a group as related to internal working models

What is spoken	A range of possible alternatives of internal working models held by Peter, a member of the group (Brackets indicate behavioural evidence of the existence of a working model rather than a working model in itself)
Peter says to Pamela, 'Pamela, you're always late to this group and that really pisses me off because you just waltz in here like a queen and disrupt the group with no apology or anything'.	The world is controllable and people are only late when they decide to be late. Transgressions of manners are OK if you apologize afterwards. Women do not treat men with respect. I, Peter, am not worthy of respect. All women constantly belittle me in front of others. Therefore women are dangerous.
Peter says to Charlie (the group leader), 'I think you should remove Pamela from this group because she is too disruptive'.	(Charlie is a person who is able to judge fairly and carry out disciplinary actions fairly.) (Charlie is punitive.) All men in authority are punitive. If I align myself with punitive people against an obvious 'enemy' like Pamela I will be safe from attack from the punitive one. Men in authority are incompetent and they need to be told – by me – what to do.

Some of the possibilities listed above contradict others. There is not enough evidence from either of Peter's short sentences to have a definitive knowledge of his working models but each of the above could form some guidelines for further exploration. The kind of working model that I might infer from Peter's discourse is likely to be different from the working model that you will infer because, even as observers of others, *our inferences about others are informed by our own working models.*

In the above example, it is very unlikely that Peter would reflect unaided on his interaction with either Pamela or Charlie. He is not very self-reflective and so he would be unlikely to come to the conclusion that his 'internalized representations of significant others has influenced his interaction in the group'! Peter is not unusual in that many participants in our groups lack the tendency to initiate self-reflection. This makes sense because self-reflection makes accessible memories that are intolerable. Cutting off of memories is a common psychological defence that results from trauma. The trouble is, the same process that is used to cut off intolerable memories also cuts off parts of self-awareness – including access to internal working models. If Peter is not willing or is not able to uncover his *own* working models, how can *we* as observers be so arrogant as to talk to each other about Peter when he himself is not aware of what he is doing? Anyway, how can he act in such a way and not be aware of what he is doing? Some tentative answers to these questions can be found in the next chapter's discussion on conscious, preconscious and unconscious processes.

Much of the interpretation that we place on the world is directly derived from aspects of our working models that lie outside our awareness. Using traditional language we could say that the patterns of expectations that form our working models are transferred to current situations and applied unconsciously. Chris Argyris outlines a view akin to that of working models in his 'ladder of inference'.

> The ladder of inference is a hypothetical model of how individuals make inferences. They begin by experiencing some relatively directly observable data, such as conversation. This is rung 1 of the ladder. They make inferences about the meanings embedded in the words (rung 2). They often do this in milliseconds, regardless of whether they agree with the meanings. Then they impose their meanings on the actions they believe the other person intends (rung 3). For example, they may attribute reasons or causes for the actions. They may also evaluate the actions as effective or ineffective. Finally, the attributions or evaluations they make are consistent with their theory-in-use about effective action (rung 4).

> If this model is a valid representation of the way individuals comprehend their everyday world, it should be relevant for designing and implementing research. (Argyris 1993, p.57)

Argyris's term, 'theory-in-use', corresponds in part to the term 'internal working model' that is used in the attachment literature. For Argyris (1993, p.65), '…there are two types of theories of action: espoused theories, those that people report or describe; and theories-in-use, those that people actually use to design and implement their actions'. Theories-in-use that do not appear also as espoused theories correspond to the unconscious aspects of internal working models. Espoused theories correspond to the conscious parts of internal working models.

We can see from the 'ladder of inference' and from the previous discussion on internal working models that the everyday process of inferring meaning from events is complex, has multiple steps and has many names depending on the author and his or her theoretical orientation. In psychodynamic psychology – which is the primary orientation chosen for this book – the most commonly used term for this process is 'transference' which refers to the transfer onto a current situation of patterns of expectations that are built from past experience. The term 'transference' is usually restricted in psychodynamic literature to refer to the unconscious transfer of expectations from parental figures onto current therapists or group leaders, but can be widened to refer to more general transfer of unconscious expectations from working models to current situations (Smith 1995). There is a risk that generalizing the concept of transference from its original formulation in the one-on-one therapeutic situation will dilute the original meaning of the word to the point that it is trivialized.

Controversy about use of the word 'transference'

Volumes have been written about the meaning and use of the word 'transference'. It seems to be one of the most controversial words in the psychodynamic literature. Some of the issues in the use of the word 'transference' are discussed by Ashbach and Schermer (1987) and Marrone (1998). Neri also cautions about using the word 'transference' in the group setting (Neri 1998, pp.20–21). Much of the discussion about transference centres on two issues: one relates to the extent to which transference needs to be completely unconscious or outside the awareness of the person who is 'transferring'. The other is the question of whether transference can occur in settings other than one-to-one. For instance can the word 'transference' be used to describe the transfer of a person's prior experience of *groups* onto a current experience of groups? I use the word roughly to mean 'the unconscious application of internal working models of the world to a wide range of current situations *involving relationships with others*'. For further discussion on the variation in the use of the word 'transference' see Bateman and Holmes (1995).

Transference is a phenomenon that involves unconscious interpersonal and intra-personal phenomena, including the projection of expectations that are built from past experience onto current situations. Projection involves a form of imaginative activity or phantasy (unconscious fantasy), but despite being informed by unconscious processes, is experienced subjectively as being real. Projections also form the basis for our interpretations of events. Projection is one of the many unconscious mechanisms that occur in interpersonal relations, and as a consequence, in groups. This family of phantasy-based processes is described in more detail in Chapter 6, but first the workings of different levels of consciousness and different communicative and symbolic processes are examined in the next few chapters.

A note on working models and implications for technique

The concepts of internal working models and subjectivity – as described in the previous chapter – fit together well. The language of internal working models helps us to understand the processes by which people can develop and maintain different conscious and unconscious views of themselves and the world that are different from the views held by others around them. When we are working with groups it can help to be able to look around and imagine that each person in the group is understanding each event in the group differently from how others are understanding each event. It is not helpful to assume that there is uniform understanding or meaning-making occurring in the group. It is certainly not helpful to assume that the meaning that *you* place on events in the group is the same as the meaning placed on those events, by everyone else in the group.

Accordingly, an essential task in group leadership is to develop an awareness of the kinds of working models that each participant might have. A second critical task in group leadership is to imagine constantly what meaning could be placed on each event and to scan the group for evidence of how each member might have interpreted events and patterns of events in the group. Thirdly, it is useful for group leaders to pay close attention to the meaning that they place on each event in the group and to check on what kinds of working model might evoke that meaning. The greater the leader's ability to access his or her internal working models or theories-in-use, the greater the flexibility of that leader.

Learning and change can be viewed as the process of changing internal working models. Therefore it can be helpful to ask oneself, 'What working

models am I enacting right now?' because the participants will be both consciously and unconsciously decoding your working models and checking to
see if they are worth adopting for themselves. Similarly, what working
models do you encourage in the group through your interventions? Again,
participants will be learning from your support or discouragement of the
working models that are being enacted by themselves and by other participants.

Finally, what we can easily see as resistance in groups may simply be one
or more participants resisting the adoption of internal working models that
are so far from their existing ones that they are intolerable. As group leaders
we need to pay attention to how far and how fast we are expecting our
participants to 'stretch'. Coercive and antagonistic behaviour on the part of
participants might be a result of our not acknowledging that we are trying to
move too far too fast for them to keep up.

CHAPTER 3

Conscious, preconscious and unconscious

No matter how low anyone's opinion of the unconscious may be, he must concede that it is worth investigating; the unconscious is at least on a level with the louse, which after all, enjoys the honest interest of the entomologist. (Jung 1968, p.18)

Introduction

In previous chapters I referred a number of times to 'the unconscious' and 'unconscious processes'. In this chapter I develop more fully the ideas related to different levels of consciousness. Common language about levels of consciousness is a bit different from the language that is used in the psychodynamic arena. For instance I have been asked a number of times in workshops, 'Don't you mean "sub-conscious" and not "unconscious"? What you're talking about is nothing like the experience of being knocked unconscious so why do you use the same word?' Good question. The short answer to that particular question is that I use the word 'unconscious' to mean both the *content* of what is outside conscious awareness and the (imaginary) *location in the mind* of where that kind of material is stored.

It is not possible to go very far into the exploration of how humans function before we are confronted with questions about the extent to which we are aware of everything that we see, hear, feel, think and imagine. In other words, to what extent are we aware of everything that goes on in our minds and to what extent are we aware of all of the sensory data that we receive? My opinion, and it has changed significantly over the years, is that there is a great deal that occurs in our minds that we are not aware of and a great deal of sensory data that we receive but do not become aware of. So we can gain a lot from working on the assumption that there are levels of mental functioning that occur beneath our awareness and from exploring the implications of this assumption. 'Out-of-awareness' functioning is generally referred to as the unconscious, although we will later introduce the notion of the preconscious which lies between conscious and unconscious. In the meantime, I will include both unconscious and preconscious in the term 'unconscious'.

Unconscious processes are of the utmost importance in determining the progress of groups of all kinds. Processes such as projection and projective identification – as described in following chapters – can only be understood in terms of unconscious functioning. Both projection and projective identification are central to group functioning. The sequence adopted in this chapter and the next three chapters is first to examine unconscious functioning in general and then, in Chapter 6, to examine in more detail specific unconscious processes. In Part 2 of the book we will apply this description of unconscious processes more thoroughly to expanding our understanding of how groups function. If you are already comfortable with your understanding of the role of the unconscious in projection, identification, projective identification, transference and countertransference and you are familiar with semiotic and symbolic processes in communication you may wish to skip the next three chapters.

In this and the next chapter both conscious and unconscious functioning are briefly examined by looking at what is involved in each, what purpose or function each part achieves and how each part of the system of the conscious operates in the overall business of human functioning. Some attention is also put into supporting the view that unconscious aspects of human functioning both exist and are significant in the overall scheme of being. Finally, I make some introductory remarks that point towards the main theme of this book, which is how unconscious processes operate in groups.

A micro-history of the concept of unconscious

Sigmund Freud was the first person to develop a full description of the mind that included both conscious and unconscious parts of our functioning. He was not the sole creator of the concept of 'unconscious' and his original ideas have been greatly extended and modified since he first put them forward. Freud himself developed not one, but three theories of human functioning, each of which included some ideas about the unconscious. One of his views of the unconscious is well summarized by Sandler, Dare and Holder who wrote about Freud's second phase of conceptualization of the mind:

> ... Freud assumed that there was a part of the mind – the 'mental apparatus'
> – which was conscious, and a further, substantial unconscious part. In this

connection, Freud distinguished between two sorts of unconsciousness – one, represented by a 'system' – the *Unconscious* – contained instinctual drives and wishes which, if they were allowed to emerge into consciousness would constitute a danger, a threat, and would give rise to anxiety or other unpleasant feelings. The strivings of the unconscious were seen as being constantly propelled towards discharge, but could only be allowed expression in a distorted or censored form. The other sort of unconsciousness was that attributed to the *Preconscious* system, and contained knowledge and thoughts which were outside consciousness but not held back by the counterforces of repression, as were the contents relegated to the Unconscious. Preconscious mental content could enter into consciousness at the appropriate time, and could be utilized by the individual not only for rational tasks but could also be seized upon by wishes from the Unconscious in their attempts to force a passage through to consciousness. (Sandler *et al.* 1973, pp.15–16)

It is important to remember that Freud wrote in times before systems theory, chaos theory, attachment theory, modern neuroscience and quantum mechanics and so his underpinning metaphors were based on Newtonian mechanics of cause and effect, and on the medical science of the day. As a result it is easy to criticize his generous use of the physical 'force and reaction' or 'hydraulic' metaphor. Despite not having modern ideas available at the time of formulation, many of his views remain significant today, which indicates that he was a remarkable thinker. Modern views of the unconscious remain based on some of Freud's original principles that the unconscious

- is a mental 'apparatus'
- contains both memories and desires or 'drives' that are repressed in order to keep the desires from being acted on, or the memories from entering consciousness because if they emerged into consciousness they would create excessive anxiety
- operates according to 'primary process' which is metaphoric and associative in its operation and is free from concepts of time, reality, conventional logic and rationality
- strongly influences what is accessible to the conscious mind
- affects our behaviour and perception without our being directly aware of its influence although we can sometimes notice the results of its influence.

In our wombat story, when the group arrived by van at Keyhole Cave
Reserve it was raining and the mood was somber. The leaders facilitated a
'warm-up' activity and then took the group caving. Very soon after entering
the caves Robert felt uncomfortable and wanted to go back to the surface.
Clive went along with him to keep him company. A short time later Vikki
and Sean also wanted to go back and this time Amy accompanied them to the
surface and stayed above ground with them for the duration of the activity.

Caves often appear in literature as metaphors for the unconscious and my
own experience is that being in a cave evokes a kind of feeling that is quite
different from being 'above ground'. The underground 'landscape' is
unfamiliar in terms of everyday life. The caver's world is fully enclosed and
everything that is outside the limited range of torches and lamps is visibly
dark and unknown. Often the sound of water provides a reminder of places
beyond the reach of vision. Even in small chambers, there is always an
awareness of passages that lead into and out of the place where one currently
sits or stands. The roof evokes images of tons of rock and earth above and for
some people, fantasies of the roof collapsing create unbearable anxiety.
Anxiety can also be evoked by fears of becoming lost in complex labyrinths
where all of the familiar landmarks of above-ground terrain are absent.
Always at the edge of group members' awareness is the knowledge that if the
groups' lights go out, there will be absolute darkness and that the probability
of escape under those conditions is very low. Images of danger are never far
away.

In terms of the unconscious, then, the caves create an evocative environment. It is no wonder that mythical goblins and trolls live in caves and that,
for instance, New Zealand Maori oral history is full of stories of both great
dangers and treasures that lie underground. The simplest analogy between
caves and human functioning is that the cave represents the repressed parts of
the unconscious mind and as such, presents a danger to those who explore
the depths. I am not suggesting that we necessarily explain this to group participants whom we take caving, but I do think that it is useful to notice who
becomes fearful in caves and to notice what in particular exacerbates their
fear and what alleviates it.

Perhaps then, Robert, Vikki, Clive and Sean had unconscious fears
evoked in them by being in the cave and wanted to avoid 'exploring the
unconscious'. This should only be treated as a hypothesis and not as a truth,
but it could have provided the group leaders with a useful form of inquiry.
After all, we see later in the story that Robert and Clive's behaviour created a

great deal of difficulty for leaders and for the group. In general terms then, we can ask ourselves how behaviour at an overt level is an indication of what is occurring at unconscious levels. The 'mapping' of unconscious processes onto language and behaviour provides us with a rich source of hypotheses about group participants – and ourselves.

The following section consists of an overview of the unconscious mind, with a brief mention of the conscious. Included in the following text is some exploration of the objections that have been raised to the view that the unconscious is a significant factor in determining human functioning. From my own experience I have some understanding of the reasons for these objections. I have in the past objected strongly to the idea that my own unconscious mind has a significant influence on what I perceive and how I act. I am aware that some readers may also be rather sceptical about the existence of the unconscious. Accordingly, I begin with a description of how I came to accept the importance of the unconscious myself, given that this acceptance has led to a much greater capacity to function as a group leader.

My own introduction to the unconscious

My own development of understanding about how groups function began with learning about the rational and conscious aspects of groups. That is, structural, rational and emotional aspects of groups – such as the need for group purpose, a pleasant environment and the more tangible signs that a group exists and is committed to working together (Johnson and Johnson 1991). However, this knowledge did not equip me to deal with the more challenging situations that I encountered in working with difficult group members and so I sought more skills. I made good progress through participating in an intensive experience of training in a particular form of 'action methods' that is usually described with the general name of 'psychodrama' (Moreno 1953; Blatner 1988; Williams 1989). Psychodramatic methods are based in part on surfacing and working with material that has been unconscious and is explored through dramatic re-enactment. In other words, the unconscious is fully utilized in psychodramatic techniques although this is not always made explicit by psychodrama practitioners themselves.

My psychodrama trainers were influenced by self-psychology and by some of the early Tavistock people – in particular Wilfred Bion and Dorothy Stock Whittaker. These 'Tavistock' people had – in turn – been strongly influenced by Melanie Klein whose work was based almost entirely on an exploration of unconscious processes. So as I progressed in my training, I got closer to unconscious processes in groups. My interest in unconscious facets of group process became much stronger as I developed my business in organizational consulting. Many of my client organizations gave great importance to rationality and conscious processes, but I found that I could only be successful in working with them when I was able to identify unspoken issues and aspects of the organisation that escaped the notice of my clients. While at times I still wanted to avoid making myself vulnerable through exploring my own unconscious processes, I was driven to self-exploration by the necessity of improving my professional ability.

I had by this time read extensively in the area of human change processes (Mahoney 1991) because I was completing a master's degree in education with a major focus on leadership of adventure-based therapeutic groups. Apart from authors and therapists whose work is based entirely on behaviourist psychology, most helping professionals believe that therapeutic change involves some unconsious process, and so I had developed a greater comfort with the existence of 'the unconscious'. By now I had also partly overcome the fear of exploring my own unconscious because I had already survived nearly three years of weekly psychodynamic/psychoanalytic psychotherapy. I must admit that for a long time I was frightened of the demons that I would discover in myself through taking part in psychotherapy but my need for integration and improved meaning in my life had led me to, and held me rather firmly in, therapy.

In Australia (and even more so in New Zealand) there is a street wisdom that psychology and things like 'the unconscious' are whacky, odd and not for 'normal' people. I was not immune to the power of this culturally supported fear of the unconscious, and whilst I respect the power that this aversion may still have over many people, I have found going against this cultural norm has been very worthwhile. Whilst I still feel fearful at times of exploring aspects of myself that are outside my awareness, I delight in the results of these explorations of unconscious processes. For instance I experience increased clarity and personal authority[1] that this exploration has led to. In particular, whilst I have great respect for the power of group process, I no longer feel overawed or intimidated by the idea of running a group. I have growing confidence in my ability to move in a dance between the unconscious and conscious processes. This reduces my fear of being 'caught out' in a shameful or humiliating way in groups and leads to a sense of competence that has increased the amount of satisfaction that I get from my work with groups.

In the last chapter I alluded to the problem that some people have with the word 'psychoanalysis'. A few times when I have been running leadership development workshops, a participant has said something like, 'I'm not interested in the Freudian psychoanalysis stuff'. A number of group members then laugh, nod, and smile in agreement. This is a powerful injunction against exploring the dynamics of what is happening in the group and it takes quite a lot of courage on my part then to find out what in particular the participant finds difficult. Any active listening, reflection, or demonstration of empathy is almost forbidden when 'Freudian' methods have been banished from the room. I believe that when group members say that they are not interested in 'psychoanalysis' or the like, they are likely to be telling me that they are scared, but they are scared to actually say that they are scared. I then need to treat this obscure expression of fear with respect and not probe the speaker in a way that would move us away from the level of psychological depth at which we have previously agreed to work (Ringer and Gillis 1995).

In summary, I now believe that a sound understanding of unconscious processes in myself, others and groups is very helpful to my work. What I need to be able to do is to make the most of this understanding without necessarily using jargon or intimidating techniques. I think the greatest art in working with unconscious processes is to be able to do so in a way which means that the people with whom we are working have no idea that that is what we are doing. I am not suggesting that we be manipulative, just that we should not act in a way that is intended to prove to participants how much we know about unconscious processes. We need to stay focused on the purpose of the group, whilst using manageable language and processes that are compatible with participants' working models.

But I use cognitive behavioural (or humanistic) processes in my groups and so all this psychodynamic stuff is irrelevant!

Unfortunately because of the age-old wars between psychodynamic, humanistic and cognitive behavioural/behavioural approaches, this cry is far too common. Fortunately it is incorrect because an understanding of unconscious processes in groups provides a strong foundation for any kind of technique or intervention. The group leader can still apply cognitive behavioural techniques as the main structure for a group, while retaining a psychodynamic understanding of the overall group dynamic

and his or her part in it. There is a huge loss of potential when dogmas
associated with any one school of psychology prevent understandings
from other schools being utilized.

Overview

There is no universally accepted view of the unconscious, so as you enter with
me into this complex conceptual world, be cautioned by the words of Blos
(cited by Sandler *et al.* 1973, p.94) when he talks about the way in which the
phrase 'acting out' has come to represent a conceptual 'forest' similar to that
surrounding the idea of the unconscious:

> ...the concept of acting out is overburdened with references and meanings.
> The rather clear-cut definition of thirty years ago...has now been
> expanded to accommodate delinquent behavior and all kinds
> of...pathology and impulsive actions. This expansion of the concept has
> reached a conceptual breaking point. I feel...[as if I am] groping my way
> through underbrush of an overgrown concept eager to find a clearing
> which would permit a wider view.

Just as the phrase 'acting out' has developed many different meanings over
the years, so has the word 'unconscious' and so the ideas that follow will
represent a particular view on the nature of the unconscious rather than any
absolute truth about the concept. (See also Bateman and Holmes (1995) for
an overview of the different ways of understanding the unconscious.)

The unconscious was an important aspect of the second phase of Freud's
thinking about psychoanalysis, and is commonly referred to as a part of the
'topographical model' (Bateman and Holmes 1995). He later moved to the
third phase – the 'structural model' – where the unconscious was primarily
located in the 'id' but was also distributed amongst 'ego' and 'superego'. So
Freud himself was not consistent throughout his life with his treatment of the
idea of unconscious (Hampden-Turner 1982; Sandler *et al.* 1973). Many
years have passed since Freud last wrote, and the unconscious has subsequently been described in a host of different ways. With that caution in mind,
I present a short development of the rationale for using the now overbur-
dened concept of 'unconscious'.

Why believe in the existence of the unconscious?

Many of you (readers) will take for granted the central role of the unconscious in human functioning. But what is true for some is anathema for others and so it is necessary to spend some time developing a rationale for the existence of unconscious processes in everyday life (Segal 1985; Power and Brewin 1997). The very idea that much of our functioning may not be visible to us can be quite scary, especially if this means that someone else can see aspects of functioning that we cannot see ourselves. If others can see parts of us and we cannot, it potentially gives them power over us and potential to shame or manipulate us. Perhaps the story of the emperor's new clothes is really a metaphor about the pervasive fear that others see our unconscious processes and we do not. In the story of the emperor's new clothes the evidence was very clear and humiliating because he looked ridiculous even though he was convinced that he looked rather grand and well presented. This led to a pretty large-scale humiliation for the emperor. So maybe acknowledging the existence of the unconscious does lead most people to recognize that we are vulnerable to being taken by surprise about aspects of ourselves of which we have previously been unaware.

Overall, there are three reasons for being uncomfortable with the existence of the unconscious. First, it contains material that is potentially shameful; second, there is an implication that others can see aspects of ourselves that we cannot even see, and third, there is an implication that we are not in full conscious control of our actions or perceptions. Each of these three implications of the unconscious can create discomfort and tempt us to deny the existence of this potentially vexing mental apparatus. In more detail:

1. Freud's formulation of the unconscious as being the storehouse of forbidden impulses and repressed memories can lead to a perception that our unconscious contains shameful things that should be hidden. I recall making friends with a psychologist when I was just developing my interest in interpersonal communication. I liked him and I found conversations with him to be really interesting and valuable. However, I felt the need to prepare myself for meeting with him and I would be terrified that unless I was careful he could use his psychological skills to see aspects of myself that I could not see. My fear was based on the belief that those hidden aspects of myself were shameful, grubby or unpleasant. A part of the fear of being involved in a group arises from our intuitive understanding that others will see some of what we

ourselves do not see about ourselves. This is one of the greatest fears facing participants in group therapy. Because the purpose of the group is to explore aspects of participants' functioning that are not working, participants know that they will inevitably have less-than-glamorous aspects of themselves – of which they are currently unaware – exposed.

2. Apart from the potentially shaming aspects of the content of the unconscious mind, there is the difficulty with co-existing with something that we can never fully experience in conscious functioning. R.D. Laing describes this difficulty with the unconscious (Laing 1971). That is, if another person claims that you are acting on some unconscious desire or impulse and you deny the truth of that assertion, there is a problem. The problem arises because the other person is claiming to infer something about your *mental functioning* that is signalled by your *actions* but that remains outside your awareness. The problem cannot be solved because who knows who is right? Can someone else know something about yourself that is not true for you? In other words, is it possible for a part of you (the conscious part) to be unaware of what another part has been doing even though it has been visible to others through your actions? How, then, can we reconcile our sense of identity if we know that a key part of our identity is present as a hidden companion, but not directly accessible to us? This aspect, too, confounds our presence in groups. Do we introduce ourselves to others, 'Hi, this is me…and, by the way, I've brought along my unconscious and although I don't know him or her you'll see evidence of him or her…'?

3. The notion that unconscious processes have a major influence on our behaviour can be difficult to accept also because of the implication that we don't control much of what we do. In a rational world where planning, prediction and control are generally seen to be desirable, the idea of being not in full conscious control may easily be mistaken for being 'out of control'. However, if rational decisions alone could change how we think, perceive and act, there would be a huge amount less crime, sickness, psychiatric illness and other maladies. The idea of being only partly in conscious control creates anxiety in group settings because we intuitively know that the behaviour of other group members will create reactions in

ourselves. If these reactions are not fully within conscious control we risk acting in ways that show us in a poor light, that evoke destructiveness in ourselves, or some other fear-evoking reaction.

What is excluded from this study: the unconscious and automatic functions of the body

Since the focus here needs to remain on how conscious and unconscious processes relate to human functioning in groups, it is helpful to exclude some aspects of human functioning that lie outside our awareness but are not directly relevant to relating to others and making meaning from that relating. Three aspects of human functioning excluded from further development in this work were identified by Gregory Bateson (1972). They are: (1) those aspects of bodily functioning that are taken care of without our conscious intervention, such as heartbeat; (2) the unconscious functioning that enables us to learn habitual patterns of motion and interaction (i.e. motor skills such as riding a bicycle); (3) the unconsciously held patterns of perception which hold the 'rules' of decoding sensory data to produce useful information, such as the ability to perceive in three dimensions and the ability to recognize a human voice. These are examined further below.

1. Bodily functioning

Many of the functions of the human body occur automatically, and in many cases beyond our conscious control. Breathing is an interesting example in that we can partially control our breath, but if the body decides that we are starving it of oxygen or too rich in carbon dioxide it takes over. This is an 'unconscious' process. Heartbeat is another physiological activity that we do not control. Whilst we can influence when we breathe, I do not know anyone who can determine when each heartbeat will occur. These kinds of physiological processes are specifically excluded from the following discussion about unconscious processes in groups.

2. Learning of habit and skills

The learning of a skill is, in its simplest terms, the committing to the unconscious what starts off as conscious. However, there are often subtleties to this process that require the suspension of previously learned or innate patterns. For example, when learning to right a kayak that has capsized, it is necessary to stay in the craft, suspended upside down in the water long enough to apply the skills necessary to right it again. In this example, being trapped under water by a tightly fitting 'skirt' in a small kayak, in the upside-down position is a terrifying experience. Instinctive messages shout 'GET OUT!' The first attempt to roll the kayak usually consists of a mad scramble out of the kayak to reach the surface for a breath. So, initially, instinctive survival patterns override the conscious wish to learn the skill of righting the kayak. The first skill, then, is to override the survival reflex and stay in the kayak once it tips over. From there, rational and cognitive learning establishes a sequence of actions. The verbal instructions that enable the paddler to roll the kayak before the body has learned the movements are quite complex. They might be, 'Reach out to the side of the kayak towards the surface of the water; push your paddle flat above the surface of the water and place the blade flat on the surface; lean forward, swing your body out, and sweep your body in an arc away from the front of the boat ending up at the back. At the end of the sweep, lean right back, flick your hips to bring the kayak deck above the water, slide your body onto the deck and end up with the back of your head touching the back of the boat.'

That is too much to learn as a script, commit to memory and 'play back' calmly while going through the actions of recovering one's body from a drowning position back to a paddling position. However, gradually, with corrective feedback from the coach and repetition to the point of physical exhaustion, the learner's body learns how to roll a kayak and instead of having to run the verbal instructions in his or her mind, it becomes an automatic sequence that is beyond words. Even years later, the person would be able to hop into a kayak, sit for a few seconds tuning into that embodied memory of rolling, and successfully complete this complex manoeuvre without a single word or instruction from their conscious mind. It would all be unconscious.

Recent progress in neuroscience and memory studies have shown that a part of human interaction is learned in a similar way to how learning of physical skills occurs (Schacter 1996). Peter Fonagy (1999) describes one aspect of memory, called procedural memory, which stores information about patterns of relating that are learned through a kind of 'absorption' into the psyche. This idea has huge implications for group work leadership and will be discussed further in the next chapter.

3. The location of codes for deciphering sensory data

As Gregory Bateson (1972) reminds us, the codes by which we decipher sensory data operate beyond our awareness. You recognize a human voice in the midst of a whole lot of noise. How do you do this? Can you *decide* not to? Probably not. Similarly, Escher's[2] playful visual paradoxes use our automatic unconscious patterns of perceiving to trick us. The tricks work because we do not have conscious access to the rules by which we decode visual information. These codes for interpreting visual, tactile, auditory, olfactory and gustatory sensory data form yet another aspect of our unconscious functioning that remains outside the scope of this study.

Whilst these three groups of processes are classified by some theorists as unconscious, their further analysis would distract from our main purpose here. An excellent summary of physiological aspects of cognitive functioning can be found in Hampden-Turner (1982, pp.72–115). In the next chapter we turn to three aspects of the unconscious that are associated more with interactive elements of human experience and therefore have greater relevance to the study of behaviour in groups.

Implications for technique

The group setting magnifies the fear that other people will see things about ourselves that we do not see. I think that most people have an intuitive awareness that there are aspects of their functioning that are outside their awareness. For example I think that shyness is partly based on a fear of being exposed. The unacknowledged fear behind shyness may be that making oneself visible through talking will expose much more than is intended and shyness is exacerbated in groups because in a group there are lots of witnesses to every action. I also think that shame becomes more of an issue in groups than it does in one-to-one situations. There is something quite shameful about being brought to awareness in the presence of a group about something previously unknown. So group participants in general will be vulnerable about working in ways that uncover unconscious material. Safety in groups depends in part on communicating to participants that they will not have aspects of themselves dredged from their psychic depths and displayed for all group members to see and comment on. Thus, the intuitive awareness in group participants of the existence of their unconscious minds means that we need to pay attention to the emotional and psychological safety in the group. (See also Ringer and Gillis 1995; Ringer and Spanoghe 1997; Vincent 1995.)

Notes

1. I use the word 'authority' here to denote the capacity to be the author of my own opinions i.e. 'author-ity' rather than to relate in any way to being authoritarian.

2. Maurits Cornelis Escher (1898–1972) was a Dutch graphic artist, who is best known for his visual paradoxes involving repeating patterns (tessellations).

CHAPTER 4

Aspects of the unconscious, preconscious and conscious that influence behaviour in groups

Introduction

The last chapter focused on the idea that the unconscious mind was probably real and relevant to our study of groups. The fear associated with acknowledging the unconscious was touched on as were some other aspects of the unconscious mind that are not discussed any further here.

Now the task is to explore aspects of mental functioning that are relevant to the study of groups. Here we take a closer look at three aspects of the unconscious; instinctually learned patterns of behaviour, 'codes' for communication and the 'storehouse' of repressed or unavailable material.

An interlude examines the role of memory in unconscious functioning and this is followed by a brief discussion about the preconscious and the conscious minds, along with some observations about the importance of unconscious functioning in groups. A further interlude examines the functioning of defence mechanisms in avoiding awareness of distressing or anxiety-provoking aspects of functioning.

The unconscious: three aspects of the unconscious that influence behaviour in groups

Three aspects of unconscious functioning that play a major part in interaction in groups are:

1. The origin of the innate, instinctual and learned patterns of behaviour that occur in humans, but that are not accessible to the conscious mind.

2.   The location of 'codes' that we use in creating acts of
     communication with others and the codes that we use in
     interpreting acts of communication between self and others.

3.   The unconscious that is the storehouse of repressed or
     non-accessible material and that is the source of impulses that we
     repress – as in the psychoanalytic view of the unconscious.

1. The location of instinctually learned patterns of behaviour and desiring

Melanie Klein, John Bowlby (Bowlby 1969, 1973, 1980; Hinshelwood *et al.*
1997; Klein 1975) and many other psychoanalytically oriented practitioners
state that infants are born with instinctual patterns of behaviour that are set
off by external stimuli. For instance, very early in life a baby will begin
nuzzling in search for a breast as soon as it is placed against a person's chest.
Instinct is

> ... an observable pattern of behaviour which follows a recognizably similar
> and predictable pattern in almost all members of a species (or members of
> one sex). It is activated by specific conditions and terminated by others. It
> involves a sequence that usually runs a predictable course. It serves a funda-
> mental function which has obvious value in contributing to the preserva-
> tion of an individual or the continuity of a species. It tends to develop
> without recourse to learning.

> Moreover, this model of instinct has an adaptive quality. This means that it
> leaves open the possibility that an instinct – having a strong adaptive
> component – can be in mutual interaction with environmental factors.
> (Marrone 1998, p.35)

In the view of Bowlby and many others, instinct is not accessible to conscious
awareness, although the behaviours that arise from some forms of instinct can
be observed and identified. Some of the ways in which instinct influences
behaviour can be excluded from further attention in this book, for example,
those relating to hunger and eating. Nevertheless, other 'drives' such as that
behind sexual attraction, or that leading to envy, can have significant
influence on participants' behaviour in groups. Additionally, while any
instinct itself remains beneath conscious reach, the phantasies arising from
instinctual drives may, with effort, be identified and can provide useful
material for groups. For a more in-depth study of this topic I suggest Segal

(1998). Other explorations of instinctual functioning can be found in Hampden-Turner (1982).

The importance for group functioning of instinctual patterns is that although these patterns are innate, they are 'triggered' by specific conditions. Some well-respected psychoanalytic practitioners, including Bowlby and Foulkes, thought that there was an instinctual drive for affiliation with others. This being the case, we could deduce that all group members would at a deep level be attracted to building better relationships with others in the group, despite any (consciously derived) protestations to the contrary on their part. This idea may increase our patience in working with aggressive or isolated group members because we could then see isolating behaviour as a defence against intimacy or a defence against some other fear-laden phantasy. Sexual attraction is too often pushed aside when working with groups. By assuming that the instinctual drive or sexual attraction will be present in groups even when it is not overt, we can notice and potentially deal with situations that would otherwise disrupt groups. As we shall see later, dealing with tricky issues such as isolating behaviour or sexual attraction does not necessarily mean directly naming its existence.

I find plenty of evidence in my own experience with groups to support the idea that there is a human instinct to form groups. Countless times I have started adventure therapy groups or training groups with a sense that participants have no pre-existing relationships and that they have a caution about forming a group. Yet after a relatively short time most of these groups have formed an identity that makes it difficult for 'outsiders' to disrupt or to enter. Being present with a relatively small number of others in a distinct space seems to activate a 'grouping' tendency so that either everyone present forms into one group or a number of groups form and develop their separate identity. When a relatively small number of people occupy the same space for a sustained period of time, there seems little possibility for all people present to remain as 'isolates' in the presence of the others. Therefore, we can consider the behaviour of participants who do isolate themselves as a defence against something. Specifically what is being defended against is almost always unconscious, and is encapsulated in the unconscious aspects of the participant's internal working models or in other unconscious mental representations.

2. The location of 'codes' for communication, interpretation and developing meaning

This aspect of the unconscious affects what we notice, what we perceive, what we believe and how we relate to others. In other words, this is the primary template for relating and making meaning from relating. One aspect of this template is the 'internal working model' referred to in Chapter 2. The contents of this aspect of the unconscious are assimilated through early experience and are then continuously modified through life. Working models are in part learned through modelling from caregivers and are in part adopted through the language of significant others. They sit mainly beneath our awareness and provide an efficient means of interpreting every event that we ever experience. Without working models life would be exhausting because we would need to consciously design schema for how to interpret every new event and everything that was said to us. Internal working models have a significant influence not only on how we interpret events, but also on what we are interested in, what we perceive and what we notice. Persistent efforts to discover our own working models are essential in our development as group leaders.

Neuro-science has given us access to a wealth of information about the way in which unconscious processes influence and are influenced by life experience (Crittenden 1995; Dreyfus 1999). Amongst recent discoveries is the notion that human beings develop expectations about the world and their relation to the world in ways that do not involve language. So, we develop expectations about some aspects of 'what people are like', 'what groups are like' and 'what I am like' simply through incorporating our subjective experience of events without necessarily talking or thinking in words about those experiences. Five different types of memory are described by Crittenden, and each includes aspects that are unconscious as well as aspects that are conscious. Utilizing each of these memory systems results in different kinds of learning.

So, we now take a diversion into the functioning of memory systems to help shed light on the functioning of unconscious processes including the location of codes for communication, interpretation and the development of meaning.

Interlude: memory systems and learning from experience
OVERVIEW

There is a strong connection between what we remember and who we are. Identity and memory are inextricably linked. In part, who I am is linked with my memories of with whom I am affiliated. As narrative therapists well know, the stories I tell about myself (which I can only do if I can access these stories from my memory) take a part in defining both who I am and how I am in the world. Processes in many groups work with either 'who I am' or 'how I am' or both[1] and so involve changes to what I will now call 'memory systems'. Given then that memory systems take such an important part in groups, it is worth looking more deeply into the structure and function of human memory.

The major point that I make here is that memory is not like a computer hard disc where data is 'written' and then later 'retrieved'. Rather than being a single 'box' into which we place mental 'things' and later recover them, memory is in fact a diverse system that stores and recovers images, feelings, meanings and cues for action in a complex way. Each part of the memory system (described below) is likely to be utilized by different people in different ways at different times – although each person develops characteristic patterns in his or her ways of utilizing memory systems.

Some types of memory have a greater 'unconscious' component than others, and some kinds are utilized by people who are psychologically mature. Other kinds of memory are more automatic, but lead to more compulsive action rather than reflective action.

Crittenden (1998) suggests that there are five or more memory systems, each of which has different modes of operation and different functions. These different modes of operation also affect the way in which learning occurs from life experience.

The five memory systems described by Crittenden are:

1. procedural

2. imaged (or perceptual)

3. semantic

4. episodic

5. working.

1. PROCEDURAL MEMORY

Procedural memory is mostly what we would call preconscious. It includes patterns of behaviour that the person learned as a child in order to stay safe.

> Most human behavior is procedural with only small bits becoming the focus of conscious thought and problem solving. As a consequence, procedures both reflect the predominant past experience of individuals and also their most probable future behavior. When conditions have been dangerous in predictable ways, children can develop procedural inhibitions or compulsions that function to increase safety. For example, when affect is punished, its display may be inhibited; when it is rewarded, it is likely to occur more frequently. (Crittenden 1998, pp.3–4/3)

Procedural memory is a major influence on personality. The nature of a person's procedural memory affects how they function with other people but this effect is beyond the awareness of the person him or herself. In groups we often see people acting in one way and describing themselves in a different way. The acting is derived from procedural memory and the description of self is derived from other memory systems described below. Influencing personality then involves influencing procedural memory. The three main effects of procedural memory are in: influencing the patterns (but not content) of discourse, influencing the quality of the interaction between people (and in particular, the transference) and influencing the way in which people manage their feelings.

2. IMAGED (OR PERCEPTUAL) MEMORY[2]

When I read what is written about imaged/perceptual memory I think of it as a kind of memory that is very closely linked to sensations experienced in the body.

> Imaged memory consists of perceptual images of past experiences, e.g., the shrill sound of angry voices, the soothing rhythm of close holding and rocking. Other images reflect contexts of safety or danger, e.g., a warm, soft bed or a dark, cold basement. Somatic images are bodily states associated with arousal, e.g., light-headedness, nausea, shortness of breath. (Crittenden 1988, p.4/3)

It seems that imaged memory is what is activated by what neuro-linguistic programmers call 'firing anchors' (Bandler and Grinder 1975). It is also involved in what I refer to later in this book as 'associative interpretation'. For example, when I hear the sound of surf breaking on a beach I am immediately transported to my childhood when almost every night I went to sleep with this sound.

Imaged/perceptual memory is relevant to group work – and in particular to experiential programmes – because during the group event itself, sensory stimuli trigger associative interpretations. These stimuli, such as smells, sounds, images, and touch, as well as other people's descriptions of events, lead to group members accessing imaged memory. Different people manage their imaged memory differently. For those who have experienced either repeated serious emotional distress or trauma, accessing imaged memory may create unmanageable feelings and so they may suppress their access either to the imaged memory or to the feelings associated with imaged memory. Other strategies include accessing or describing images in a chaotic way.

3. SEMANTIC MEMORY

Both procedural and imaged memory function before language develops in infancy, and so are described as implicit memory systems (Schacter 1996), but semantic memory requires language and so first develops in the second year of life. Semantic memory involves generalized language-based 'learning' about life and is accessible to consciousness. As such, semantic memory is described as 'explicit'. The activity of 'processing the experience' or 'reviewing' as described in experiential learning enables participants to develop verbalized generalizations from their recent specific experiences and so to build learning that will be retained in their semantic memory system. In other words, 'reviewing' transforms episodes that have just been experienced into generalizations: episodic memories (see below) are used to build semantic memories.

Semantic memory involves a *verbal transformation* of cognitive information. In its simplest form the transformation is an if/then statement where what follows the 'if' refers to an event or condition and what follows the 'then' refers to the consequence. For example, a programme participant may understand from a recent experience that 'if I express my feelings then people will relate to and support me'. This may update learning from earlier life when the generalized transformation was 'if I express my feelings then my mother/father/teacher will avoid me'.

4. EPISODIC MEMORY

Episodic memory is the most sophisticated of the four types described above, and does not function until about three years of age. Episodes, as the 'content' of episodic memory, are built from integrating aspects of imaged memory in a time sequence, involving both cognition and feeling.

> Thus, full episodes consist of an integration of cognitive (temporal) information about dangerous (or safe) sequences of behavior with affective information about dangerous (or safe) contexts and somatic responses. Such an integration requires...considerable information, generated by disparate parts of the brain... (Crittenden 1998, p.4/3)

Episodes are the basic element of what is worked with in narrative therapy, and they often form the majority of the discourse during 'processing' or 'reviewing' experiential exercises. The experiential learning cycle is based in part on the assumption that verbalizing 'episodes' will engender learning.

SO FAR, SO WHAT?

There are a number of consequences for group work of the existence of these four types of memory system.

First, the existence of the procedural memory system implies that learning can occur without any post-experience discussion or deliberate cognitive processing. The learning is translated, without any cognitive mediation, directly from an experience into a 'behavioural disposition'. For example, a young person who has recently completed a long arduous journey in wet forest may learn – at a procedural level – that being in the forest is an intensely unpleasant experience. This learning cannot be overridden by subsequent verbal explanations that the journey was a success in terms of – for instance – achieving something more difficult than the participant had previously thought possible. This kind of non-verbal learning is not enhanced or even affected by 'processing' or 'reviewing' experiences. It occurs in the thick of the action. So what we might end up with at the end of a reviewing session is a participant whose procedural memory system informs him or her that forests are unpleasant but whose semantic memory system informs him or her that he or she has recently had a personally successful experience. Both can be true at the same time.

The existence of imaged/perceptual memory means that our bodies learn, just as our minds learn. Some people describe this as 'learning at a cellular level' and others describe the 'embodied mind' (Valera, Thompson and Rosch 1992). Again, learning can occur without cognitive processing or verbalization when it involves the imaged/perceptual memory system. If we make the mistake that learning has only occurred if it can be verbalized then we may miss a great deal.

Learning that involves either procedural or imaged/perceptual memory systems occurs while the person is involved in an activity. This means that experiential educators need to pay attention to the quality of the lived experience of the participants at the time that they are having the experience, rather than expecting to be able to leave it until later to facilitate learning through reflection and discussion.

There is another major implication of there being a number of different kinds of memory functioning. That is that the utilization of different memory systems impinges directly on behaviour. Procedural and imaged/perceptual memory operate faster than do the verbally based memory systems of semantic and episodic. So, if a person is in a frame of mind where instant action is required (for example if physical or emotional danger is perceived), there will be negligible reflection on that person's own experience. Instead, the more immediately accessible procedural and imaged/perceptual memory systems will provide the cues for action, with a consequent loss of access to 'knowledge' that is accessible through either the semantic or episodic memory systems. This idea leads to a brief exploration of the relationships between sensory stimuli and memory systems.

5. WORKING MEMORY

The term 'working memory' is the very short-term memory system that enables a person to remember a phone number between reading it in the phone book and dialing the number. Working memory also manages the process by which new experiences derived from sensory stimuli are related to the four memory systems and the way in which the four memory systems operate in relation to each other. Anxiety and danger affect working memory and so situations perceived by the learner to be of high danger will result in different 'routing' of information to the memory systems than if the same event occurred in a low anxiety situation. Different people have different anxiety thresholds and so their working memory systems will function differently, resulting in different types of learning from the same situation.

CONCLUSION

An understanding of the nature of different kinds of memory system enables experiential educators and group leaders to plan and execute processes that assist participant learning through a range of memory systems. It will be seen that different approaches to group work address different memory systems. For example, narrative approaches are strong in working with integration between episodic and semantic memory systems. Leaders need to keep in mind that learning through the implicit memory systems (procedural and imaged/perceptual) occurs without the mediation of conscious thought and that it occurs during the activity or experience. Such learning is said to influence personality or 'how I am' (Schacter 1996). On the other hand, learning through explicit (semantic or episodic) memory systems is probably mediated by verbalization, such as is achieved during post-experience discussions that are often called 'reviewing' or 'processing'. Explicit memory systems influence identity or 'how I describe and see myself' (Schacter 1996). Perhaps, too, the most valuable thing that we can achieve as group leaders is to provide a space for participants to enable the full exercise of working memory. This requires a perception on the part of participants of emotional and physical safety, and so requires attention from the group leader to facilitate conditions for safety.

Resuming the discussion on the location of 'codes' for communication and interpretation, and developing meaning

The saying 'Happiness is largely a matter of where you place your attention' suggests that we can make a conscious and rational choice to focus on some things and ignore others. However, if rationality was the major factor influencing how we placed our attention on events most people would not pay attention to distressing events and so could live reasonably happy lives. Rather, it seems that the selection of what we notice and what attracts our attention occurs beneath our conscious awareness and is often beyond our control. We learn as a part of our early experience what is noteworthy and what is interesting and so the part of our mind that directs our attention is located in our unconscious. Each member of any group is influenced to a great degree by their working models and these working models establish what Wilfred Bion (1961) described as the group member's 'valency' (where the word 'valency' means a tendency towards, or attraction to, a way of being) for specific patterns of relating, projection and projective identification. This theme too, is expanded on later. These valencies are probably influenced strongly by aspects of procedural memory systems as described in the interlude about memory systems.

No doubt, you will know at least one person who, regardless of what occurs in his or her life, manages to see doom and gloom in everything. Others see threat or danger, and some see what seems like a ridiculous degree of joy and hopefulness in every situation. The same world evokes very different responses. We attribute this vast difference to the fact that people have significantly different templates for interpreting the world and their place in it, as was described in the last section.

> The leaders' report for the trip in the wombat story described that around the campfire on the first evening, the leaders attempted to elicit from each participant their personal goals for the trip. Jack and Clive went first and second respectively with two well-considered and mature goals. They had obviously thought about their place on the trip, what they wanted to achieve and even a little about what they might need to do in order to achieve that. Next Daniel asked Robert to talk about his goals because Daniel had seen Robert as relatively mature and therefore likely to set a positive direction for other group members. In fact, Robert only talked briefly about his situation at 'home' and then when pressed for a more definite goal for the course 'flew off the handle' with a loud outburst of verbal abuse directed at Daniel. Robert then retreated to his tent and Clive joined him soon afterwards, saying that he was going to offer Robert support. Later that night the leader group decided that Robert had been really uncomfortable because he had revealed more of himself than he was comfortable with. It seemed that Robert's fundamental interpersonal strategy was based on very low levels of trust of others. He defended himself from what he saw as the threat of abuse by disclosing as little of himself as was possible. The goal-setting task had required him to disclose too much and so he felt acutely threatened, though he did not have conscious access to the specific nature of the threat, probably because it was accessed at an unconscious level through his procedural memory.

It seems then, that most 'codes' for understanding communication and for understanding the meaning of events in the world are included in unconscious functioning.

3. The storehouse of inaccessible, repressed or unwanted material and the source of repressed and denied desires

Another aspect of the unconscious is like a storing place for all of the material that for many reasons we cannot keep conscious. We keep it unconscious because of the potential danger to our emotional equilibrium that this material poses. In most cases having this collage of memories and impulses in conscious awareness would create too much anxiety. In Bowlby's terms some material is kept unconscious because it clashes with our predominant working model (Bowlby 1991a). Bowlby asserted that we have a resistance to changing our working models and so information that challenges an existing working model may be repressed to avoid the anxiety that would result in questioning the working model. Thoughts, feelings, affect (emotional tone) and memories are repressed as a defence against anxiety and are stored in this aspect of our unconscious.

In the view of many psychoanalysts, we keep other material – such as primitive impulses – out of awareness because of the fear that we would act on them. It is surprising how difficult it is to differentiate between an impulse and an action that arises from the impulse. For instance, a fear of heights is sometimes a result of an unconscious impulse to jump. The mind does not differentiate between the impulse and the real action of jumping, and so the fear results from the unconscious belief that the person *is commencing the act of jumping*. Also, it is only after about four years of age that we are able to understand that our thoughts are not visible to others (Meares 1992), and some of the unconscious fear that others can 'see' our primitive impulses may also lead to their being relegated to the unconscious. Imagine if people could see what we are thinking when we see a person in public to whom we are sexually attracted! Imagine what would happen if the neighbour could see what we are thinking when their dog has barked incessantly all night! These difficult-to-accept wishes and impulses are stored in the unconscious because of a decision (that is made out of awareness) to exclude them from conscious awareness.

> For all of us, there exists a whole world of ideas that we are not normally conscious of: an unconscious part of our mind that exerts a very strong influence on us. Furthermore, this part of our personality sets up a resistance to most of these ideas coming into consciousness and therefore they tend to remain unconscious. All of us contain an internal phantasy world, first developed as a child. (Stapley 1996, p.38)

> An idea may be unconscious because it is actively repressed owing to its unthinkable nature – a memory, fantasy, thought, or feeling which conflicts with our view of ourselves and of what is acceptable, and which could cause too much anxiety, guilt or psychic pain if it were acknowledged. (Stapley 1996, p.23)

Impulses to act are also repressed when they conflict with the person's view of what is acceptable. For example, one member of a couple may be angry with the other and may at an unconscious level wish to hurt the other, but the anger and the impulse to hurt are both kept out of awareness. In a training group for managers we sometimes do an exercise that results in participants having their emotional 'buttons pushed'. We ask what their impulse was at the moment that they first felt their buttons being pushed and many reply that they felt like running away. Often, when that is explored more fully, the first impulse was actually to physically attack the other, but that was pushed out of awareness and what was first accessible to the person was the psychological defence against doing something unacceptable – the act of running away.

Whilst in this case it is not helpful to act on the impulse to hurt the other, it can be helpful for the angry person to be aware that he or she has that impulse and then it can be discussed and potentially resolved. A general term for the mechanisms by which we deal with the unbearable anxiety that would be created by becoming aware of unconscious material is 'defence mechanisms'. These defence mechanisms occur at a number of different levels, ranging from those relating to social interaction to those that repress primitive impulses such as the impulse for physical violence. (See the interlude about defences below.)

There remains a great deal to be learned about memory systems, but clearly most people are influenced by past events even though they do not have any explicit memory of those events. Daniel Schacter (1996, p.233) goes so far as to say that, 'While our sense of self and identity is highly dependent on explicit memory for past episodes and autobiographical facts, our personalities may be more closely tied to implicit memory processes'.

In terms of memory systems, there is potential for everything that occurs and is perceived to be encoded in our memory systems, which means that everything that is not kept in the conscious or preconscious may be kept in the unconscious. There are major differences of opinion about the way in which material that has been encoded into memory is made accessible, but it is apparent that the conceptions of memory as a single 'container' for remembered material are incorrect. The accessibility of memories depends on how and when it was encoded into memory, what is occurring in the life of the person who is (or is not) remembering and a range of other factors. Without going into detail, it is useful to consider that each person has a complex array of memories encoded into a complex memory system and much of what is present in this memory system can be considered to be 'unconscious' material. Some of this is unconscious because of psychological defences and some is unconscious because of the foibles of memory systems, encoding, and accessing memories (Schacter 1996).

Defences are interesting and relevant to group work because the means by which we repress and keep repressed unwanted material has a great impact on how we relate to others, both individually and in groups. Some of the defence mechanisms that support the repression of unwanted material include denial, idealization, splitting and projective identification, and displacement (Agazarian 1997; Segal 1988).

Interlude: defences

INTRODUCTION

To call someone 'defensive' is a criticism and so the word 'defence' when used in a psychological sense – as it is here – is often misconstrued as being something wrong or bad. On the contrary, psychological defences are an essential part of normal human functioning because they enable us to match the psychological demands placed on us with the resources that we have available at any given time. As such, defences are the processes that we learn in order to manage our emotional and psychological integrity and well-being. Defences are mobilized when we perceive that events in our own internal functioning or in the environment around us create too much demand on our emotional and psychological resources. Classical views of defences are that they are against internal phantasies and desires that, if acknowledged consciously, would threaten our emotional stability. More recent views are that defences also protect against the otherwise unbearable effects of external events and relationships.

DEFENCES: A SUMMARY

Defences occur mainly as unconscious processes and are primarily protection against anxiety. They are primarily patterns of cognition that provide a protection for the person from experiencing or becoming aware of aspects of their experience that may disturb their mental or emotional well-being too much. Some models of defences also include patterns of feeling and of behaviour, and not just cognition. Defences can occur in response to intrapsychic and/or interpersonal events.

However, defences do become problematic when the defence stays in place after it stops being necessary. Two things make defences unnecessary.

1. As human beings grow up, they develop more robust and sophisticated emotional and psychological functioning – after all that is what the non-physical aspect of growing up is. So, events

that created a threat to emotional and psychological well-being for an infant or a child often will not create any difficulty for a mature adult. Witness, for example, the acute embarrassment that most adolescents feel in many social situations. A few years later those same social situations pose less of a threat because of the maturity that the person has gained.

2. An (intrapsychic or interpersonal) event that was in the past experienced as a threat to psychological or emotional wholeness may no longer occur in later life. For example, if a person has been living with a very intrusive parent, he or she may have developed a withdrawn demeanour in order to avoid intrusion. When the intrusive parent is no longer present in the person's life, the withdrawn demeanour is no longer necessary.

Defences become a problem in individual functioning when they restrict the range of responses that a person may have to the world or they become a habituated response. For example, the following dysfunctions are all a result of the inappropriate use of defences: obsessive/compulsive behaviour, promiscuity, habitual lying and the inability to form intimate relationships.

In summary, the main features of defences are as follows:

- They may be normal and adaptive as well as pathological.
- They are a function of the ego.
- The are usually unconscious.
- They are dynamic and ever-changing but may coalesce into rigid, fixed systems in pathological states and in character formation.
- Different defences are associated with different psychological states, for example repression in hysteria, and isolation and undoing in obsessional neurosis.
- They are associated with levels of development, with some defences being seen as primitive and some mature. (Bateman and Holmes 1995, p.80)

Three main types of defence are considered: primitive/immature, neurotic and mature, as shown in Table 4.1.

Table 4.1 Mechanisms of defence		
Primitive/Immature	**Neurotic**	**Mature**
Autistic phantasy	Condensation	Humour
Devaluation	Denial	Sublimation
Idealization	Displacement	
Passive-aggression	Externalization	
Projection	Identification with the aggressor	
Projective identification	Intellectualization	
Splitting	Isolation	
	Rationalization	
	Reaction formation	
	Regression	
	Repression	
	Reversal	
	Somatization	
	Undoing	

Source: Bateman and Holmes (1995, p.81)

Primitive defences occur in all adults under duress, but become pathological when they are used habitually and repetitively. Neurotic defences are present in all adults relatively often and, in moderation, enable people to carry out normal lives without experiencing too much stress. However, habituated and excessive use of neurotic defences creates problematic personalities. For instance, a person who constantly intellectualizes so as to avoid feeling strong feelings becomes a bore and has difficulty in developing intimate relationships with others. Mature defences are a necessary and useful part of human functioning and make society more interesting to live in. However, even these, when used compulsively or to excess, create difficulties for people in building and maintaining relationships.

Readers wishing to explore in more detail the defence mechanisms listed in Table 4.1 will find fuller descriptions in Bateman and Holmes (1995, Chapter 4) and Tyson (1998, pp.72–74).

GROUP LEVEL DEFENCES

The presence of a group tends to create conditions that promote primitive defences. Not only are the so-called 'individual' defence processes listed in Table 4.1 more predominant in groups than in pairs, but also group-level defences occur. Three quite different understandings of defences in groups are separately described by Wilfred Bion (1961), Didier Anzieu (1984) and Yvonne Agazarian (1997).

Bion and subsequent authors who wrote in the same vein described 'basic assumption' functioning of groups, all of which is intended to defend against group-level anxiety. Basic assumption functioning takes participants away from the task of the group and involves them in states of mind that avoid the work of the group. Anzieu described the 'group illusion' which is a group-level phantasy that helps to alleviate anxiety in the group and may distract the group from its task. The group illusion feels comforting and reassuring, but may not represent a helpful state of mind in terms of the purpose of the group. Agazarian, using what is described as 'systems centred therapy' created an almost step-by-step approach to group therapy that is based in part on working systematically through participants' defence mechanisms. Systems centred therapy is based in part on the principle of identifying, confronting and working through the defences of members.

A further defensive process that groups engage in is that of role fixation where each group member over time reduces his or her range of behaviour to comply with the emerging norms that are expected of him or her. This defence at an extreme leads to scapegoating, which is well described by Wells (1995) and Colman (1995).

Much of the literature on the functioning of the group-as-a-whole is derived from principles that can be traced back to origins relating to defence mechanisms in groups. Some of these views are addressed in Chapter 8.

What does the unconscious do? How does it operate?

In summary, the aspects of the unconscious that have been explored because they add to the understanding of group behaviour include: the origin of instinctual patterns of behaviour, the means by which we interpret and make meaning from communication and events, and the storehouse of inaccessible and repressed material. If this comprises the contents of the unconscious, what then happens to the contents? What functions does the unconscious perform, and how does understanding this help us as group leaders?

The rules by which the unconscious operates are somewhat different to those of the conscious. The unconscious operates by 'primary process' which does not follow the logic or rationality of the conscious mind. Primary process is more like dreaming, where the connection between things is through association rather than logic. 'Free association' is the classical form of primary process. Here, one concept leads to another through whatever association occurs to the subject at the instant that the first concept appears. The reason for linking one concept with the next may be quite different from the reason for linking the next two. For instance, in primary process a person may link 'ice cream' with 'hot' because what instantly came to mind when they thought of ice cream was a childhood memory of buying *ice cream* at the beach in *hot* summer weather. So in this case the association was through temperature of the environment and through childhood memories. But then what might come to mind in response to 'hot' might be the place name 'Hotham' because the person has a visual recall of the word. So the second association is linked through the visual relationship between 'hot' and 'hot ham', which is a very different form of logic from relating through memory of temperature. Again, the association to the word Hotham/hot ham may follow the 'ham' path or many other routes. In any case, during free association one thing follows another in the unconscious because of the symbolic link between the two – in the mind of the thinker. Often the symbolic link for one thinker may be absolute nonsense for another. This is because the connections in the unconscious mind are intensely personal (whilst retaining a group and social element).[3]

For example, the smell of burning kerosene immediately evokes in me vivid pictures of tussock-covered river flats, with steep bush-clad hills rising to snowy mountains above. Concurrent with that image is a sensation of cold air in my nostrils and a feeling of happiness. Maybe you do not have the same response? That is because burning kerosene for me symbolizes camping, where my childhood memories of camping during winter in New Zealand were associated with kerosene pressure lamps. It is in this way that primary process differs so much from secondary process.

Primary process can also resemble a dream-like functioning where rationality and logical sequential reasoning are absent. The frustration about primary process is that, because it occurs primarily in the unconscious, it is seldom accessible to conscious awareness so we can relatively easily retain the illusion that the only thinking that we do is what we consciously experience as thinking. Deliberately thinking something over or puzzling about something occurs in secondary process. Letting the mind drift and seeing what comes to mind is more akin to primary process.

So to summarize, thinking as we normally envisage it is not present in the unconscious, where both rationality and the logical development of thought are absent. The main characteristics of primary process are that:

- time no longer follows the clock
- ideas follow each other because of symbolic association
- the concept of 'reality' becomes meaningless in that imagined phenomena comfortably co-exist with 'real' phenomena.

Despite the hackneyed nature of the phrase – attributed to Sigmund Freud – it is worth repeating that, 'Dreams are the language of the unconscious'. You can probably recall dreams where you were a grown-up in a dream even though the setting was from your childhood, or where you could fly and you were quite content with the fact that you could fly. Having a discussion about how to fly (without mechanical aids) is fine in the context of a dream but it would put us into an asylum if we had the same conversation in real life. The phantasy-related functioning of primary process also occurs in our unconscious while we are awake but remains outside our awareness. Flashes of intuition occur when, in times of waking, primary process intrudes into secondary process. In other words, intuition occurs in part through the relaxing of the boundary between conscious and unconscious.

Trance and hypnosis blur the distinction between secondary and primary process. I once attended a five-day residential workshop in Ericksonian trance where we spent more than half the time in varying degrees of trance (Watzlawick 1978). This resulted for me in the line between conscious and unconscious becoming much less definite. Ever since that workshop I can more easily drop into a dream-like state and access images, snippets of imaginary conversation and other 'flotsam' of the unconscious. Also, when on the edge of sleep I notice images, snippets of conversation and impressions floating past my awareness – almost accessible but not quite. These fragments are presumably connected together in a way that seems coherent according to the rules of primary process. They are the start of my dreaming for the night. If I fully wake up and so move out of the semi-sleeping state to look back on these snippets they appear just as disconnected fragments because my review of them is conducted in conscious – and therefore secondary – process.

Spoken puns are another example of primary process thinking. In a pun the meanings of the two words are not linked by logic, but rather by the quality of the sound that each makes when it is pronounced aloud. Visual puns rely on reading the word. The example of 'hot/Hotham' is a kind of visual pun rather than auditory because the pronunciation of the 'th' in Hotham hides the word 'hot'.

The active unconscious

The unconscious mind is not just a passive receptacle. It is constantly active and is both responding to *and generating* events. Some of the events generated are phantasies that remain out of awareness, but some are more noticeable like 'Freudian slips' in our language. Sometimes when our conscious mind is distracted our unconscious directs our actions so that we end up (for instance) driving a car to somewhere that is present in our unconscious or preconscious but totally different from the place that we had consciously decided to go. Sometimes the unconscious reminds us of what we had chosen to push aside. Have you ever found yourself driving (for example) to a place where you used to live or work rather than to where you currently live or work? In such cases you may be at an unconscious level seeking something from visiting that place in your history or your unconscious may just be repeating patterns that have become stored in your procedural memory.

It is also possible for something to evoke feelings without any of the unconscious stimulus ever becoming conscious unless there is a deliberate attempt to 'get to the bottom of the feeling'. You might get grumpy when there is nothing to get grumpy about. If that is the case it could be useful to sit and talk with someone else and to quietly explore your thinking and the events of the few hours prior to your becoming grumpy. Often you can extract from your unconscious mind the stimulus that triggered the grumpiness and then do something about it. I have learned that I get grumpy mostly when I am sad but I have suppressed the sadness. So now, to deal with the grumpiness I first try to find if I am sad but have pushed the sadness away.

The presence of a group of other people has an impact on the way in which the unconscious mind operates. In broad terms, being enveloped in a group evokes some unconscious processes that are more typical of early life (infancy and childhood) than of mature functioning. Hence the widespread agreement that unconscious processes become very significant in groups. For instance, 'My thesis is, that in terms of psychological dynamics, the group is a dream' (Anzieu 1984, p.129). Because of the amplified presence of uncon-scious dynamics in groups, understanding unconscious processes becomes a powerful tool in understanding the functioning of groups. Not only do we need to understand unconscious processes in general, we also need to understand some of the peculiarities of our own unconscious processes if we wish to be effective as leaders. Remember that our implicit guidelines on how to perceive and interpret events lie in an aspect of our unconscious. These guidelines or 'templates' as I have described them earlier are central to how we behave in groups, because they include the codes for relating to others both individually and collectively. I will return repeatedly to this aspect of the unconscious in other parts of this book. But having described three aspects of unconscious that are particularly relevant to group work, I will move briefly to an examination of the preconscious and conscious aspects of mind.

The preconscious

In Freud's original formulation the preconscious was the place in which 'material' was stored when it was no longer in direct conscious awareness but was readily accessible for recall. In our lives we accumulate a huge number of experiences and therefore memories of experiences. Some of these are repressed and so become unconscious, some are generalized to create our working models and some remain instances of episodic memory or imaged/perceptual memories (Marrone 1998; Schacter 1996). The episodic and imaged/perceptual memories that remain accessible can be said to remain in our preconscious and are accessed when a stimulus occurs or when they become linked with a current experience. Carl Jung explains further:

> Forgetting, for instance, is a normal process, in which certain conscious ideas lose their specific energy because one's attention has been deflected. When interest turns elsewhere, it leaves in shadow the things with which one was previously concerned, just as a searchlight lights upon a new area by leaving another in darkness. This is unavoidable, for consciousness can keep only a few images in full clarity at one time, and even this clarity fluctuates.

> But the forgotten ideas have not ceased to exist. Although they cannot be reproduced at will, they are present in a subliminal state – just beyond the threshold of recall – from which they can rise again spontaneously at any time, often after many years of apparently total oblivion.

> I am speaking here of things we have consciously seen or heard, and subsequently forgotten. But we all see, hear, smell, and taste many things without noticing them at the time, either because our attention is deflected or because the stimulus to our senses is too slight to leave a conscious

impression. The unconscious [preconscious in my framework], however, has taken note of them, and such subliminal sense perceptions play a significant part in our everyday lives. Without our realising it, they influence the way in which we react to both events and people.

An example of this that I found particularly revealing was provided by a professor who had been walking in the country with one of his pupils, absorbed in serious conversation. Suddenly he noticed that his thoughts were being interrupted by an unexpected flow of memories from his early childhood. He could not account for this distraction. Nothing in what had been said seemed to have any connection with these memories. On looking back, he saw that he had been walking past a farm when the first of these childhood recollections had surged up in his mind. He suggested to his pupil that they should walk back to the point where the fantasies had begun. Once there, he noticed the smell of geese, and instantly he realised that it was this smell that had touched off the flow of memories.

In his youth he had lived on a farm where geese were kept, and their characteristic smell had left a lasting though forgotten impression. As he passed the farm on his walk, he had noticed the smell subliminally, and this unconscious perception had called back long-forgotten experiences of his childhood. The perception was subliminal, because the attention was engaged elsewhere, and the stimulus was not strong enough to deflect it and to reach consciousness directly. Yet it had brought up the 'forgotten' memories. (Jung 1968, pp.20–22)

There is a wide range of opinion as to the existence of and importance of the preconscious and so my compromise is to consider the preconscious to be the link between conscious and unconscious. There are no hard lines between conscious, preconscious and unconscious; each merges into its neighbour, and each has gradations within itself.

The conscious: what is in the conscious?

Paradoxically, there may be relatively little in the conscious mind. It may be the poor cousin of the unconscious. This is paradoxical because of the great deal of value that western culture places on rationality and consciously accessible knowledge. Societies that retain more of an Earth-based spirituality seem to have retained also their valuing of unconscious processes, although they use different terms than are used in western psychology.

We seem to have the capacity to be conscious only of what is occurring at this moment, with a sense of what has just happened and an expectation of what will soon happen. As soon as we focus in detail on memories or on the future, our awareness of the present diminishes temporarily. Similarly, as soon as we focus intensely, say, on one sense such as vision, our awareness of the sounds and smells around us diminishes. In other words, consciousness may be a very thin slice off the top of what is potentially available to us: a narrow window on the full richness of our internal and external worlds. Within reach of conscious awareness and at a slightly deeper level, we have ready available for recall a host of memories and of expectations for the future. This readily accessible material that is not the current focus of attention lies towards the conscious end of the preconscious.

Gregory Bateson says that very little is known about the conscious mind, but:

> Consciousness operates in the same way as medicine in its sampling of events and processes in the body and of what goes on in the total mind. It is organized in terms of purpose. It is a short-cut device that enables you to get quickly at what you want; not to act with maximum wisdom in order to live, but to follow the shortest logical or causal path to get what you next want, which may be dinner; it may be a Beethoven sonata; it may be sex. Above all, it may be money or power. (Bateson 1972, pp.433–434)

In other words, the fullness of our sense of self lies in the preconscious and the unconscious. The conscious mind simply provides a moving window on our current experience, on our memories and on our dreams – depending on where we focus our attention. This leaves unaddressed the question of what level in our functioning (unconscious, preconscious or conscious) directs our conscious mind to focus on one thing in preference to another, but that is beyond the scope of this book and may even be beyond what is comprehensible to human beings.

What does the conscious do?

The conscious mind rationalizes the decisions that the unconscious has already made, though some decisions do seem to originate through almost purely rational and conscious means. Our consciousness provides the main interface between ourselves and the world, in that our deliberate actions are directed by the conscious mind. The rational mind also applies logic and sequence to put ideas into 'sensible' order and juxtaposes old ideas with new to achieve some conceptual progress.

The analogy of the conscious mind as being a moving window on sensory data as well as on the preconscious and on the unconscious may be useful. It can be seen as a window that selectively makes accessible to our waking selves the results of what is going on in the outside world and what is going on in areas that would otherwise be beneath our awareness. The conscious may be the boundary manager between what is inside ourselves and what is outside, that is the rest of the world. It also seems likely then, that the location of this window is not even fully within conscious control. So what seemed at first to be a simple concept – that of consciousness – is in fact very complex.

I do not intend to degrade the value of the conscious mind. It provides humanity with probably its greatest tool for manipulating the environment to create comfort and survival. What is important though, is that we recognize that unconscious functioning is probably even more important than conscious functioning in directing behaviour, perception and the making of meaning when we are in groups. Western society seems well endowed with ways of thinking in conscious rational ways and so in this book I spend minimal time specifically focusing on the conscious. Largely, I will focus on the ways in which unconscious processes support or undermine the taken-for-granted capacity of group members to reason at a conscious level.

Groups as a challenge to the conscious mind

Groups provide a number of significant challenges to the conscious mind that results in much of the processing of group experience occurring at an unconscious level. The conscious mind is not well equipped to deal with the complexity of group situations whereas the unconscious, through the use of primary process, is well equipped. To explain, the main invitations toward unconscious functioning occur from over-stimulation of the senses and the need to manage paradoxical realities that are difficult for the conscious mind.

OVER-STIMULATION

Try to focus on six different things at once. Try to feel the temperature of the air on your face, hear the sounds around you, think about what you will be doing tomorrow, notice what colour the ceiling or the sky is, check what you are feeling at the moment and keep reading! If you are like most people, your conscious mind cannot cope with these multiple inputs. But your unconscious can. While you are reading, at some level you are noticing what is going on around you and this information is being processed in your unconscious and 'stored' in one or more of your memory systems. As I say elsewhere in this book, the level of stimulation in a group far exceeds what can be dealt with using conscious processes and so unconscious processes are very active. For example, when you are in a group of ten people sitting in a circle, you see any movements made by most members, and you hear even faint noises made by all members. You are smelling the smells, feeling your body, and so on. What is more, you are intuitively keeping track of the relationships between group members and there are 90 relationships in a group of ten people – nine involving you and 81 not directly involving you. That is an overwhelming number of sources of information. Your conscious mind cannot cope and so your unconscious mind processes the information and it becomes accessible to you as intuition, feelings, premonitions, and so on. In other words, perhaps the most important part of your mental apparatus in any group is your unconscious mind.

PARADOXICAL REALITIES

There are a number of confusing kinds of reality that occur in groups that quickly befuddle the conscious mind but are dealt with better by the primary process of the unconscious mind (Berg and Smith 1995). These include the paradoxes between:

- group and individual
- difference and similarity
- safety and threat; comfort and anxiety
- task and relationship
- newness and familiarity.

Group and individual
When in a group we see a number of other individuals and we experience ourselves as individuals, and yet our subjective experience is often that of being a small part of a unit. This is confusing if we try to reason it out.

Difference and similarity
We are attracted to people who are similar and yet our existence as distinct individuals exists only because we are different from others. So difference is simultaneously essential and uncomfortable.

Safety and threat; comfort and anxiety

The group environment simultaneously has the potential to be a warm nurturing container – somewhat like a 'mother' – and a dangerous place where our difference can be attacked and our needs may be overruled. This is an uncomfortable realization.

Task and relationship
Sometimes to achieve the task of the group it seems necessary to override the needs of individuals and to put relationships at risk. Yet the group can only survive long enough to do its task if relationships are adequately catered for. This gets difficult at times.

Newness and familiarity
Each group and each group situation is new and unique. No participant has experienced exactly the same in his or her life before. On the other hand the experience of being in a group is so universal that the mental representations of 'group' that participants bring with them create an illusion of familiarity (as conveyed by internal working models). There is a constantly occurring process of comparison between what is expected and what is actually happening. Most of the world models (Parkes 1975) of 'group' that people bring to groups are held at an unconscious level and so the tension between newness and familiarity is played out primarily at an unconscious level.

Groups, then, create an environment that evokes high levels of unconscious functioning. While rational and conscious functioning is still possible, it is constantly underpinned with unconscious processes. We ignore these unconscious processes at our peril.

The relationship between the conscious and the unconscious

There is not a hard line between conscious and unconscious. Some memories lie deeply repressed in the unconscious. Victims of abuse are the greatest testimony to the ability to repress memories. When a child is abused he or she does not have the emotional capacity to experience the abuse fully as real and so the experience is split from 'reality' and memories are buried deeply behind strong defences. Whilst this 'repression' process is strongly present with some victims of abuse and trauma, all human beings push out of awareness some experiences and aspects of themselves that threaten their peace of mind. Sometimes people repress material that might be seen as 'good', if that good material threatens their dearly held internal working models and so creates anxiety. In the wombat story, Sean had been particularly helpful one evening in tidying the camp site, doing the dishes and gathering firewood. When Amy briefly commented to him that she had seen him being very helpful he became angry and told her that he had only been pretending. His firmly held working model of himself as a rebel against all forms of authority was threatened by Amy's feedback.

We all have repressed material in our unconscious. Most people repress impulses that, if acted on, would lead to such things as murder, greed, rape and violence. Not only do most people not *act* in murderous or violent ways, but many are not even *aware* of the fact that they are capable of such acts. I believe that there is a great deal of energy and creativity released in people when they understand and can tolerate the thought that they are *capable* of horrendous acts, but that they *choose* not to carry them out. Though distressing, it can also be comforting to see war atrocities on television: the comfort comes from the unconscious reminder that it is not 'us' who are killers; it is 'them'. We can retain the fantasy that 'we couldn't do things like that'!

Still unconscious, but less repressed, lies the kind of material that Jung referred to in his story about the professor. This material may not even be distasteful, it is just no longer relevant to day-to-day life and so is moved away from the main arena of conscious mental activity. Soon after visiting the farmyard and seeing the geese, Jung's professor had moved material from the preconscious across the boundary to the conscious. Even more accessible are the recent memories and the impulses that can find acceptable expression in action. Whilst these are not constantly at the front of the mind, they can be readily and freely accessed by conscious will. For instance, if I asked you if you saw any food yesterday that you wanted to eat but decided not to, you would probably be able to recall, thus (again) moving material from the preconscious to the conscious.

A puzzle remains, how do we uncover deeply repressed unconscious material, and how do we move between levels of consciousness?

The state of trance is a graphic demonstration of the human capacity to move freely across boundaries of consciousness. Free association, as used in psychoanalysis, is another means of moving deliberately from conscious material to unconscious. In fact, persistent use of free association, combined with a safe environment, can unearth very deeply repressed or hidden material. Free spontaneous drawing or painting provides a direct route for unconscious material to be represented in a graphical form. Poetry, fiction, psychodrama, free dance and even sometimes just walking, as well as many art forms, enable direct expressions of unconscious material that subse-

quently become available for conscious scrutiny. Membership of and participation in groups can quickly provide access to material that was previously
unconscious. The group environment itself encourages regression to younger
states of mind, which in turn gives access to previously inaccessible material.
This is true even when the purpose of the group is quite rational and task
related. Also, a group that feels emotionally safe provides the kind of
emotional containment that intrinsically encourages self-exploration and
self-disclosure. We return to these group themes later.

A danger in western societies is that conscious and unconscious are seen
to be irrevocably split. Some express this as a split between 'right-brain' and
'left-brain' functioning (Zdenek 1985). However, there is an essential partnership between conscious and unconscious. Preoccupation with conscious
leads to lifeless and passionless rigidity. The conscious mind is well adapted
to enact rules, and therefore easily creates routines and predictable systems. In
contrast, primary process – the mode of functioning of the unconscious mind
– appears chaotic and unpredictable even though it has its own internal
'logic' to the person whose mind is engaged in the associative processes
involved. Nonetheless, preoccupation with unconscious leads to lack of deci-
siveness and becoming lost in intuition at the expense of action. Respect for
all levels of functioning is enlivening and leads to productive creativity. Many
studies on creativity describe the need for 'incubation' time for ideas (Neville
1989). At first an idea seems little more than a niggle in the mind (or even
stomach). If deliberate focused thinking fails to develop the idea any further,
then 'sleeping on it' is likely to give the unconscious primary process a
chance to work.

This primary process works in an associative way and can make
'abductive' leaps where previously unrelated ideas come together in some
new symbolic representation (Bateson 1988). The discovery of the structure
of DNA is one of many major scientific breakthroughs that is said to have
occurred in a dream or in abductive forms of reasoning (Neville 1989).
Similarly, in the midst of a difficult occasion in a group, one problem-solving
technique is to attempt to think it out using models and theories of groups
and human behaviour to identify interventions. Usually, any intervention is
then subjected to an intuitive test; does it feel right? Another technique is to
maintain free-floating attention, and to allow intuitive processes to work
beyond conscious awareness. When an idea arises, it can then be tested in a
more rational mode, using models and theories. Both of these means of
developing interventions utilize a synthesis of rational and unconscious

processes. Neither system is necessarily superior to the other, but having a range of strategies is more versatile than relying on one only.

Unconscious processes in experiential groups

The human psyche is a complex dynamic interdependent system of levels of consciousness, sensory systems, somatic systems, memory systems and physiological systems. Groups too, are complex dynamic interdependent systems, where each participant is a component of the group system. Each person brings to the group his or her own ways of constructing reality and means of interacting with others. The individual unconscious contributions of each participant interact with each other through a host of different conscious, unconscious, verbal and non-verbal communication channels. The rational representations of self that we normally use may no longer be fully helpful when thinking about groups. For instance, it is possible that under some conditions there are stronger links between one person and another at an unconscious level than these same people have between their own conscious and unconscious minds. In other words, there could be occasions in groups when the unconscious-to-unconscious linking between group members is momentarily more significant than other aspects of group functioning, even intra-personal functioning.

Conscious and rational thinking *alone* is a woefully inadequate way of dealing with this myriad of stimuli and information. So unconscious processes are absolutely central to the functioning of groups. Examination of unconscious processes enables sense to be made of the *system* rather than only seeing each individual as an independent agent. Most important, unconscious processes provide a window on the evolving relationship between the leader's subjective experience and the dynamics of the group. The primary means of interaction in groups incorporate unconscious processes. These include projection, introjection, projective identification, transference and countertransference. They will be examined in more detail in the next two chapters.

Implications for technique

Leaders who act as though conscious processes are the only ones present in groups will be experienced as clumsy, rigid and inappropriate in their leadership. In contrast, leaders who have a tolerance for the idea that much of what goes on in groups will not reach their conscious awareness or the conscious awareness of group members are likely to be experienced as more responsive and appropriate in their leadership styles. However, to be able to accept the ubiquitous nature of unconscious processes in groups means being able to accept the prevalence and significance of unconscious processes in our own (the leader's) functioning. To reach this acceptance requires the leader to have had a sustained experience of exploring his or her own unconscious processes. This can be achieved by many means including personal growth groups, psychotherapy, psychodrama, and many other systems of self-exploration.

Simply reading this book, or other books about unconscious processes, without having a personal experience of exploring your own unconscious processes, is likely to make you more dangerous rather than more skilled!

Notes

1.   We also work with 'how I am perceived' but that is beyond the scope of this short overview.

2.   At the point of copy-editing this book I found Damasio's original work on imaged/perceptual memory. I stongly recommend the interested reader to two highly relevant and readable books by Antonio Damasio (2000a, 2000b).

3.   My temptation here is to qualify this statement by expanding on the idea of the social unconscious and the forms of association that occur through social dreaming. Unfortunately these topics do not fit well within a book of this nature.

CHAPTER 5

Unconscious processes: language and symbolism

...we appear to have no option but to maintain [the view that] self's knowledge of other's experience, of any kind, conscious or unconscious, is based at any age of self or other entirely on inference...(Laing 1971, p.20)

In my experience, self does not experience the experience of other directly. The facts about other available to self are actions of other experienced by self. (Laing 1971, p.19)

Introduction

This chapter and the next describe in more detail the specific nature of unconscious processes in human functioning and describe some of their implications for groups. This chapter explores the process by which unconscious events are processed and acted on by the unconscious mind. An event can be interpreted by the unconscious mind and then responses can emerge from the unconscious interpretation of that event all with no conscious mental processing. This is a core process in everyday human functioning because if we consciously decided the significance and meaning of every event, no matter how tiny, we would be exhausted. Much of our meaning-making is habituated and occurs mostly beyond our awareness. This has implications for how we behave in groups, both as leaders and as participants.

Many of the concepts presented here are derived mainly from the study of language, signs and symbols which together is encapsulated in a field of philosophy called semiotics or semiology (Cobley and Jansz 1999). Semiotics offers ideas about how actions, visual signs such as pictures, auditory signs such as speech and written signs such as text convey meaning in individual and collective senses. As such, semiology provides some useful explanations of the processes by which communication occurs in groups and relates well to the study of the unconscious. Indeed, a significant part of the body of knowledge in semiology has been derived from psychoanalysis.

In Chapter 2 I outlined the notion that all persons have their own idio-syncratic ways of interpreting events, and this 'subjectivism' was described mainly in terms of internal working models. Then Chapters 3 and 4 developed some notions about unconscious functioning, and now we are ready to examine in more detail some more of the processes that occur in the human psyche that lead to individuals having such a variable view of the same event. The processes described in this chapter and in the next are all unconscious and so all involve primary process, which is mainly associative in its nature and does not involve the rationality and logic of conscious thought.

For many of the unconscious processes described in this and in the next chapter, what happens is:

- One person – the subject – has some interaction with another person or persons. Other persons may be 'real' in the sense that an independent observer would see them. Sometimes the other persons are memories or fantasies.

- The subject's working models of him or herself and the world shape his or her response to the event or situation.

- The subject is unaware that his or her response to the 'event' could be any different from what it is. In other words he or she is not conscious at the time that other people may interpret that event or memory (real or imagined) quite differently.

- The whole process of responding to, understanding and making meaning of the event occurs in the unconscious of the subject – that is outside the awareness of the subject.

The wombat story now continues and provides an illustration…

On the second day the group leaders had intended to run a series of 'trust exercises'. These are physically active group exercises that only succeed if all group members co-operate, and if the main player has some trust that the group will act safely and responsibly.

'Wind in the willows' (Rhonke 1988) is one such activity, where group members stand around in a circle facing inwards, with one group member standing in the middle, eyes closed and arms folded across the chest. When it has been established that everyone is ready, the person in the middle falls, keeping his or her legs straight and body rigid. The other group members are close enough so that the centre person's fall is relatively slight before one person in the outer circle pushes the falling person back upright. The person in the middle deliberately stays off-balance, constantly falling, and so the outer group members constantly gently 'pass' the falling person around the group or across from one side to the other.

However, the group leaders assessed that the level of negativity in the group on the second morning was so great that trust activities were likely to fail because at least one member of the group would be likely to act in a destructive or untrustworthy manner. Instead, they travelled by van to a local river for kayaking. In the van, Jack began complaining that he had not slept well because his tent was pitched on a sloping and rocky piece of ground. Daniel asked why he had chosen that particular place instead of a more suitable place. To which both Jack and Sean – who shared a tent with Jack – responded that the group 'bosses' had always intended that the group members would have a bad night and that the 'bosses' had taken the only good camping spot because they knew the area well. Daniel, Amy and George looked at each other with wry smiles because they had, in fact, chosen a less-than-perfect place to camp so that the others could put their tents together in the best place. What had actually happened was that each pair of group members had gone to great lengths to avoid having their tent anywhere near any other tent. Jack and Sean had avoided an excellent camping site so as to be as far as possible from the other tents.

Clearly, then, the logical argument put forward by Jack and Sean was not founded on facts or logic shared by the leaders. But Jack and Sean were aggressive, hostile and committed to their view. In their minds they were on solid ground – if you excuse the pun. No other group members contradicted them.

How might the unconscious processes of the type that we focus on in this chapter have been present in this scenario?

Jack and Sean both seemed to have a mental representation of the leaders as 'bosses'. A 'boss' was, for them, someone who was punitive and manipulative; so their world models of authority figures led them to see Daniel, Amy and George as punitive and manipulative, regardless of their real motives. This mental representation was likely to be outside Jack and Sean's awareness in that if one asked either of them if they thought 'bosses' were mean people, they might have agreed after some thought, but until asked would not have realized that this was their view. This process of association is one of the unconscious processes that we explore further in this chapter.

The main ideas presented earlier about internal working models and their more generalized form, 'world models',[1] are relevant to this chapter:

- Our entire history of interaction with others and the world leads us to build 'world models', which are durable patterns of perception, interpretation and meaning-making about events of all kinds. *Jack and Sean's histories had led them both to perceive people in authority as punitive.*

- These 'world models' exist partly in our conscious awareness and partly beyond our awareness. Many cannot be modified by conscious decision because we are not aware of their existence. *Neither Jack nor Sean were aware that they habitually saw leaders as punitive.*

- Even though many of our world models exist beneath our awareness, they are a major influence on how we interpret events. *Despite the fact that Jack and Sean did not 'know' that they saw leaders as punitive, they acted as if it was true.*

- Our world models are constantly being modified by new experiences, even though we may not be aware of the changes that are occurring. *One possible outcome of the adventure therapy expedition could have been that Jack and Sean might have had such powerful experiences of Daniel, Amy and George that they might have started to revise their habitual views that all leaders are punitive.*

- Our conscious awareness of ourselves and the world is only a thin slice through the full range of complexity of our existence. Much activity exists outside our conscious awareness. *Jack and Sean probably thought that they were fully conscious of every aspect of themselves. This is a common view of psychologically naive people.*

This unconscious process of interpreting, responding to and making meaning of events is almost taken for granted by psychodynamic psychologists and so it is not widely described in psychological literature. Although there does not seem to be a single widely accepted term that encompasses the phenomena, they are all based on what could be called 'associative' systems and what Laing (1971) refers to as 'inference'. Mark Freeman (1993) uses the term 'interpretive' to indicate that we interpret all events. However, the word 'interpretive' implies a degree of consciousness in the process of interpreting and the focus here is on unconscious processes. Here, semiotics comes to the rescue. The basic principle of semiotics is that every event or object in the world can take the function of a 'sign'. The main characteristic of a sign is that it 'signifies'. Signifies what? you might ask. Well, that depends on who perceives the sign. Taking the example of an inanimate object as a sign: two people are standing looking up at the sky. A dark cloud appears on the horizon, moving quickly towards the observers with heavy sheets of rain beginning to stream from the cloud towards the ground. One observer stands silently in awe, tears of joy and relief streaming down his face. This cloud (the sign in this case) clearly signifies something wonderful. The other observer's face shows distress and disappointment at seeing the same sign (the rain cloud). So the same sign signified fundamentally different things for the two observers. Clearly there is a complex relationship between sign, signified and observers. (You can make up your own story to make sense of this event.)

Human communication, whether spoken, acted, enacted, drawn, painted, sculpted, printed, fabricated, worn (as in clothes, jewellery, make-up, perfume, and so on), played, sung or written, is based on a system of signs. So, human existence can be seen primarily as the process of constructing and interpreting signs (Barthes 1993). In all human interactions we are constantly generating and interpreting strings or sequences of signs (Bateson 1972). A spoken sentence is a string of word-signs combined elegantly and simultaneously with a string of non-verbal signs, all conveyed in a context that is laden with signs that are often generated by others (furniture, floorings, and so on). Given this complexity how do we describe this complex process of sign, signified and interpretation?

I will use the term 'associative interpretation' to describe the whole family of processes that is involved in receiving signs, interpreting them and placing meaning on them. I will assume that the vast majority of this associative interpretation occurs beneath our awareness and so can be described as unconscious and therefore involving the implicit memory systems described in the interlude in the previous chapter.

When an event occurs it triggers associations with other events through one or more of the five memory systems described in Chapter 4. *The professor in Carl Jung's story walked past a farmyard where there were geese.* That is, the event is associated through unconscious processes (primary process) with other events that have been retained in conscious or unconscious memory. Similarities and differences between this current event and prior events are noticed – still at an unconscious level. It is necessary for our everyday functioning that this association occurs outside our awareness, otherwise we would be flooded with information about our past every time one of our senses was stimulated –

which is all the time we are awake. Some of the new sensory data reaches our consciousness and some does not. *The professor's conscious mind noticed images of his childhood because his unconscious mind had already carried out the associative process.* We have already discussed the fact that our unconscious minds need to screen us from receiving all sensory data to avoid overload, and that in some cases our unconscious minds screen out events that would create excessive anxiety. So, by the time we become conscious of an event through seeing, hearing, touching, and so on, our unconscious mind has already associated the event with prior material and so has established the event in a context. This placing in a context is a form of meaning-making. *The professor re-traced his steps and found the origin of the stimulus – the smell of geese – and was then able to make the conscious link with his childhood experience.*

An important observation that is relevant to our work in groups is that if the professor in Jung's story was a member of a group we were working with, and we did not know anything of his history, we would have no inkling that the farmyard had evoked images of his childhood. The same stimulus as the professor had would have evoked for me images of walking, as an adult, past geese on the shores of Lake Monger in the city of Perth. So, one of the keys to successful group work is to be able to hold in mind constantly that each group member could at all times be creating, from events in the group, very different meanings and associations from the meanings that you and other group members are creating.

Summarizing what happens every time one of our senses is stimulated by an event occurring around us: *Jack hears Amy say, 'OK, find yourselves a place to pitch your tents. There's a nice flat place here with room for all the tents'.*

1.   The unconscious compares/associates the sensory data with prior data and 'decides' what sort of event this is. *Amy's voice appears in Jack's unconscious as a bossy punitive voice.*

2.   The unconscious allows some sensory data to be 'noticed' by the conscious mind, but some does not reach awareness. *On the edge of his awareness, Jack feels anger and a reaction against Amy's suggestion. Without thinking, he picks up his tent and looks for a place a long way from others.*

3.   By the time we do notice an event, it has already been placed in a context and so already carries some meaning. *As he pitches his tent, he talks with Sean, and they agree that the leaders are trying to keep the*

participants in one place so they can supervise and control them. They are controlling and manipulative leaders.

What needs to be emphasized is that the majority of these processes *need to* occur beyond our awareness. We need to avoid overloading the limited resources we have in our conscious minds with too much stimulation. Secondly, we need to protect ourselves from excessive anxiety. Because of this, our vision, hearing, smell, taste, and touch are already tuned to some events and tuned out from other events. We do not just see 'reality'; we see what we already believe to be possible. This selective perceptual 'blindness' is not a fault, but a necessary adaptation for survival in a world that is very rich in sensory stimulation.

Given, then, that our response to events is very subjective and varies widely from person to person depending on our histories, what other aspects of life are intensely subjective? There is widespread support for the view that all forms of communication whether verbal or non-verbal have similar characteristics. If you are in a group and someone says, 'I went to the beach yesterday', you will have a mental picture of a beach, or a sequence of mental pictures of different beaches. Someone else who comes from a different part of the world will have mental pictures of beaches but they will be different beaches from yours. Even someone who comes from the same area and who pictures the same beaches will have differences in the detail of his or her pictures. Furthermore, some persons' emotional response to the word 'beach' will be different from others. The signification can be vastly different for each person depending on his or her prior experience. So what in everyday life we take as a single class of 'objects' such as 'beach' is in fact a sign for a class of objects. The word 'beach' exists to give the listener access to his or her own personal memories (from the imaged/perceptual register) of beaches. The word in itself means nothing, it only has meaning when the listener has heard it and has made the necessary unconscious association with his or her own imaged/perceptual memories of beaches.

Thus, interpersonal communication is a constant process of associative interpretation. Associative interpretation occurs when the unconscious makes a link between one thing and another through the kind of unconscious association that occurs in primary process (as described in Chapter 4). This can lead to conscious images or words, but does not necessarily. Successful communication with others only works because of what I describe here as associative interpretation. However, associative interpretation is not only necessary for communication, it is necessary for the act of thinking itself.

(For those interested, books by Steven Pinker (1995), Paul Cobley and Litza Jansz (1999), Roland Barthes (1993), Perry Hinton (1993) and Gregory Bateson (1972) provide further information on these topics.)

Associative interpretation and the process of thinking

Here, we need a short diversion into the evolution of thinking as an infant grows into a child. It has been demonstrated that in order for thought to occur, the subject needs to be able to tell the difference between a thing that exists in the world and the mental symbol that the thinker has for that thing. As mentioned earlier, it is thought that the very tiny baby is not aware that its thoughts of its mother are different from the real mother. This is a difficult concept for us to understand because as adults we take it for granted that when we think of a tree, what is in our minds is not a real tree. We know that having a real tree inside our heads would be fatal! The baby has no concept of what is 'in its mind' so there is no difference to it between the thought-of-mother and the real-mother.

Thought, then, involves the mental manipulation of symbols-for-things (or, in the language of semiotics, signs-for-things). We are very well aware that when we are thinking of adding twenty dollars to forty dollars, we are not actually moving dollar bills around inside our heads; we are moving *signs* for dollar bills around in our heads. So, in order to think about adding dollar bills, we need to have understood that the signs for the dollar bills are different from real dollar bills. Now, just as we use signs-for-things inside our minds in order to think, we use signs-for-things to communicate with others. I write a phrase 'dollar bill' on this page and when you read this phrase, you create a picture in your mind of something that you believe is a dollar bill. Communication through signs is tricky though, because the sender of the communication needs to assume that the receiver mostly has the same mental representation for each sign. The dollar bill is a good example, because at the time of writing, in the USA there is a dollar bill that is green and is 'paper' money. In Australia and New Zealand there are no dollar bills. The dollar is a coin in both countries. So the phrase 'dollar bill' creates for most Australian and New Zealand readers or listeners a bit of confusion in that there is no local real-life equivalent for the phrase. There is a similar potential for confusion with the use of words or phrases that represent concepts such as 'generosity', 'love', 'security' and so on. Different people have different associations to the same word or phrase. The reason that communication works at all is that social systems and the languages that go with them enable members of a society to learn the generally intended signification for each word, gesture or sign.

The purpose of any word or phrase is to enable both the speaker and the listener to create a mental picture or association in response to the word or phrase. Communicating with others always involves one party generating communicable symbols that are conveyed to the other on the assumption that the other will associate with the symbol what was intended by the person who originated the symbol in the first place.

Language is used to create rich pictures that are built from a mosaic of associations. Our first action on becoming aware that we are meant to be receiving communication from another is that we create a mental 'frame' that says to ourselves, 'Get ready to fill in this space with associations in response to the communication that you're about to receive'. This instruction to create an empty frame usually occurs outside our awareness. As soon as a person starts to speak, the intended listener creates a mental space or screen in preparation for constructing the picture that will be communicated. Often in a group a person will signal the intention to speak with a distinct body movement or sharp audible intake of breath. This 'intentional movement' will create in the minds of other group members a mental space ready for receiving what will be signified by the speaker.

Communication as a process of building a frame and then painting a picture

So, on receiving the start of any communication we first build a mental frame with a screen inside and then we use words and other non-verbal symbols, such as tone of voice, posture of the other, to paint our pictures on the screen. *Let me tell you a bit about myself.* Now you have created a frame that has a label on it: 'Martin's story'. *I grew up in the country.* That provides a screen in your mind onto which you paint something of your own idea of what 'country' means. I could add the details by describing more about what I mean by 'country'. But if I stop there and tell you no more, you will attempt to paint a picture with enough detail to satisfy you. You will fill in details from your own world model of what countryside is like. Is it forest, grassland, crop-growing country? Is the climate warm or cold, dry or wet? What kinds of trees grow there? What kind of cars and roads are there? Are there traffic lights? Are there shops in your picture of my country home?

In that example above I provided what I like to call a 'blank screen' on which you painted your own image. The blank screen is created by using words that describe only classes of items or events. Phrases like 'grew up' and words like 'country' encompass a huge range of possible details and so provide a frame without a picture inside the frame. Used in this way, language that creates blank screens can be helpful. The problem arises when a speaker is attempting to be clear with a listener but unwittingly uses generalizations in his or her language and so accidentally creates ambiguity in the communication. The deliberate use of generalizations is the basis for trance formation or trance induction, a topic that is thoroughly described in literature about NLP (Neuro-linguisting Programming). For example see Bandler and Grinder (1975), Cameron-Bandler (1985), Lewis and Pucelik (1993) and Watzlawick (1978).

Language, whether verbal or non-verbal, whether spoken or written, is a code that only works if the sender and receiver share the same code-set for encoding and decoding messages. However, the code has multiple levels because it changes depending on the context in which statements are made. For instance a jibe, 'You're a fool', has the same words as the insult, 'You're a fool', but the context that exists in terms of relationships and non-verbal expressions tell the recipient which code-set to use in understanding what is meant (Bateson 1972; Pinker 1995). If your best friend smiles, jabs you in the ribs and says, 'You're a fool' you will probably take it in fun and laugh. However if the context is quite different – your professor asks to meet with you and opens with a frown and the words, 'You're a fool' – that is likely to have an entirely different meaning because you use a different code for interpretation in each case. (This is the basic problem with email communication; the content of the message is usually lacking a frame or code that enables the reader to construct accurately the meaning that the writer intended.)

These codes are an integral part of our world models and because of the variation between individuals in world models there are variations also in the way in which we code and decode language. It is impossible to clarify continually what we mean by each word as we use it, because we could only do so by using more words and would end up in a loop of explanations about explanations about explanations… So we have to act *as if* the other shares our code for language.

Communication then seems a rather haphazard and potentially lonely business where the originator sends verbal signs to the other(s) who apply their own decoding set to interpret what was meant. Each person develops his or her own idiosyncratic view of what is meant and then acts *as if* this is true! In other words, *every act of communication is an act of associative interpreta-*

tion that has embedded in it inevitable misunderstandings and 'errors'. In everyday life this haphazard process works well enough for us to get by most of the time because errors in interpretation can easily be redressed. It is when we are working in a responsible position with groups that it becomes important to hold at some level the awareness that we can never be *certain* what any person in the group really means by what they say. The role of group leader then involves the tension of knowing that we do not know but having the courage to act on our hypotheses. More importantly, we need the humility to re-visit mismatches between our associative interpretations and what was intended when a group member asks to be heard again.

In summary, every situation that involves human communication occurs through a process of one person applying his or her own rules for decoding the communication. In other words, the recipient applies a process of associative interpretation to all communication that he or she receives. The rules applied by the recipient in decoding the communication will inevitably be different in some aspects from the rules that were used in encoding the communication. Thus, all human communication has embedded in it significant 'error' or mismatch between what was intended and what was received.

A story from a training group

I was conducting a four-day training group in 'group process' for helping professionals. Day 3 was progressing well but when one student led an experiential exercise to elicit conversations about competence, a woman began to cry. The student leader spent a small amount of time exploring the crying and then closed her session. About half an hour later, the same woman began crying again and talked about her anxiety that she would never become competent enough to lead groups in her work place, and that she '…should not be crying in a training group because it's not a therapy group'. Other group members seemed anxious and I wanted to ensure that there was space for participants to express authentic feelings. I responded rather too quickly, saying something like, 'Well, what you say sounds distressing. To feel incompetent at something central to your work must not be fun…and anyway you weren't doing a full-blooded cry with great gobs of snot!'

A woman sitting next to the person to whom I had addressed my comment looked shocked and avoided eye contact with me, resting her eyes instead on the man next to me. I felt embarrassed that I had overstepped the mark by talking about 'snot' (catarrh) and I was anxious that I had jumped in too soon with reassurance (matching the group-level anxiety about incompetence). We talked a while about the fear of not being competent and some of the unhelpful levels of anxiety seemed to disperse.

About half an hour later, we were about to stop for a tea break when the woman who had earlier avoided eye contact with me firmly addressed the man next to me: 'Alex, are you OK?' I looked at Alex and he was pale, clearly distressed and looked very withdrawn. I had not noticed this before! I then did a kind of 'emergency care' focus of attention with him. He clearly needed much stronger containment than he had been experiencing. It transpired that his aunt was in hospital and was dying of cancer of the throat. She was constantly streaming catarrh and was a very distressing sight. Earlier in the group Alex had been overwhelmed with grief about this when he heard the word 'snot' from me. He had felt afraid to talk about his grief because he was in a training group and not a therapy group (which was already a theme in the group). Alex's associative interpretation from the word 'snot' had taken him into a private world of grief. I had not noticed (which was embarrassing too) and so he had felt abandoned in his grief and without permission to deal with it. This was a great reminder to me of the unpredictable nature of associative interpretation in groups.

Note

1.   Parkes (1975) generalised Bowlby's idea of internal working models to apply more widely to areas of human behaviour additional to trust, safety, and so on. At times I use the wider term "world models" in preference to "working models".

CHAPTER 6

Projection and other phenomena
of the unconscious[1]

The previous chapter dealt with unconscious aspects of everyday communication. This chapter addresses some 'deeper' unconscious processes that have a protective function – serving in part as defences – and a communicative function. Specifically, this chapter addresses a 'family' of unconscious processes that all involve the broadly defined term 'projective processes'. These processes have a lot of influence on how people interact in all settings, one-to-one and in groups. However, in order to keep a reasonable level of simplicity in this chapter, I focus mainly on one-to-one situations and refer in later chapters to the group equivalents of the mental processes described here. There is not a direct transfer from one-to-one situations to group situations of all of these phenomena, but the descriptions of the processes that appear below form an essential basis for descriptions for those related to groups.

A 'deep' form of projection occurs to protect us against both acknowledging and acting on impulses that would lead to unacceptable self-image if we became aware of them. Impulses to rape, kill, cheat, and so on would be in this category. Instead of acknowledging these impulses in ourselves we see them in other people but not in ourselves.

Projection at another level occurs when we unconsciously *cannot tolerate aspects of ourselves*. In this case we disown what we do not like by failing to see those aspects in ourselves but projecting the disowned part of ourselves onto others and therefore seeing these characteristics in others. The shorthand for this is 'splitting and projection'. In the example below, Jack could not tolerate becoming aware of his own destructiveness, so he projected it onto others around him.

More from the wombat story:

Jack had previously shown a consistently destructive pattern of behaviour. He would squash any beetle, butterfly or fly that he could catch. A number of times he had 'inadvertently' bumped or pushed other group members, and he had often talked about incidents where people got hurt or killed. It is possible, then, that Jack had a strong destructive element to his functioning that he was not able to see. It would have been too threatening for him to see that in himself. Instead, he constantly saw destructiveness in others around him. In this way he protected himself from becoming aware of his own destructiveness and suppressed anger. In this chapter we will describe such patterns as 'splitting' off his own destructiveness and 'projecting' it onto others.

The family of unconscious mental process that will be examined below includes:

- projection
- identification
- projective identification
- transference
- countertransference.

Projection

Projection is a process by which an individual reduces his or her anxiety by unconsciously disowning a part of him or herself and imagining that the unwanted feeling or characteristic belongs to someone else. As for most concepts that have been derived from psychoanalytic fields, the word 'projection' is used by different authors to mean different things. Tyson captures the basic elements of projection in the following passage:

> Projection is an intrapsychic [intrapersonal] event whereby a person unconsciously splits off and gets rid of a bad feeling or an unacceptable aspect of their personality by attributing it to another person or, in some cases, an object. Projection can also involve the splitting off and projecting of positive feelings. In either case, the other is said to be the 'container' for the split-off and projected material. As this process occurs at the unconscious level of fantasy [phantasy], with both projector and container unaware of the process, it is difficult to detect, yet it may have a profound influence on interpersonal behavior. (Tyson 1998, p.34)

In its simplest form projection involves three conditions all being met:

1. The person projecting believes that another person is experiencing some kind of emotion or has some kind of characteristic or behaviour.

2. The other person is not actually experiencing that emotion or does not have that characteristic.

3. The person doing the projecting does have that same emotion present or does have that characteristic but it is pushed out of their awareness.

The term 'projection' implies that the person doing the projecting has disowned and projected (as in throwing a projectile) the unwanted emotion 'onto' the other. It is still a projective process when the other is not aware that the person doing the projection has this inaccurate expectation of them.

For example, a busy consultant is trying to do more than she can possibly achieve in the time available. She is not conscious that she is rushed. The traffic is slow and she is using the time to plan how to approach the client. She parks, then on arrival at the client's premises, rushes into the client's office. She says, 'I'm sorry to take your time when you're so busy'. The client is mildly amused, because she is feeling relaxed, having wound down for the holidays ahead. Sometimes both people may be stressed, but the projective aspect is that one person has identified the unwanted feeling of stress in another person *before* they realize that they themselves are in the same state.

Projection is a universal phenomenon. We often project aspects of ourselves onto animals, such as our pets, or onto our children. A figure wearing a balaclava on a hot day collects projections of fear, as does a group of motorcyclists riding together. Royalty attracts projections of authority and benevolence. Our liking of different plants, cars, house styles, and so on depends on the kind of projection that we place on each. Group leaders use projection deliberately in some exercises. The following group exercise is based on the use of projection:

> Step 1: 'Go outside and walk around until you find an object that is small enough and clean enough to bring back inside. The object should appeal to you in some way.'

> Step 2: 'Now get into pairs and talk to the other person as though you are that object or as though that object is a part of yourself. For example, if I had brought back this soft-drink bottle I might say, 'Hi, I'm a soft-drink bottle and I'm the part of Martin that seems quite hard and cold, but is necessary to contain and protect the more exciting and fizzy part of him.'

In choosing the object initially, the participants do not rationalize why they like it and they do not know why they are being asked to choose an object. This means their choice is based on some aspect of themselves that they project onto an object. The specific nature of the projection remains outside their awareness until they are asked to explore it through the description in Step 2 of the exercise. However, this exercise could also be said to involve elements of the mechanism of identification. That is, the person identifies with some characteristic of the object of their choice.

Identification

When a person fully identifies with someone else they lose the distinction between themselves and the other. When we cry in movies it is us who is crying, but that crying occurs because we experience emotions that are being expressed by someone else (or the image of somebody else). We identify with the person who is crying and act as if that person is us. Identification occurs at other levels too. The function of a role model is to provide a sustained opportunity for us to identify with another so that we can gradually become what we perceive them to be. We identify with this talented person and so gradually imitate their talents until finally we have introjected the talents and possibly no longer need the role model. Jacques Lacan believed that the first development of a baby's sense of self occurs through identification with others (Leader and Groves 1995). Yet another form of identification occurs when the television news shows a person who has been persecuted or treated unjustly. We may feel the outrage for the other person though a phantasy that we are that person. At a conscious level it is possible to rationalize the strong feelings by saying things like, 'We can't let that sort of thing happen. What if it happened to us?' However, seeing the television report creates the phantasy that this terrible event has already happened to us – through the unconscious process of identification.

As members of a group, when we see another group member being treated unfairly or inappropriately by the group leader we often decide not to trust the leader. This decision is made by identifying with the unfortunate group member and feeling what we imagine to be the feelings of the person who was mistreated. Then, on the basis of our feelings *as if we were the other*, we decide not to risk acting in the way that they did. The experience of identifying with another is the same whether or not we are correctly identifying with feelings that are actually experienced by the other. Sometimes we might identify with another and on checking, find that the other was not experiencing the feelings that we identified with. The two most relevant forms of identification in groups are, first, identifying with the leader, and hopefully attempting to emulate his or her abilities and, second, identifying with other group members and thus evoking aspects of ourselves that had previously not been accessible to awareness.

Projection and identification work together in powerful ways, both in one-to-one interaction and in groups. We will return later to this subject in the exploration of group-as-a-whole patterns.

Projective identification

Melanie Klein originated the idea of projective identification. As you can see from the name of this phenomenon, it involves both projection and identification. Projection and identification are intrapersonal phenomena – involving only the person who is projecting or the person who is identifying, whereas projective identification involves both interactive and intrapersonal elements. That is, two or more people are involved in some form of interaction and each of the persons involved has associated intrapersonal processes occurring outside their awareness. Bullying is a clear case involving projective identification. The victim is a person who has some visibly submissive characteristics but also has some suppressed aggressive tendencies. The victim cannot tolerate the idea of him or herself being aggressive or dominant. The bully is a person who has visible dominant characteristics – which are often accompanied by a sadistic streak. The bully has suppressed the submissive aspect of him or herself because this is unacceptable to him or her. The active bully/victim pattern occurs because each sees embodied in the other very distasteful characteristics and so they intuitively dislike each other. The bully's characteristic behaviour is to dominate and humiliate and so he or she starts to do this to the victim. The victim's characteristic response is to be submissive or run away from such unacceptable behaviour. The victim's response exacerbates the bully's dislike for the victim and so both parties' behaviours fuel the other.

In the language of projective identification, the bully projects his unwanted submissiveness onto the victim – who introjects it and acts it out. The victim projects his unwanted aggression onto the bully who introjects it and acts it out. This is an especially powerful form of projective identification because it involves two mutually reinforcing processes of projection and identification.

Marrone viewed projective identification as occurring in four steps:

Step 1 is the subject's projection of a part of himself on to another person. Step 2 is an interpersonal interaction whereby the projector actively pressures the recipient to think, feel and act in accordance with the projection. In Step 3 the recipient complies with the pressure exerted on him to fulfill the projector's expectations and behaves accordingly. A further step, often described, is that the subject reinternalizes the projection after it has been processed by the recipient. These processes can also be observed in small groups, between the subject and part of the group or the whole group. (Marrone 1998, p.132)

Some authors emphasize the role of projective identification in groups, and view this projection/identification dynamic as the most significant influence on the development of all groups (Wells 1995). This unconscious dynamic occurs because the group setting creates the perfect conditions for the kind of regression that leads to projection and identification. Furthermore, there are many people in a group, each of whom can both project and/or identify with material that others are projecting onto them (Wells 1995). Thus, in a group we have multiple 'projectors' and multiple 'identifiers' for each 'projector'. We will look much more closely at this key dynamic in the next chapter on 'group as a whole' phenomena.

Transference

Transference is another intrapersonal phenomenon where one person transfers expectations derived from his or her past onto a current situation that involves another person. Historically the term 'transference' was restricted to the unconscious association of figures from the past with group leaders and therapists. For example, a client in therapy who habitually treated his therapist with suspicion could be seen to be unconsciously transferring his experience of his father onto his therapist. A second use of the word 'transference' occurs amongst experiential educators in the USA and it is important to be clear which usage I apply to the word. This peculiarly American (although grammatically correct) use refers to *transfer of learning* from a training or therapy group to everyday life (Kimball and Bacon 1993). My usage in this book follows the language of psychoanalysis and relates to unconscious expectations about significant figures in a person's earlier life, and in particular to persons in authority. As such, transference is an associative process whereby working models of significant others – such as parents – are unconsciously applied to current experiences of leaders, therapists and sometimes other group members. It is important to remember that much more is transferred than the individual is aware of because the transfer is derived from working models that are mostly outside awareness. A second important feature of transference is that it is based on the transfer of the symbolic or psychic realities that were repeatedly experienced in early life, and not on real people or single incidents in childhood. An individual will change his or her patterns of transference as he or she resolves or re-works early life struggles with significant others. Conversely, working deliberately with transference patterns can lead group participants to revise their working models to create new ones that are more helpful. It is my view that transference is derived mainly from aspects of procedural memory, but that has not been validated by any studies of which I am aware.

As with most concepts that originated in the field of psychoanalysis, transference has been reinterpreted many times in many different ways. Mario Marrone and Nicola Diamond have written an excellent summary of some of these different views in Chapter 9 of the book *Attachment and Interaction* (Marrone 1998). For those who wish to explore the idea of transference further, this is an excellent place to start. Marrone describes the extreme variations between Klein's, Lacan's, Kohut's and Bowlby's views on transference. I choose Bowlby's view that 'transference is the direct manifestation in current interpersonal situations of the individual's working models' (Marrone 1998, p.128). This is a rather middle-ground approach in which little attention is given to primitive defences against anxiety. However I do approach these primitive defences later when describing unconscious phenomena in groups. Furthermore, in this stated view of transference I pay little attention to the dynamic that sets up the transference – in other words, the way in which group leaders' behaviour actively encourages participants to transfer unresolved issues with authority onto the leader and onto the group situation (Ashbach and Schermer 1987). More about this later.

Gosling provides an excellent description of transference and practical examples:

> From the psychoanalytic point of view, states of mind are seen as deriving from the impact of a present situation on a mind already patterned by previous experiences, each of which has had its impact that has left some residue. Thus, the impact of earlier experiences is seen as equipping the mind with residues, expectations or fantasies that affect subsequent experiences in important ways. The new experience is perceived to some extent in terms of the old and is interpreted in the light of it. Thus the impact of the

first experience is *transferred* to the second. To give some rather crude examples: a boy who has been brought up by a harridan of a mother might well have built up within him a firm expectation that all women he meets will turn out to be harridans. A girl who has in part experienced her childhood as one in which she and her mother were constantly being humiliated by her father might grow up to have a profound conviction that men will always humiliate her sooner or later. And, finally, to carry the experience back into even earlier childhood, an infant who repeatedly experienced his mother as becoming perplexed and worried and then as withdrawing from him every time he got furiously angry might well grow up to have a gloomy foreboding that his angry feelings are dangerously destructive to security and affection. (Gosling 1968, pp.1–2)

From Gosling's passage it is easy to see the similarity between the unconscious application of internal working models and/or patterns of attachment with the idea of transference. In the group situation it is generally considered that the main transference occurs between the group member and the leader. There are two aspects to this transference. First, the group member attributes greater powers, or a punitive approach, or wisdom or some other attributes to the leader purely because this person takes the position of leader. Alternatively, the group member attributes a particular leader with specific attributes such as being gentle, being punitive or some other attribute, because of the unconscious association that this group member has with other significant people in his or her earlier life. We could call the first form 'role-specific transference' and the second 'person-specific transference'. There is also room in the participant–leader unconscious relationship for splitting and projection, and for projective identification that can occur in both directions. For a thorough, if somewhat dense, explanation of transference phenomena, see Chapter 8 in Ashbach and Schermer's (1994) book.

Whilst transference is often talked about as though it occurs all of the time in groups, König and Linder (1994) remind us that the intensity of transference (and countertransference) phenomena changes rapidly with time and with specific events in a groups. König describes the idea of 'transference triggers' which are specific events that occur and that evoke transference in participants. For instance, a period of conflict and the leader's response to that conflict could trigger a transference reaction in one or more participants. (This idea can be extended to the idea of 'anchors' in neuro-linguistic programming (Cameron-Bandler 1985).)

Finally, group members transfer their working models of group experience onto the group-as-a-whole. Participants who have had traumatizing family experiences may have generalized their view of 'family' to that of 'group' and so may find groups terrifying places to be. This is a form of transference to the group. The group leader, too, has responses to the group and to individual members that occur outside his or her own awareness. These responses are of the same nature as transference as described above, but through the history of psychoanalysis these responses have been referred to as 'countertransference' because the therapist was originally construed as having reactions against the patient's transference. I will stay with the word 'countertransference' when referring to the transference reaction of group leaders and therapists (Ashbach and Schermer 1987).

Countertransference

Countertransference is the sum of the leader's unconsciously evoked reaction to the group experience. This definition is rather more general than the original Freudian idea of countertransference in one-to-one psychoanalysis, which was the analyst's unconscious resistance to the conflicts aroused in the analyst by the patient's work. This widened view of countertransference in the group situation leads to a greater complexity. There are three major aspects of countertransference that have importance to us in the group setting. One is the transfer of unhelpful or pathological aspects of the leader's working models onto the group-as-a-whole, subgroups or individuals in the group. This could result in the leader acting in ways that are damaging to him or herself and the group. It is important for group leaders to avoid 'acting in' as a result of this form of countertransference by having a very thorough understanding of the self and preferably of one's own working models. The second is the transfer of the leader's working models where these are functional and helpful – such as reflecting back to a participant that he or she has overstepped the boundaries for the group. Third is the leaders' response to transference and projections from group members and to the unconscious themes that evolve in groups. The ability to notice and interpret these themes is probably the core competency for leaders who wish to work sensitively at depth with groups. In fact throughout this book I emphasize the importance of leaders' capacity to use their own feelings and intuition as information about what is really going on in the group. The leader's emotional experience in the group is influenced by both helpful and unhelpful factors from his or her past experience. As a result, a leader will only be able to work effectively with difficult issues in groups when he or she has learned to manage the strong feelings evoked by these issues in him or herself. Failure to manage

these feelings results in the leader avoiding key issues or acting inappropriately by attempting to use the group to resolve his or her own discomfort.

This may seem like a stern warning to ensure that you do not experience
feelings evoked by countertransference, but countertransference is the core
means by which the leader reads the unconscious processes in the group. The
key is to acknowledge that the leader is an integral part of the unconscious
processes in the group and that the leader experiences feelings and intuitive
responses that derive directly from the 'group unconscious'. Then the artistry
in group leadership is to use these feelings and intuitive flashes as *information
that inspires interventions*, rather than attributing them solely to the functioning
of one's own internal world or trying to make them go away. We will re-visit
this important point later.

Complications

There is a significant danger in taking concepts that were originally derived
from one-to-one situations and applying them to group situations. Claudio
Neri (1998) believes that the use of the terms 'transference' and 'countertransference' should not be applied to groups for this reason. Farhad Dalal
(1998) cautions against the unthinking application of the ideas of splitting
and projection in group contexts because many of the phenomena generally
attributed to splitting and projection can be explained in more sociological
ways. I consider these to be useful warnings and urge interested readers to
explore them.

Implications for leaders

It may be possible that the most powerful form of emotional communication
in groups occurs through projective processes. Some authors claim that group
participants 'place' emotions into others and into leaders through projective
identification and that this results in many of the feelings experienced by
leaders. If this is the case, the subjective experience of the leader could well be
a very direct read-out of the kind of emotional experiences that group participants do not want to experience for themselves. The leader may become a
'container' for unwanted feelings. A positive side of this is that next time you
are feeling terrible while leading a group you can comfort yourself with the
thought that you are containing the unwanted feelings of group participants
– you are not a terrible person!

On a less extreme scale, leaders need to pay close attention to the way in which they are experiencing themselves and containing difficult emotions. Even if some of the feelings of group leaders are their own 'original' feelings, projection, identification, and countertransference are also always present in groups and are always influencing the leader's experience of him or herself and of the group.

Notes

1. This chapter is a broad summary of a huge range of knowledge derived mainly from psychoanalysis. Many concepts have been simplified without specific acknowledgement that such gross simplification has occurred. For an expansion on some concepts see Bateman and Holmes (1995) but the interested reader should go back to the original sources.

CHAPTER 7

Patterns in the group-as-a-whole

If people can think of countries as entities or sports teams as entities then perhaps they should be able to think about groups as entities? For some there is a fear that talking about the group-as-a-whole will deny the existence of the individual. On the contrary, I am of the view that focusing on the group-as-a-whole neither takes away from nor adds to the existence of the individual(s) in the group. Both individual and group-as-a-whole co-exist and both are essential elements of consideration.

Introduction

An important power in psychodynamic theory about groups is the ability to think about and describe patterns of perceiving, believing and behaving that occur in the group-as-a-whole. This empowers the leader to work with the *group* as distinct from working with individuals in a group setting. In this chapter the overall issue of group-as-a-whole functioning is introduced by extending the views of the previous chapters about unconscious functioning from individual or dyadic interactions to interactions involving the whole group or subgroups. Four levels of the group-as-a-whole will be examined, with emphasis being placed on unconscious elements of group-level functioning. These unconscious phenomena will be shown to rely heavily on fantasy and phantasy that involves groups and their leaders. The usefulness of group-as-a-whole models and theories is examined and applied to the practice of group work leadership.

The nature of silence

I think times of silence are some of the most interesting in groups and teams. Every person in the team or group sits thinking without speaking. What is it that holds thought from being voiced? When groups are actively engaged in conversation there is usually a sense that there is not enough space for everyone to speak. So what occurs in the collective mental representation in a group that keeps thoughts private rather than public?

I think that there are many different kinds of silence in groups and teams. Each type emerges from the interaction prior to the silence. One type that is quite common in staff groups or work place teams is what I call the 'devouring' silence. Prior to this silence what has usually happened is that each time a person has spoken, another person has soon afterwards discounted what they have said. The discounting may be disguised in warm and accepting language or it may be hostile. It does not matter. What matters is that people in the group build from the interaction an unconscious (and sometimes conscious) expectation that their verbal 'offering' to the group will be destroyed. Anzieu (1984) refers to this as the collective phantasy of the 'group as a mouth' where the mouth destroys what is put into it. Such groups can feel stuck and passive after a while. There seems to be little energy and life in them. Often there is an underlying hostility in the group or team that is being kept hidden and appears only through discounting that is justified in rational terms without addressing the underlying anger and destructiveness.

Another team or group might be silent but with a very different kind of mental and emotional functioning. If the group has been grappling with a problem and there have been many ideas put forward and a lot of discussion, most group members might just need quiet time to think. In this case the silence is busy with individual thought that has all been 'seeded' by the previous discussion. This is what I refer to in Chapter 10 as a 'group reflective space'. Such times of digesting information and feelings are essential in the functioning of most groups and their absence can reduce the quality of thinking in the group or team. Leaders need to learn not to interrupt them prematurely.

There are many other kinds of silence. Groups at times will be silent so as to prevent destroying a feeling of euphoria. Here, the 'ideal' group has been created (Anzieu 1984). It becomes sacred and must not be destroyed by someone saying the wrong thing. The prolonged silence enables the ideal to be soaked up by group members for their enjoyment. A different kind of silence occurs when a group member has presented some very moving disclosures and there is a sense in the silence that the significance and value of that material is being respected. What becomes important in working with any silence in a group is to learn how to determine what the silence is achieving. If it is leading the group to denial or avoidance then it usually needs to be challenged. On the other hand, if a silence is building something it should be left well alone. For me, silence is an excellent illustration of a group-as-a-whole phenomenon.

Does the group-as-a-whole exist?

Some well-respected group theorists have been firm in their views that there is no such thing as a group-as-a-whole. 'How,' they ask, 'can anyone be so silly as to claim that what is visibly a gathering of *individuals* is an entity in itself; something that has a "group mind" or any other similar folly?' Perhaps the same objectors would happily talk about 'an organization' or 'a cricket team' without flinching. There seems to be something frightening about the idea that a person in a group could be considered to be a part of an entity that is bigger than him or herself. Perhaps it is the term 'group mind' that scares people? I think that there is a fundamental fear of being consumed or over-powered by 'the group' and so talking about group-as-a-whole evokes that fear. On the other hand, I am afraid that not talking about the existence of group-as-a-whole phenomena gives them more power because they are denied. Something that exists but is denied is very powerful so I believe in the usefulness of naming and working overtly with group-as-a-whole phenomena. If such things do not actually exist then the worst we do is waste our time discussing and working with something that does not exist. If they do exist then we gain much more ability to do effective work in groups.

But does talking about group-as-a-whole mean that you think that everyone in the whole group is expected to be thinking or feeling the same? No. Focusing on group-level patterns of thinking, perceiving, believing and behaving still allows that different individuals and different sub-groups within the group will do these things differently. What is understood is that there are patterns that recur within the group-as-a-whole that may move from one individual or sub-group to another. So, the individual or sub-group can function in ways that are engendered by group membership.

Before moving on, I want to clarify the difference between functioning *in a group context* and *group-level* functioning. Some people will happily acknowledge that people behave differently when in groups than when in one-to-one relationships, but will still claim that there is no such thing as group-as-a-whole. I agree that thinking, perceiving, believing and behaving in a group context is different from the one-to-one equivalent. I am also convinced that there are other phenomena that occur in groups that can only be explained by group-level analysis. These group-level phenomena all involve unconscious communication of issues and concerns that form patterns in the group-as-a-whole. Examples include Anzieu's group illusion, Bion's basic assumptions and Neri's genius loci all of which are briefly described later in this chapter. In contrast, there is the commonly intuited pattern where the level of disclosure is much 'lower' or at a less personal level for participants in a group compared to the level of disclosure that occurs in equivalent situations where there are only two people present. Groups engender cautious behaviour on the part of participants in comparison to one-to-one situations and this is a result of the group context rather than being a group-as-a-whole phenomenon (although the particular phantasies that exist in groups that are unusually cautious can be seen as a group-as-a-whole phenomenon). There is even a parallel in terms of individual functioning. That is, when working in psychotherapy with a person who is, for example, suffering from depression, we do not attempt to work only on the isolated experience of depression. This one aspect of a person's functioning only makes sense when it is understood as a part of the person's overall functioning. Our level of analysis is 'person-as-a-whole' in order to understand the depression. Few people would claim that it is useful to focus only on the depression and so it seems curious to me that people could wish to focus only on how individuals function without taking into account patterns in the group-as-a-whole.

The falsely constructed problem of 'individual versus group'

Common language about groups is paradoxical. On one hand there are many figures of speech that signify the group as being a single entity. Commonly we hear statements such as 'The group was difficult this morning' or 'A member of a group gave me a nice compliment' or 'I belong to a group'. The reference to 'the group' indicates that it is a single entity in the mental representation of the speaker. The phrase 'I belong...' could be seen to imply that the group is a life form that can 'own' me. Reference to 'members' indicates a metaphor of individuals being connected to, and a part of, a single entity which is 'the group'.

Again, in the literature, there are unacknowledged – and in my view incorrect – premises about groups and individuals in society which I think befuddle and even corrupt our thinking about groups.

1. One premise is that the individual exists outside any group and that entering a group is in some form doing something different from everyday life.

2. A second premise is that entry into a group will take away the autonomy of any individual who enters a group.

3. A third premise is that there is something 'God given' about the 'individual' and something less than satisfactory about the power or influence of a group.

4. A fourth premise is that it is possible for the psychological functioning of an individual to exist independently of the groups to which the individual belongs.

These premises are derived from a highly westernized world view that is rooted in an unconscious fear of the group, supported by the illusion that human beings are autonomous individuals who can act with 'free will' without reference to or constraint from others. Such criticisms can be seen to be psychological defences of the western obsession with individualism. This western 'disease' of individualism is so embedded that, whilst I am aware of it, even some of my own writing has embedded in it the assumption that individuals in the group should be seen as 'free agents'. By implication it could be (falsely) seen that I am supporting the view that the group is only a collection of individuals, no more and no less. A further complication to the debate about the group-as-a-whole is that some authors consider sub-groups to be the smallest subdividable unit of a group – rather than individuals (Agazarian 1997).

An example of 'free will' in the life of an 'individual'

A nurse in an intensive care unit has been looking after the victim of a serious road accident. The young patient was in the prime of his life and now lies on life support. There have been a few flickers of life in the patient but after a long period there is no sustained improvement and when the life support is turned off briefly, the patient does not breathe on his own. After considerable discussion between medical experts and the patient's family, the nurse is asked to turn off the life support system. With the decision made, he feels very distressed. As a nurse, he has dedicated his life to saving others' lives. What will his colleagues think? When he meets his friends at the pub this evening what can he say about today on the ward? Is he a 'killer?' What will happen now in the staff team on the ward – how will they grieve the death of the patient who represented hope for them?

This nurse could claim to be an individual with 'free will' but we see from above that he or any member of a profession and/or work group carries elements of those groups in his or her psyche. The mental representation of 'reference groups' is present in the minds of all people at all times and so the so-called 'individual' is in part a mosaic of mental representations of the groups to which he or she belongs. Malcolm Pines writes of the 'self as group' in contrast to the illusion of the individual 'self' existing as a free entity. Rather than thinking of the self as an entity that is independent of others, it can be very useful to think of 'self as group' (Pines 1998).

It seems that the problem we are grappling with is not whether groups are entities unto themselves, but the limiting nature of the view that groups can only possibly be one thing. Instead, it is useful to consider that groups can be considered simultaneously to be collectives of individuals, collectives of sub-groups, and entities in themselves. Each view provides different possibilities to the conductor of the group. Focusing on individuals justifies certain types of interaction, focusing on the group-as-a-whole justifies other forms of interaction and focusing on sub-groups justifies still further types of interaction. It is also useful to pay attention to the nature of patterns of human behaviour that seem to be inextricably linked with the fact that they emerge in *the context* of a group setting. The following view on group-as-a-whole is presented on the basis that group-level analysis is one of the many equally true perspectives on life in groups.

Levels of group-as-a-whole phenomena

Group-as-a-whole phenomena have been written about very extensively and a full review of the literature is beyond the scope of this book. The most comprehensive view of 'group-qua-group' phenomena that I have found is presented in Ashbach and Schermer's book *Object Relations, the Self and the Group* (Ashbach and Schermer 1987). This book has been largely ignored by many subsequent writers but in my opinion, is the most thorough and significant work published in English on group phenomena. Ashbach and Schermer describe three levels of functioning in the group-qua-group system, each of which contains two categories. The levels and their corresponding categories are shown in Table 7.1.

Table 7.1. Group-qua-group levels and categories

Level	Category
Regressed	Primordal
	Primitive
Individuated	Transitional
	Oedipal
Mature	Task-oriented
	Self-actualizing

Source: Ashbach and Schermer (1987, pp.284–5)

The regressed level functions primarily at an unconscious level and is not related to the group task. The individuated level functions more consciously but is still largely anxiety driven and preoccupied with power relations and other unconscious dynamics. The mature level is creative and work-oriented with minimal contagion from unaddressed unconscious material.

While Ashbach and Schermer's schema provides some excellent insights into group functioning, it is too complex to be adopted by the average person who wishes to understand group-as-a-whole functioning. I do not believe that there is any ideal conceptual map for understanding how groups function as entities. In the remaining part of this chapter I present a range of schemata that fit my way of thinking about groups and will I hope give some readers enough stimulus to develop further their own way of thinking about group-qua-group phenomena.

There are four aspects of group-as-a-whole functioning that I want to pay attention to. The first two of these are extensively dealt with in most group work literature.

1. Procedural

Structures, arrangements and procedures that provide the frame within which a group functions. This procedural aspect is dealt with in some detail in Chapter 11 under the headings of 'task and activity' and 'structural' levels in a six-level analysis of group functioning and therefore the procedural level is not explored any further here.

2. Conscious thematic / Informal

Patterns of interaction such as norms that provide some of the 'personality' of the group.
This aspect involves that of shared values and shared patterns of interaction –
much like the 'norms' that are described in conventional group literature.
Some of these occur at a conscious level and most of them can be observed by
group members once they have been named. The literature abounds with
descriptions of how group norms develop and function and how values are
negotiated between group members. Therefore, this aspect will not be dealt
with any further here.

3. Unconscious thematic

*Concerns, issues, doubts, hopes and fantasies that move through the group and are
constantly changing.* The unconscious development of themes, concerns and
issues in groups occurs mainly through projective processes and so is dealt
with quite fully below. This aspect deals with the existence of shared signs
and ways of making meaning. The focal conflict model as described in more
detail below is an example of this. Here, specific patterns of anxiety and
concern will hold a group's attention for a period and then the group will
move to another concern. A typical example is the often unconscious
group-wide anxiety that exists in adult groups that are gathered to learn
something new such as group work leadership. Groups that gather to learn a
skill (training groups) often unconsciously work on the issue of how to learn
and at the same time not look incompetent.

4. Unconscious primordial

Myths, phantasies and primordial themes. This is the almost unknowable aspect of
group functioning that eludes the group leader unless he or she is highly
attuned to his or her own intuitive functioning. This fourth aspect is what I
would call the symbolic level that can seldom be addressed using conscious
rational language but can be influenced by associative and symbolic interventions. The unconscious primordial level responds to symbolic communication and so is rarely responsive to rational analysis. In fact rational analysis
can interfere with the healthy development of the primordial (Neri 1998).
This aspect and the one above will be the main focus of the remainder of this
chapter. An example of a primordial group is one that acts as if it is waiting for
a messiah to arrive so that all of its problems will be solved. (This is very
common in modern work places!)

Language as an example of a group-as-a-whole phenomenon

On a grand scale language is a group-as-a-whole phenomenon. The process involved in a language-group (usually called a culture) sharing a common language involves the largely unconscious process of sharing and learning the shared signs and symbols that enable speakers and listeners to make sense of communication in that language. The language is embedded in what has recently become known as the 'social unconscious' of a culture (Hopper 2001). Therefore, members of the language group unquestioningly see themselves as being a part of the same group because there is so much commonality in their unconsciously held sign and symbol systems – including language. Small groups share some of these characteristics in that group-as-a-whole phenomena occur mostly through an unconsciously shared set of commonalities in the group that are communicated effectively and efficiently amongst group members at levels that are primarily beneath their awareness. Some group-as-a-whole phenomena are versions of 'languages' in that they are sign and symbol systems that develop specific to the group and that do not make sense to people who are outside the group. 'In-group' jokes are one example.

Each group theorist has developed his or her own language and focus when describing group-as-a-whole phenomena in groups. Most of these models are based on the principle that group members act on unconsciously held principles *as if* the group represents something – such as a mother – or exists to do something – such as save them from anxiety. Group-as-a-whole models about unconscious thematic and unconscious primordial levels rely on the principle that group participants, including the leaders, develop mental representations of the group and of their place in the group that are primarily unconscious, and that these unconscious maps of the group provide the templates that influence their perception, making of meaning, and behaviour. Some models of group-as-a-whole are founded on the phantasy generation of participants as defence against anxiety, and others are based more on the idea that participants act to defend their personally held and constantly evolving internal working model of the group and their place in it. All models incorporate some unconscious processes, and in particular splitting, projection and projective identification. All models describe processes that can either assist with or detract from effective functioning of the group. A summary of models is given in Table 7.2.[1]

Table 7.2 A selection of models of group-as-a-whole

Authors	Name of model	Synopsis of model
Unconscious thematic group-as-a-whole models		
Wells (1995) Guetzkow (1953)	Role fixation and scapegoating	Repetitive patterns of projective identification result in various group members enacting in an exaggerated way particular personality characteristics. The extreme form is scapegoating.
Foulkes and Anthony (1990)	Group (dynamic) matrix	Groups function as a network of interrelationships that can be said to resemble a neural network in a human brain. That is, the communication and behaviour of any member is interdependent on all others present. No one person can be singled out as the focal point.
Whitaker and Lieberman (1964)Whitaker (1989)	Focal conflict model	There exists in the group a central concern (tension) and participants' 'solutions' (responses) to that concern range from defensive to generative. The nature of the concern changes with time.
Unconscious primordial group-as-a-whole models		
Lawrence, Bain and Gould (1996) Bion (1961)	Basic assumptions	Unconscious defences result in some group members acting as if an unconscious assumption is true, and this 'as if' mode of functioning distracts from the group working on the primary task. Bion introduced three basic assumptions and two more have since been identified in the English language literature, while others are described in the French literature (Kaës 1993; Pigott 1990).

Neri (1998, 2001)	Genius loci	There exists in the group a person or theme that hold the 'spirit of the place' and carries an essential function for the group. This function is implicitly acknowledged by group members but not named. Naming the genius loci can destroy its effectiveness.
Anzieu (1984)	Group envelope (phantasy-based)	In order to exist, a group must develop a psychic envelope that is built from a shared phantasy on the part of members about the nature of the group. Examples given by Anzieu (1984) are phantasies of breaking apart, of group-as-machine, and group as a breast–mouth.
Anzieu (1984)	Group illusion	A specific form of group illusion where a part of the individual sense of identity (ideal ego) of group members is replaced by an idealized collective unity. This provides a transitional space from which progression can occur. (Compare with the basic assumption oneness' above.)
Foulkes and Anthony (1990) Brown (2001)	Group (foundation) matrix	There exists in all groups a collective unconscious representation of the pervasive 'realities' that exist in society and that are unconsciously acted on in the group.

The pervasive theme in the unconscious primordial group models is that the theme is communicated entirely unconsciously through 'primitive' modes of communication such as projective identification. Some models are based on the assumption that the primordial group-as-a-whole functioning occurs as a defence against primitive anxieties in group members. The unconscious 'associative chain' in the group transfers primary process communication throughout the group, between individual mentation and the collective mentation. (See Neri 1998, in particular Chapter 4.)

The pervasive theme in the unconscious thematic group models is that the group solves a problem or enables its functioning through communicating at a largely unconscious level about anxieties that are present at any given time. For instance, in a training group the leader needs to make room both for the expression of the fear of looking dumb, stupid or incompetent and for the wish to learn. If a person expresses fear and the leader reassures them without acknowledging the underlying fear, this reassurance is experienced as a disallowing of the fear. All group members notice this and therefore experience the need to suppress the expression of (and possibly the experiencing of) fear. Such 'forbidden' topics lead to a wooden and preoccupied feel about the group. On the other hand, if the group leader emphasizes the difficulty of learning and the likelihood that participants will look and feel stupid, then the group is likely to become paralyzed with fear. The art is to be able to shuttle between fear and hope by paying selective attention to participants who express each of these sentiments.

This sample of group-as-a-whole models is only a fraction of all the possibilities and does not explain the way in which each model can inform the practice of group leaders. A full analysis is beyond the scope of this book. The material in Table 7.2 is intended only to show that there are many different ways of thinking about how groups function as entities.

Some benefits of group-as-a-whole views

On a practical level, considering the group as an entity can save endless vacillation. Consider the problem of negotiating to change the timing of the lunch break in a group. For example, as facilitator I might suggest to the group breaking at 12.30 instead of 12.00. If I am treating the group only as a collection of individuals, I will hold one-to-one conversations with each person until a decision has been reached. No change will be possible until every person has agreed. If I treat the group as an entity I will make the suggestion, listen to the conversation that emerges in the group, perhaps make comments or answer questions, and then I will tell the group of the decision that I believe that the group has made. In this second mode, I will acknowledge that not everyone feels fully supportive of the decision, but that in the view of 'the group' that decision is best. The second situation also indicates an implicit agreement about what constitutes a decision in that group. For those interested in group decision making, there was extensive research done on power, influence and decision making in the 1950s. A good example of this appears in Cartwright and Zander (1970).

The group-as-a-whole and the group-in-the-mind

Having dealt briefly with group-as-a-whole phenomena it now seems useful to relate this idea to some of the ideas about the subjective experience of the individual that were presented in Chapters 1 and 2. This is done by expanding on the idea of the group-in-the-mind.

It is pretty obvious when we look at a group that there is no such thing as a 'group-as-a-whole'. Our eyes show us a number of individuals whose bodies are clearly not joined together in any way to form an amoeba-like blob that could be called a group-as-a-whole. Given that a primary 'reality checking' device is our vision, the visual evidence of the separateness of each person makes it potentially very difficult to conceptualize an entity that is common to the whole group.

The term 'group concept' may not mean much to you right now so before describing group concept itself I will relate the idea to a more familiar one – that of 'self-concept'. There are probably hundreds of psychometric tests that attempt to measure the way in which people view themselves. These tests (such as the Tennessee Self Concept Scale) attempt to measure the reasonably constant aspects of how people view themselves. For instance the test item 'I am a moral failure' asks the respondent to assess how much he or she believes that he or she lives up to his or her expectations of being a moral person. These tests are based on the assumption that we all carry in our minds a fairly constant set of pictures, feelings, thoughts and expectations about ourselves – in other words internal working models. All together this jumble of images, sounds, fears, wishes, dreams, thoughts and memories forms our 'self-concept'. There is general agreement amongst psychologists that self-concept changes over time, but that each person's sense of self has core elements that in normal circumstances change only slowly. I am suggesting that we also carry mental representations or internal working models of ourselves in relation to groups. Some of these will be episodal memories, some will be procedural and some will be semantic.

Prior to entering a group we have some expectation of what that group will be like for us. That expectation is built up from 'facts' about the particular group we are about to join and from our generalized expectation about what groups are like. Information about the specific group may have been obtained from the promotion material, conversations, reading or enrolment information. Information or expectations about groups in general is built up as an accumulation of experience of groups in our lives. Our original family was one very important setting where we learned what it was like to be in a group.

Of course when we were children we were not aware that we were building an image in our minds of how groups function but later in life it usually becomes apparent that our behaviour in groups is strongly influenced by what we learned from being in our families. Other sources of information that add to the generalized picture of the group-in-the-mind include school groups, social groups, work groups and committees.

So, even before we enter the room or location where we join the others, we have built a tentative group-in-the-mind. From our first contact with the real group we start moulding our internalized group to fit our actual experience. The modification of the internalized image of the group continues right through the actual group meetings. We continue to change our memory of the group even after the last time we meet together (Freeman 1993). Key aspects of the group-in-the-mind include our images of:

- other members
- the relationship between ourselves and other members
- the relationship between other members – not including ourselves
- the leader
- the relationship between ourselves and the leader
- the relationship between the leader and other members
- the nature, atmosphere, and so on of the group-as-a-whole
- the nature of the task that the group is undertaking
- the environment in which the group meets.

This dynamic set of expectations and internalized experiences shapes the core of each participant's experience. Broad aspects of each participant's group-in-the-mind include their sense of:

- emotional safety
- interpersonal trust
- enjoyment
- excitement.

This group-in-the-mind is clearly a complex phenomenon for each group member. I believe that it is the group-in-the-mind for each group member that provides the core of the experience and that enables the educative, developmental or therapeutic process to occur. It is my intention in this book to pay close attention to how group leaders can be attentive to the ways in which actions in groups may influence the group-in-the-mind for participants and how those influences can shape the outcomes achieved by group members.

A 'fishing line' to help participants find their own group-in-the-mind

Each group has a distinctive 'feel' that can be difficult to put into words. Rational explanations are not enough to distinguish why some groups feel different from others. We need ways of conceptualizing groups that go beyond the observable and rational. We need techniques that enable us to work directly with the ephemeral aspects of groups. What follows is an exercise that I sometimes use as a tool for surfacing representations of the group-in-the-mind for participants in training groups. Each group member identifies a different symbol and from free association on that symbol comes up with different characteristics of the group. It is important to be aware that this visualization tool does not identify the 'group-in-the-mind' for each participant, all it does is give participants a 'fishing line' to access from their unconscious a symbol and some associations for their own 'group-in-the-mind'. When I am working with groups to assist them to build an understanding of the collective nature of the group-in-the-mind for their team or group, I write summaries of their individual responses on a whiteboard and ask them to identify commonalities or patterns in the symbols and the associations. This exercise can create a fundamental shift in the ambience of the group. It surfaces unspoken perceptions of each individual's experience of the group and so can have a powerful effect on the feeling of understanding that group members have for each other and for the context in which they operate. In short, the collective examination of the individual mental representations of the group helps to clarify the nature of the group-as-a-whole.

The exercise: a group-in-the-mind visualization

Place yourself at some moment in time when this group is meeting but you are not at the meeting. I want you to imagine that you are approaching this group from a long way away. You are not particularly searching for the group but you are moving in that direction. You may be out in the middle of a field or paddock, out to sea, I'm not sure where, but somewhere where you are perhaps walking slowly towards the group. At first there is no sign of the group but gradually just on the edge of your awareness you realize that you become aware of something. Pay attention to that first vague notion of the existence of the group.

As you get closer that first impression of the group starts to become clearer. But it is an unexpected image that somehow fits the real essence of the group rather than a pictorial image of the group. This symbolic image may seem odd at first and even be a bit unsettling. It may be a line from a song, a piece of art, a book, a scene from a movie, television show or video, an opera, a plant, an animal, a snippet from real life, a figure from a fairy tale...whatever it is, it has a sort of life and quality of its own.

Now you come even closer and the image takes on a life of its own and it grows in clarity...

Write down or draw the image or symbol that came to mind. If more than one appeared, write them all down.

Now spend a few minutes writing down whatever comes to mind, whatever is evoked by your original symbol or symbols for the group. What do you feel, what floats into your mind? This might be words that describe the most obvious characteristics of that image or impression or it could be words that seem completely unrelated.

A member of one group I worked with likened his group, which was a work place team, to the symbol of a revolving door. People constantly moved in while others were moving out. For him, this had associations of being mobile and dynamic, but also associations of having difficulty with keeping track of all the changes. Other members of the group had strong associations to that same symbol that were more negative, such as the sense that people did not stay in the organization any longer than they had to. When a group sees all of the symbols that emerge from each other's visualizations the response can be a very powerful cross-association that leads to a significant shift in the group's perception of itself.

Earlier in this chapter I reflected on the relationship between each participant's internal working models and the group-in-the-mind. What starts to emerge from exercises such as the group-in-the-mind visualization is a group-level 'internal working model' that is implicitly and explicitly negotiated through discussion about the symbols that emerged for each person. This collective mental representation or group-level internal working model is built from conscious and unconscious memories, fantasies, expectations and phantasies about the group's functioning. Working with any aspect of the group will make some changes, even if only small, to the group-as-a-whole.

Implications for practice

There are too many models of group-as-a-whole to derive here implications for practice for each of them. Instead I step back and take a practical look at what can be achieved by taking any group-as-a-whole perspective whilst leading groups. I also look briefly at some of the challenges for leaders that result in taking the group-as-a-whole seriously.

While I was grappling with the challenge of writing about group-as-a-whole phenomena, the following thoughts provided a useful clarification:

- I find it relatively easy to experience group-as-a-whole characteristics of a group in my *memory*. That is, the pervasive memory of groups is often a collective one of impressions and feelings rather than a disparate set of episodal memories.

- I find it much less easy to experience group-as-a-whole characteristics of a group *when I am actually in the presence of a group*. When I am surrounded by people in the flesh what dominates is the experience of being in relation to a number of individuals and the generalized impression or feeling tone of the group is less accessible to me. In other words, the immediacy of the sensory experience of seeing and hearing *individuals* in the same room as me makes it difficult to retain awareness of group-as-a-whole phenomena.

- In exceptional cases individuals and specific events do dominate my memory of a group. For example an arrogant, defensive garrulous person dominates my memory of a recent group experience. My recall of the overall feeling tone of the group is less dominant in this case.

- If I can generalize my experience, it seems that group-as-a-whole phenomena are mental representations rather than specific sensory impressions. Therefore, the flooding of my senses with pictures, sounds and smells whilst in the midst of a group is likely to reduce my ability to get access to the mental representation of the group-as-a-whole phenomena. Furthermore, the conductor's attempt to keep track of thoughts and feelings that occur in response to each group member's contribution can reduce the ability to develop awareness of group-as-a-whole phenomena. It is necessary to shuttle awareness constantly between group-as-a-whole, interpersonal and intrapersonal levels.

- In that case, effective group work leadership probably means finding ways of accessing our semantic memory and the associated unconscious/intuitive parts of our being whilst in the midst of the sensory bombardment. In psychoanalytic terms, this access is created by 'free floating attention' where the specific events in the group are not attended to. Rather, the conductor enters a trance-like or dream-like primary process state so that the group is experienced as a series of waves of impressions. No one person or one statement is specifically attended to (Foulkes and Anthony 1990).

There are two particular quirks that I have that create tension for group participants. These both arise from the strategies that I adopt to keep my attention on group-as-a-whole phenomena rather than constantly attending to individual participants. These two quirks emerge from the stories that I tell next.

After facilitating a particularly intense group work training workshop of two days duration in a country many miles from where I lived I was standing outside my hotel waiting for a friend to pick me up. It was early evening and a few hours after the group had ended. I saw a participant from the training group emerge from the hotel, see me, pause in her stride and look very uncertain. Clearly there was something amiss. I smiled briefly and looked away to give her a chance to decide what to do. She remained fixed to the spot so that when I thought enough time had passed and I looked again in her direction I once again caught her eye. She was clearly waiting for a signal. I smiled again and asked if she was looking for someone. She moved quickly across to stand beside me. A short period of small talk ensued and then she said, 'I want to ask you a question about the group today'. I gave my usual short speech about confidentiality and so on, but was less rigid than usual because something seemed to be different about this occasion. She then asked me why I had not looked at her when she had been talking at the end of the group. She told me that I had made eye contact with everyone except her. Did I not like what she said? Did I not like her?

My response was quite simple. I said that there were many times during the two days when I had not made eye contact with someone who was speaking. In fact, most people would have thought that I was staring fixedly at a spot on the floor in the centre of the circle of chairs. This was simply a strategy that I used in order to keep focused on the feel of the group-as-a-whole rather than get caught up in the story or content of what any particular individual was saying. I asked her to reflect on her overall sense of whether I had valued her input during the two days. She said nothing and after a perceptible pause, visibly relaxed. We stood in silence until my friend arrived.

A second incident that occurs about every four or five times I work with a group is that in the middle of saying something that seems quite important to the speaker he or she will pause, look uncertain and ask something like, 'What's wrong? Did I say something wrong?' When this first happened I was quite puzzled but now I understand what evokes this question. When I am deeply considering what a person is saying and at the same time trying to relate it to what is going on in the group my brow furrows and some people interpret the furrowed brow as a signal of disapproval. (This is an internal working model that is not shared by everyone, fortunately.) I was relieved when I saw Claudio Neri doing exactly the same thing, and in fact some people who knew me quite well and who participated in a workshop with Claudio and myself subsequently called an informal group to which they belonged 'the furrowed brow'. The lighthearted theory was that having a furrowed brow must lead to some kind of wisdom about groups! The serious side of this story is that group leaders will be perceived at times as not being fully responsive to group members when they (the leaders) are focusing on group-as-a-whole issues. This disadvantage is counterbalanced by the fact that a leader who is well attuned to group-as-a-whole issues can be much more effective than a leader who works only with interpersonal or intrapersonal issues.

The usefulness to you of the above thoughts will vary from reader to reader, but it seemed important to debunk the myth that most group leaders are omnipotent and can focus on all things at once. I do not know any group leader who is able to respond effortlessly to individuals, monitor the group-as-a-whole, manage their own feelings states, and retain sharp focused thinking – all at the same time. Group work leadership is much more messy and challenging than that.

A fable to help shift the way we think about groups and individuals

Given that I spend a lot of time working with groups in corporate settings, I am constantly looking for ways to translate psychodynamic ideas into language that makes sense to people with no background in psychology. The following myth is one such attempt to provide an alternative way of thinking about groups (or teams) and individuals.

The fable of the 'Grerson'

A large flying saucer landed in an isolated and remote country town. The door opened and a group of strange looking humanoids came out together and stood, looking around. Soon, a second group of the same kind of humanoids came out, moved towards the first, and began a conversation in a language that was unintelligible to the townspeople who had gathered around.

One brave person from the gathered crowd moved forward and tried to hold a conversation with one group of aliens but it was hopeless.

For days the aliens moved around the flying saucer within earshot of the local people. Then one day one of the aliens began a stumbling conversation in the language of the townspeople. After a few more days of conversation, the aliens became amazingly fluent in the language of the townspeople and both races started to get visible enjoyment from each other and began to teach each other about their respective worlds.

However, it was not long before a disturbing pattern of behaviour became apparent. Whenever one or two townspeople approached a group of aliens the aliens would not respond to them. No amount of shouting, persuasion, manipulation or any other strategy would evoke a response from the aliens. This was clearly rude and unacceptable behaviour, and so the town council met and decided to protest to the aliens about their bad manners.

The whole council dressed in their finest formal attire and marched as one down the street to where the alien's vehicle rested. To their surprise, the aliens responded with a great deal of respect. Two groups of aliens listened and responded carefully. When the mayor demanded that the aliens respond to (rather than ignore) one or two townspeople on their own, the aliens laughed. They said that the word 'person' was not in their language. The smallest component of any society was a 'grerson' which in human society was called a 'group'. For the aliens to respond to a single person would be like a human talking to someone's foot or belly. In human society one does not talk to a part of a person as though the other parts are not present and in this alien society a grerson does not talk to a part of a grerson as if the other parts do not exist. A grerson only exists if there are at least four aliens present and no conversation is possible with less. They explained that a grerson has

- a grersonality
- moods
- competencies
- intelligence
- and all of the characteristics that humans mistakenly thought that individual persons had.

The town council protested that a 'grerson' could be made up of different people at different times. The aliens were not worried about this. They explained that when one or more 'members' of a grerson changed then all that happened was that the grerson then had a slightly different grersonality because its components were different. It was still a grerson and it still had all of the characteristics of a grerson. They explained that a lot of communication goes on between the elements of a grerson at a non-verbal level and at a level that is not visible to humans. So what looks to humans like a collection of individuals is in fact a coherent whole.

So what of the wombat?

This is the final episode in the wombat story. We pick up the narrative on the second day of the trip when the group is preparing to go kayaking…

> Participants had plenty of time to prepare lunches for during the day, but only half managed to get organized well enough to do so. Once on the water,

Jack and Sean behaved in an intimidatory and aggressive way. Others such as Robert and Clive had a lot of trouble with paddling and it was quite a challenge to keep the group together. Difficulties were increased by the leaders' unfamiliarity with the area and the lack of suitable landing spots on the steep-sided lake.

Eventually the group turned around more or less together with the exception of the two, Jack and Sean, who had earlier on abandoned the rest of the group and headed back on their own. While the rest of the group pulled in at the first available landing for some food and discussion, Jack and Sean paddled all the way back to the boat ramp and carried their boat back to the vehicle for a presumably cold wait for the rest of the group.

Once the whole group was back at the vehicle warm clothes and drinks were the priority. In the midst of these arrangements Jack and Sean set off with their bags and without a word to the instructors, obviously intent on a long walk back to civilization. This sparked off a generalized group gripe session, at the end of which Jack and Sean were still adamant about wanting to leave. Confronting feedback, this time from the instructors, inspired another walk-off, before Daniel led the next round of negotiations and it was agreed that the group would be dropped off at the slalom camp site before Jack and Sean were driven to Big Bluff where Sean's father would pick them up and take them home. In short, they were leaving.

Once at the slalom camp site it became apparent that the two female participants, Katrina and Vikki, were also thinking about leaving the course. Much to Sean's credit he did not attempt to convince them of this course of action and eventually George and Daniel convinced them to stay on. Still, rather than reintegrating with the rest of the group they chose to light their own fire and sit away from the instructors for the night.

In the meantime George drove Jack and Sean into Big Bluff where Sean's father picked them both up. On the drive all animosity was dropped and the three had an excellent discussion of what went wrong on the course. Sean attributed his main difficulties to the fact that he was known to everyone else on the course. He seemed insightful and self-aware and George's final impression was that he would no doubt reflect deeply on his experience with the programme. Jack just said that he missed his pillow and so that was why he needed to go home.

That night back at the now reduced camp, the group was quiet, though clearly not well motivated to do the scheduled bush walk the next day.

Day 3

The next day began well with a thorough brief for the bush walk given by Amy. The group decided on a two-day walk instead of the three-day one that was previously planned. The group packed and sorted food well, although a number of them still left essential items behind despite the exhaustive discussions on what would be required.

Robert created a minor scene when he discovered he had left his raincoat behind. At first he refused to go back and get it, then threatened anyone who offered to get it for him. Dennis and Clive defused the situation with tact and generosity. They went back for the raincoat and another minor item but left the coat a little way up the track when they returned for Robert to pick it up.

After lunch at the river the group walked consistently and well, making good time into Burnt Clearing before dark. The final creek was crossed and a beautiful camp site, balmy evening and generous pile of dry wood represented tangible rewards for their efforts. Nonetheless the group remained as determined as ever not to enjoy the experience. Vikki and Katrina had left their stove behind and dined *once again* on snack food before retiring to their tents, cold, hungry and grumpy but unwilling to do anything about it. Robert and Clive were in bed within an hour of arriving at the camp site and Barry followed soon after.

Day 4

George opened a bleary eye to see Clive visiting the other tents obviously gathering support to abandon the walk that morning. Upon getting up, the group mood was quite hostile and little disposed to discuss options. After three days of doing the 'hard sell' the instructors were all drained and at a loss to fathom the group's lack of motivation and absolute unwillingness to engage with the challenges of the walk that they were so obviously up to. The group had decided to quit and walk out to the vehicle instead of carrying on with the trip.

George and Amy sat the group down and attempted to get them all as individuals to account for their decision to walk out but the whole group all walked off *en masse* without meaningfully engaging in a conversation about the issues. The instructors were left in the company of Dennis, who remained as calm and well disposed as ever. Shortly afterwards they were rejoined by Barry, who had lost touch with the group, fallen into the creek and generally lost his confidence to go on alone. Throughout the walk out he was transformed into a meek and congenial person, rather than the unpleasant ball of negativity he had been in the group's company. However, once he caught up with the rest of the group he quickly transformed back into his previous unlovable persona.

The group ate lunch together and a degree of cordiality returned to group relations, possibly because the decision had been made to end the trip. Obviously they were already in two minds about their decision and came up with the option of returning to the slalom camp site and basically hanging out or even doing a short day walk for the final day. The instructors were all agreed that this was a pointless option. It seemed important that the quitters experience the consequences of their decision not to engage with the challenges of the week, and so back to the vehicle they went.

Ironically the group did the clean-up quite well, demonstrating their ability to work towards goals they perceived to be in their self-interest. The final 'discussion' was short and tinged with a degree of bitterness from both sides. The group got into the vehicle, George just managed to persuade them to do up their seatbelts and they were off on the journey. Shortly thereafter, the 'wombat incident' occurred, as described at the start of the book.

Making sense of the wombat incident and trip

It is not possible for any of us who were not present throughout the trip to know what really happened, but I will use this story as a basis for conjecture about what might have been happening given a psychodynamic view of groups. This final analysis is greatly aided by information from all three of the group leaders.

What was happening in the van before and during the time that the 'van hit a wombat'? Some conjecture follows:

- Jack and Sean had probably carried the projections of the others, 'It's too hard' and 'I can't change who I am' being two major issues during the trip. After all, the overt intention of the trip was to enable participants to make positive changes in their lives.

- Once Jack and Sean had left, this negativity had nowhere else to go but onto other group members, hence the reluctance of some to go bush walking. Meanwhile, Dennis retained his positive image and so remained split from the group and more overtly aligned with the group leaders who were by now clearly identified as being the people who wanted this trip to occur. That is, the motivation to do the trip had been completely projected onto the group leaders and Dennis.

- The phantasy of the 'perfect trip' that had been present at the pre-trip day was by now completely ruined. This created a psychological loss but there was no place for grieving. Instructors saw the fault as being with the participants – and in particular with Jack and Sean who had left and therefore publicly made the trip a failure.

- The splitting and projection of badness was occurring both ways. Group members were projecting their 'badness' onto group leaders and group leaders were projecting their 'badness' onto the group members.

- The end of any trip is a difficult time. Successful trips need to be grieved. For some disaffected youth a successful trip can be one of the most positive emotional experiences of a lifetime and going 'home' represents the loss of a treasured group. For this 'wombat' trip the loss was more of a dream than of a reality. Nonetheless, the loss needs to be grieved. Group participants had not left the space for the leaders to do the 'processing' required for grieving.

- So, in the van on the way back to 'civilization' time was running out for any kind of resolution of what by now were very high levels of projection and projective identification, along with unresolved grief. The emotional tone in the van was a bomb waiting to go off.

- These conditions are ripe for what many people would call a 'psychotic episode' where reality becomes distorted and events are experienced by some that are not experienced by others.

- The event that sparks off a psychotic episode can be quite small such as a group member getting a fright from a bump in the road.

- In the right conditions, once a psychotic idea is voiced, and if it fits the group climate, it will spread through the group in an instant and will become a powerful group phantasy that is treated as real.

- The anger, loss and mourning about the trip could well have been displaced onto the 'wombat'. The belief that the driver killed a wombat and that the group participants had to bury it because the 'heartless' leader would not stop the van perhaps provided a bizarre form of resolution for the group members – but not for the group leaders.

Was there really a wombat? I do not think anyone really knows. What we do know is that this kind of 'extreme' behaviour is much more common in groups and organizations than most people would wish to acknowledge. Many corporations and even more executive teams build their functioning on an elaborate set of propositions that simply do not hold up under the light of day, but members of the organization all act as if they are real.

'Reality testing' in groups and organizations requires close attention to be paid to unconscious processes and in particular to a whole range of group-as-a-whole phenomena as have been outlined in this chapter. Further conditions for reality testing in groups and teams are outlined in Part 2 of this book.

Note

1.   I do not deal here with the rationalistic models of group-as-a-whole that were put forward by Lewin, Bales, Moreno and Mayo (see Chapter 5 of Anzieu 1984). An excellent rationale for this decision can be found in Anzieu (1984). Nor do I deal with Sigmund Freud's original conceptualization of the group's unity being derived from identification with the leader because this concept has been developed and refined by Wilfred Bion (1961).

Part 2

Introduction to Part 2

Application of principles

The previous chapters build for the reader a picture of the various components of human functioning in groups. Subjective experience and internal working models are linked with ideas about levels of consciousness and then related to language and semiotics to build a view of communication in groups. The specifics of projective processes are then built on this foundation and finally, a brief summary of group-as-a-whole phenomena is assembled from the previously described components. The use of the wombat incident and other shorter anecdotes provides some illustrations of the ideas presented.

From here on the wombat is largely put to bed and each of the subsequent chapters builds on the foundation of Part 1. It is assumed in Part 2 that the reader has a reasonable grasp of the concepts in Part 1. Nonetheless, in some of the chapters that follow I have repeated in a summarized form some of the ideas that are more fully examined in Part 1. This is in part because repetition can improve learning and in part because some of the latter chapters are intended to be suitable as handouts for teaching about specific topics.

We start in Chapter 8 with a critical review of the theory of experiential learning in the light of psychodynamic views of group functioning. Some of the conventional assumptions underpinning experiential learning are questioned. Also, some of the conventional assumptions about the link between action and acting out in psychodynamic groups are critically appraised. Chapter 9 provides a conceptual framework for thinking about the essential elements for establishing effective groups and teams. This is achieved by identifying ways of creating safe, bounded and purposeful groups through paying attention to boundaries, intra-group links and the idea of group members' affiliative attachment to the group-as-a-whole.

The scene is then set for creating a 'reflective space' in groups so that learning, change and effective decision making can occur in the presence of high quality collective thinking. As such, Chapter 10 works against Janis's pessimistic view of 'groupthink' as a collective intellectual impairment (Hartley 1997) and even Wilfred Bion's (1961) assumption that basic assumption groups are by necessity always present. Chapter 11 provides a conceptual framework for integrating most of the material that occurs up to this point in the book through examining the competency needs of group leaders. Six 'windows' on group functioning are described and the corresponding group work leadership competencies are discussed. Nonetheless, Chapter 11 is rather too rational to be adequate as a full summary of the book and so Chapter 12 takes the perspective of the artist and compares group leaders with artists and groups with works of art. Here, nothing is certain and the reader is invited to make his or her own conclusions.

CHAPTER 8

A psychodynamic view of experiential learning in groups

This book is intended to be useful to people who want to develop a deep understanding of group dynamics in educational, therapeutic and organizational settings. The application of action-based experiential processes such as adventure-based learning runs through the whole text as a theme because I believe in the power of adventure-based experiential learning as a result of having worked with groups in the outdoors over a period of nearly twenty years. Action-based experiential learning rests on a strong tradition that is seldom articulated in psychodynamic books and papers and so I have endeavoured in this chapter to summarize the key points of experiential learning that are relevant to groups in a wide range of settings.

The chapter begins with the comparison of assumptions about experiential learning and assumptions about psychoanalytic groups. This is followed by discussion about the compatibility of the two sets of assumptions, illustrated by some examples, including one drawn from psychodrama which is an action-based mode of learning. The overall intention of the chapter is to enable the reader to identify his or her own assumption sets and to help with the loosening up of previously held assumptions so as to open new possibilities.

Assumption sets in conventional[1] experiential learning

In the introduction to this book I used the diagram below as a basis for an introductory description of experiential learning. This time I will use it as a basis for a critical appraisal of experiential learning.

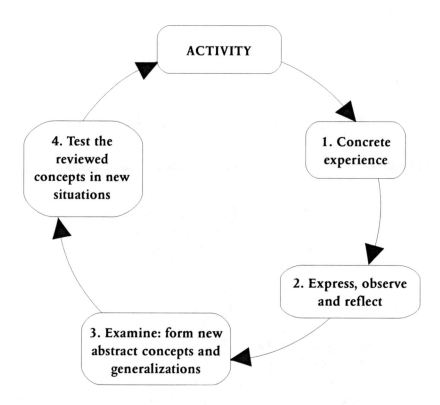

Figure 8.1 The experiential learning cycle
Source: Greenaway (1993) and Kolb (1984)

The cycle in Figure 8.1 is based on the assumption that a group participant takes part in an activity that forms concrete experience (1) and that this is followed by a period of talking, reflection and thinking (2) with other group members. This second 'step' is sometimes called 'reviewing' in adventure education literature. The third phase (3) of the cycle involves the formation of new ideas or working models that arise from the previous two. New action plans are then formulated that incorporate the learning from these three stages. The new action plans are tested (4) in another concrete experience, and so on.

Table 8.1 compares assumptions that are commonly held by practitioners of adventure-based experiential learning with assumptions that are commonly held by leaders of psychodynamic group work. The experiential activity implicit in Table 8.1 could be, for example, a group that climbs a rock face and then gathers around in a circle to talk about their experience. (This differs from experiential personal development groups such as those run by the NTL or group relations 'small study groups' where having a group experience and talking about it all occur in an integrated fashion.) Now to a quick review of the assumptions that are commonly associated with the stages in the experiential learning cycle.

Table 8.1 A comparison between assumptions about experiential learning and assumptions about psychodynamic group work	
Assumptions in traditional experiential learning about each stage	Parallel assumptions in psychoanalytic group work
Stage 1: Activity and (resulting) concrete experience	
Physical activity will result in personal experiencing, which is then called 'concrete experience'. Just sitting around and talking does not create 'concrete experience'.	Physical activity is a means of avoiding verbal expression of important emotional and cognitive material. Any physical activity in a group is a defence.
An activity that is planned, prepared and implemented deliberately by the group leader can be powerful and effective if it matches the group's developmental needs at the time.	There is no differentiation between action that is planned by the leader and action that is spontaneously initiated by the participants because activities are not included in the allowable group programme.
Expression, observation and reflection occur after the concrete experience has been completed. Learning does not occur to any great extent during the activity. In other words classical experiential learning does not acknowledge the role of procedural memory in learning.	Expression, observation and reflection occur at all times in the group. Learning occurs at all times in the group. Different schools of psychoanalysis conceptualize differently how this learning occurs (Bateman and Holmes 1995).

Physical activity and consequent interaction with others and the physical environment leads to authentic personal and interpersonal behaviour that is minimally modified by psychological defences.	Action is a defence: physical action hides the 'true self'. Such action is likely to be less authentic than the interaction that occurs when physical movement and action are restricted.
Talking about 'what I would do' allows defences to remain in place, but being confronted with having to actually do something removes the possibility of hiding behind verbalization and posturing.	Talking is the means by which intrapsychic material is transformed from undifferentiated and conflictual material.

Stage 2: Express, observe and reflect

This step occurs after the physical activity has ended.	Expression, observation and reflection are an integral part of the whole experience and occur at all times in the group.
Expression, making observations and reflection are not concrete experience: only physical activity provides concrete experience.	Expression, making observations and reflection constitute real and significant experience that is the raw material of the psychoanalytic group.
Consolidation of experience, awareness and insight occur through this step.	Consolidation of experience, awareness and insight occur at all times during the group after the initial group forming.

Stage 3: Examine: form new abstract concepts and generalizations

New abstract concepts will be formed from expression, observation and reflection on the prior concrete experience. Therefore, participants will identify shortfalls in their existing internal working models through having experienced different results from their behaviour from what they had expected.	There is no need to make special provision for the formulation of new abstract concepts. These are formed continually during the analytic group experience.

Stage 4: Test the reviewed concepts in new situations	
Transfer of learning from the current situation to 'real life' occurs primarily either through practical testing of new concepts in old situations or through the 'thought experiments' that can be carried out whilst still talking with others in the learning group.	Transfer of change from the therapy group to the rest of the world occurs through changes to intrapsychic 'structures' such as ego strength, sense of identity, and reduction of unhelpful defence mechanisms.

I do believe that some of the assumptions in both columns are contestable. Looking across from left-hand column to right-hand column creates some challenges too. Some assumptions of traditional experiential learning are not compatible with group analytic and psychoanalytic views and vice versa. For instance, the views about the psychological significance of language as articulated above are very different across the two columns. In hard core experiential learning, language without action is considered to be defence. In psychoanalysis, action without language is considered a defence! That is, action constitutes either 'acting out' or 'acting in' (Bateman and Holmes 1995, p.195). 'Acting out implies a regression to prereflective, preverbal level, a belief in the magical effects of action, and a desperate need to get a response from the external world' and 'on the positive side, the act may be a communication that becomes a useful source of analytic material…' Either way, in conventional psychoanalytic views, action is used as a defence against anxiety and so language is the most reliable way of accessing the undefended self.

On the face of it, the difference in opinion between psychoanalysts and adventure-based experiential educators is too large to bridge. Whilst this may be true, I attempt in the remaining parts of this chapter to make some links between the two fields because I believe that each field offers something to the other. Adventure-based and action-based interventions create moments of spontaneity that are difficult to emulate in talk-therapies. A downside of the experiential approaches is that they can be used to provide a rationalization for defences against anxiety both for participants and for leaders. Psychoanalytic group approaches can, through the relative absence of physical activity, effectively force the symbolization and verbalization of deeply experienced internal psychic material that would not otherwise become accessible to either the participant or the leader. A downside of the verbally dominated approaches is that action as a form of communication is ignored and therefore useful information is lost. For instance, physical interaction in a group – even when it is focused on an activity such as kayaking – can quickly evoke transference and countertransference that can be dealt with in any combination of physical action and verbalization.

The traditional view that acting out is unhelpful needs to be re-visited. 'Acting in', which is the use of action by group participants to defend against anxiety, can provide direct signals that a participant needs to address some underlying issue that has not yet reached his or her awareness. Such 'acting in' can be useful when it is noticed and eventually addressed. So acting in can provide a shortcut to unconscious material that might take longer to reach by purely verbal means (Hopper 2001, p.637). The challenge for the leader is to find a way of bringing the information that is conveyed by acting in to the attention of the participant(s) at a time and in a way that makes it useful to the participant(s).

I would challenge the traditional psychoanalytic 'verbal-only' practitioners to learn to communicate in a more flexible fashion. It may even be that the analytic group leader's insistence on verbalization as the only legitimate group-level activity is also a defence against the analyst's anxiety about his or her competence to use activity-based modes to communicate with clients. A group that is designed to involve activity and movement then provides a challenge for traditional group analysts. The relatively neutral or 'blank screen' of the therapist or group leader cannot be maintained in an activity-based group (Larned 1996). In adventure-based groups the leader spends many days and nights full-time with the group, walking, making camp and eating, and so the personality of the leader becomes visible to the participants. Real life relationships inevitably form between leader and participant. Activity-based and adventure-based experiential learning groups make it impossible to maintain the kind of boundaries between participants and leaders that are required in analytic groups. Transference and countertransference become much more complex and, in the view of traditional group analysts, unworkable.

Conversely I would challenge the traditional adventure-based practitioners who insist that useful learning only occurs in conjunction with a physical activity, because new behaviours emerge during the activity and subsequent talking through consolidates these new behaviours. This claim may cover a fear that they (the leaders) have limited ability to deal with the intense anxiety that can occur in groups where action is forbidden and talking is the main modality.

Many experiential learning practitioners are critical of groups where there is reliance on talking, especially groups for adolescents whose identity and world view is often centred around action (Bateman and Holmes 1995). In my own words, a summary of this limited view of experiential learning is that

> an experience provides the basis from which the learner develops new understanding of themselves and the world. Effective experiential learning involves activities that result in participants having new experiences. These new experiences are reflected upon, described and discussed in a group setting. Reflection upon and verbalization of a new experience then forms an integrated basis for the learning of new ways of thinking, feeling and perceiving.

A fundamental flaw in the design of action-based groups where the cyclic model of experiential learning dictates that action precedes reflection is that experiencing of self-in-action can be lost for participants (Ringer 1996b; Schon 1995). Adventure-based group leaders will set up an activity, allow the activity to be completed, and then facilitate a discussion with participants about what they noticed, learned, decided, and so on. In such cases participants are taught that action is different from reflection, that one should only become mindful of one's own experience *after* the experience has occurred. This contrasts strongly with the implicit rule in analytic groups that one is constantly mindful of one's experience of self, other and group. Fortunately, there is a growing questioning of the idea that concrete experience can only lead to learning if it is later described and verbally analyzed (Handley 1993; Haskell 2001). This, in turn, leads to some interesting possibility for reconciliation of ideas about experiential learning and psychoanalysis. The next short sojourn will use ideas about memory systems as an integrative framework.

Reconciling experiential learning with psychoanalysis

When experiential learning is related to memory systems (which were described in the interlude in Chapter 4) it appears that the activity and consequent concrete experience will already have influenced both procedural memory and imaged/perceptual memory. So, even before any verbalization occurs, some changes or learning will have occurred. This strongly parallels the idea in group analysis that experiencing oneself in the group is in itself an important factor in learning and therapy. My observations of effective adventure group leaders show that they provide linking and containment in their groups. They provide constant non-verbal and minimal verbal responsiveness to the group during the activity and they maintain sound standards of physical and emotional safety (Ringer and Gillis 1995; Ringer and Spanoghe 1997; Vincent 1995). So, group participants have positive lived experiences of themselves, the activity, the group and the leader. These experiences are internalized (in procedural and imaged memory). Additionally, positive stories are retained in episodal memory.

In experiential learning, the reflective conversations that follow the activity will firstly consolidate the encoding of episodal memory and then assist memories of episodes to be generalized into semantic memory. Semantic memory is then consolidated with the application of principles to plan or anticipate new actions. This schema also fits narrative therapy which works to transform episodes into semantic memory as 'new narratives'. As an aside, it seems that sound implicit and explicit memory systems are necessary for healthy functioning. Implicit memory systems (imaged and procedural) form the basis of personality as it is enacted in-the-moment whilst explicit memory systems (episodal and semantic) form the basis for identity (Schacter 1996). See Figure 8.2.

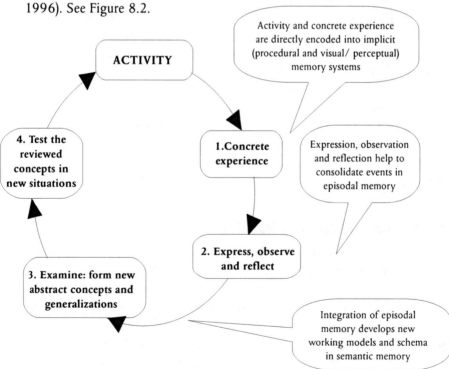

Figure 8.2 The experiential learning cycle in relation to memory systems
Source: Adapted from Greenaway (1993) and Kolb (1984)

Action as distraction?

There has been considerable progress made by group analysts in finding ways of integrating action with analytic approaches to groups. Psychodrama is one approach that has been successfully adapted to psychoanalytic group work. Although in some countries, such as Australia, psychodrama (an action-based approach) is mainly shunned by group analysts, the French have for years been successfully integrating psychodrama and psychoanalytic work with groups. For more detail, see Anzieu (1984) and Kaës (1999) who describe 'analytic psychodrama' which was recognized in France from 1956 and is still an accepted form of analytic group work (although Anzieu emphasizes that analytic psychodrama differs from traditional Morenian psychodrama but retains some of the core elements).

Whilst few traditional experiential educators would see themselves as psychodramatists, some of the same principles apply in the effective leadership of adventure-based work as in effective leadership of psychodrama groups. In the following section I will draw some parallels between psychodrama and adventure-based group work and at the same time explore in more detail the issue of when and whether action is beneficial to the group and when it is a distraction from the group's real task.

Action

As shown in Figure 8.3 psychodrama can lead directly to verbalization from action, without the classical 'reflection/processing' stage that is advocated in experiential learning. In psychodrama, thinking, feeling and action appear together in an enactment that is imaginatively related to a specific context (Williams 1989). The words uttered by the main actor (protagonist) during the drama articulate the content of the actor's mental representations. Others can link his or her words with the actions and demonstrated feelings, to put the action into context and so to make meaning of the words and actions. During the drama this meaning can be reflected back to the protagonist by auxiliary actors and by mirroring from the leader. The protagonist then relates the group members' comments and reflections to his or her own understanding of the drama in his or her world. The action and words emerging from the drama may be 'raw' in that the protagonist has not made any sense of them at the time they emerge. (For a very thorough description of the use of psychodramatic techniques for psychotherapy see Kipper 1986.)

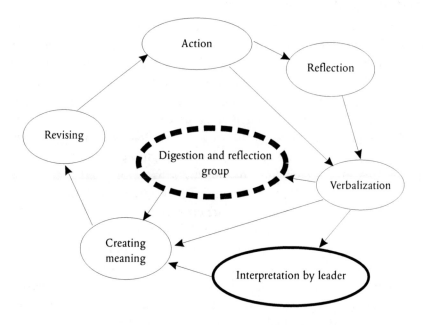

Figure 8.3 Multiple paths for learning from experiences in groups

The strength of the feeling may be too great for the protagonist to tolerate. In this case, containment occurs through the combined emotional capacity of the group and the leader to tolerate the strong feelings, to 'digest' them and to transform them into words – with the associated interaction – that the actor can tolerate as shown in Figure 8.3 by the line between the 'Action' ellipse and the 'Verbalization' ellipse. A strength of psychodrama and role training is that the actor is not alone in the drama. Others have taken an active part and have been moved by the emotion involved. These people, when they talk to the actor, are likely to have a great deal of empathy and are likely to have 'digested' some of the difficult feelings and therefore will be able to help the actor re-introject the feelings that were projected outwards during the drama.

Action in psychodrama or in adventure-based activities can be either authentic – often arising directly from the unconscious – or defensive, which is sometimes mediated by the conscious mind to create a desired impression to self and others. Verbalization is similar, it can be defensive or authentic. When a person verbalizes directly from the activity, the group and leader can assess the congruence between action – non-verbal language – and verbalization. They can then reflect the congruence or lack of it back to the actor. This then stimulates another step in the associative chain for the actor. So, learning about self can come from many paths involving self, other, group and leader. (See Figure 8.4)

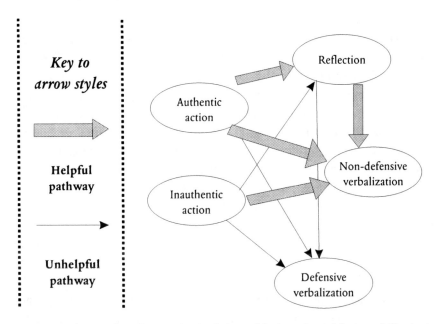

Figure 8.4 Authentic and inauthentic action in relation to defensive and non-defensive verbalization in experiential learning

Although experiential exercises such as simulations, games and initiative exercises are somewhat different to psychodrama, there are some of the same elements present. For instance, all group members will provide mirroring for others (verbal and non-verbal reflection back to the other of their experience of the other) simply through the way that they interact. When participants are distracted by a challenging physical or psychological task, they have less capacity to apply interpersonal defences. Their non-verbal interaction is likely to be relatively authentic. (Incidentally, the same undefended authentic action often happens in work place teams when there is intense activity or discussion.) So, mirroring occurs frequently. Second, each micro-interaction in an activity group can have very visible consequences. For example, if a person consistently refuses help when climbing out of a deep pool in a cold cave and fails in their own attempts, the physical consequences – intense cold – create strong sensory information that something is not working. This, in turn, can create the kind of 'cognitive dissonance' that leads to reassessing one's own behaviour.

Expression and reflection

In experiential learning, when all of, or one stage of, the activity has been completed, the group stops the action to talk together about their experiences. This talking is often called 'processing' in the experiential learning literature. Processing has many forms, but usually consists of a structured discussion amongst participants, and is facilitated by the group leader. A simple framework for these discussions is to focus first on the events that occurred and for each participant to describe the events from his or her perspective. Second, the discussion focuses on the 'so what' or on making sense of or meaning from the events. This may involve the leader in an interpretive mode, or the leader may maintain a strictly facilitative role. Third, the group focuses on what they will do differently as a result of the insight gained from the action and processing to date (Schoel, Prouty and Radcliffe 1988).

Reflection in experiential learning can be used as an opportunity for further defensive verbalization or it can be used to explore congruence and authenticity. When a group member is in action, he or she is unlikely to be aware at the time whether his or her actions and verbalizations are authentic or not. The challenge is to use the resources of the group members and the leader to discriminate between authentic and inauthentic action and to draw useful learning from the activity. Learning can also be originated by the actor when he or she is prepared to identify unease and anxiety that was experienced during the action but that did not become apparent or was not acknowledged at the time.

Making meaning and developing new ways of being

The leader and the group reflect on the actions, the verbalization and the complex relationships between them. No other group member can know which actions or which verbalizations are authentic for a group member who is actively engaged with the group ('actor'), and no other group member can know which actions are authentic for this person who is currently active ('speaker'). Claiming to know the actor/speaker's internal reality is both disrespectful and arrogant. What can be legitimately commented on and challenged is the apparent degree of congruence between the actions and the verbalization. It is this discrimination that can be most helpful to the actor/speaker. However, even as we reflect to the actor/speaker our observation about what we perceive to be the lack of congruence between action and speech, we need to keep in mind that in doing so we are still applying our own working models of congruence. Our working models may not apply to the other person. On the other hand, astute reflection and interpretation by the leader or other group members can trigger significant learning for participants. Furthermore, the leader has the opportunity to interpret and reflect at four main levels: the level of the individual, the level of relationships between participants, the level of the group, and the level directly involving the leader's own experience in the group. Given the significant power that the leader has, especially through normal transference, there is a responsibility on the part of the leader to act in ways that are primarily intended to further the learning of group members rather than to alleviate the anxiety of the leader him or herself.

Action as a relief from anxiety for the group leader

In action-based experiential learning, the most accessible and *apparently* legitimate way that a leader can alleviate anxiety during difficult moments is simply to introduce another activity!

In this section I explore the paradox that activities in groups – particularly developmental or therapeutic groups – can both assist learning to occur and simultaneously distract the group from achieving useful learning. If the group leader uses activities to allay his or her anxiety about what to do with a group, then the action is very likely to result in the leader and the group members acting out. However, if a group leader is finely attuned to him or her self and the group and thus introduces an activity as a result of careful consideration, then some powerful learning can occur.

When the primary task of a group involves learning about interaction between people and learning about one's reactions to others, then interpersonal interaction and self-reflection are the two activities that achieve these outcomes. If the leader introduces an action-based activity, the whole group can then act as if the primary task is to achieve success in that activity, and so avoid experiencing the tension that is inevitably involved in simply addressing the question, 'How do we fare at relating to each other?' For the leader, it is usually much easier to provide instructions for an activity than it is to create the silence or minimal questions that create reflective space. In this reflective space participants could fully experience the nature of their interactions with others and expose themselves by talking about what it is like to be in 'this' group when there is no structured action. Not only does the trained experiential group leader often find action a relief, but also most group participants will seek plausible ways of avoiding relatively unstructured reflection on their immediate lived experience of being in the group. I could not count the number of times that group participants who expect physical action have – at least initially – expressed discomfort at relatively long periods of quiet and reflection. Sometimes, with constant questioning of 'slow' starts to groups, I even start to doubt my own judgement about the usefulness of these periods that do not involved structured activities.

I know that as leader of corporate developmental groups I am often given strong implicit encouragement to provide a continual stream of activities that enable participants to create the belief that they are learning something. Despite rhetoric about the importance of the 'learning organization', corporate life is usually a constant stream of activities that are driven by demands that originate from outside the individual actor in the scene. In western corporations – although not necessarily Japanese corporations – sitting to reflect quietly at one's desk is seen as being 'not busy' and is frowned upon. This expectation, learned at work, that one should be in constant action, translates easily into an expectation that we as facilitators of learning will provide the client group with a roller-coaster of activity. Even though I am aware of this trap, I still find myself falling into it because it can be too demanding to challenge such a fundamental belief system. I fear that if I do not meet the clients' basic desire for action then they will find some other consultant for the next assignment. Adolescents too, are typically oriented towards action and shun reflection on the interpersonal and the intrapsychic and so groups of adolescents will find ways of communicating to leaders that this sitting around talking stuff is 'boring', 'just like our health education class', or unsatisfactory in some other way.

At a more personal level, providing a group with a reflective space can be quite threatening for ourselves as leaders because the reflective atmosphere itself creates an environment where we as leaders will be drawn to consider how we are doing in the role of leader. Simultaneously holding the space for inquiry and facilitating the group's reflective dialogue calls for considerable personal clarity. What, for example, if we uncover a previously out of awareness concern about our leadership of this group? Who will hold us and contain our distress? This is one reason why I advocate professional supervision. Even when we are physically in the presence of a group that we are facilitating, having regular supervision builds in our minds a safe space that helps to hold our anxiety. It matters little that we may not actually see our supervisor for another week because we have internalized that safe space.

How do we avoid introducing action at times when reflection is more useful? I think by carefully examining each impulse that we feel to introduce another activity. A useful test question is, 'In what way would an activity improve the chances of achieving the primary task of this group?' or, 'What would an activity detract from or add to what is going on right now?' Conversely, how, when facilitating psychodynamic groups, do we avoid using inaction as a defence against our own anxiety? We probably need to be constantly asking ourselves, 'What am I achieving by being silent/maintaining inactivity in the group?' Your role of the leader is to assist the group to achieve its primary task and at times that may mean acting in ways that increases rather than decreases your own anxiety. That may also mean acting in ways that most group members do not initially agree with.

Notes

1. There are two main 'schools' of experiential learning in the English-speaking world. The one to which I refer is derived from ideas originally articulated by John Dewey (1938), Kurt Hahn (Kimball and Bacon 1993) and David Kolb (1984). The American-based Association for Experiential Education (AEE) is a peak body for many people in this school. The other, international group takes a wider view of experiential learning and includes more political and social factors. The International Council for Experiential Learning (ICEL) is an international organization representing many people in this school.

CHAPTER 9

Linking, containment
and affiliative attachment in groups[1]

Introduction

This chapter outlines three vital aspects of the facilitation of groups. These aspects, linking, containment and attachment to a group (affiliative attachment), are important in all types of group whether they are for recreation, education, development or therapy. Linking refers to the existence of links at both conscious and unconscious levels. These links involve each group member, the group-as-a-whole, the leader, and the primary task of the group. Adequate containment refers to group members having the conscious and unconscious sense of being firmly held in the group and its task, and yet not immobilized by the experience. Affiliative attachment refers to the group members' durable expectation that the group and the leader will provide safety, security and responsiveness. The leader has a vital role in facilitating linking and containment, but to do so requires a sound level of skills and a degree of emotional and psychological maturity. Affiliative attachment is more subtle in that it cannot so easily be deliberately created, but leadership behaviours are vital in assisting the growth of affiliative attachment by group members. Some aspects of leader competencies are examined in relation to linking, containment and facilitating affiliative attachment.

As we have seen from the chapters to date, groups are complex. They involve the interdependence of a number of human beings whose actions, interactions and perceptions are constantly changing. The leader of a group is an integral part of the dynamic system that involves both conscious and unconscious processes of all present. Accordingly, he or she is strongly influenced by the emotional tides that move through the group. Being a member of a group challenges participants and leaders alike to maintain adequate emotional independence and behavioural autonomy, whilst simultaneously being influenced to act in ways that meet the needs of the group. Leading groups, then, is a challenging and complex business, but one that is as rewarding as it is difficult (Neill, 1977a, 1977b, 1977c). Some components of group leadership that can facilitate satisfying leadership experiences and the development of effective groups are addressed below.

The group leader is the facilitator of three major functions in groups. The first function is what I will call 'containment'[2]. This involves creating boundaries around the group that enable it to conduct its business with a reasonable sense of security and without interference or harm. At an unconscious level, containment enables participants to experience anxiety associated with being in the group whilst the intuitive sense of security that acts as a 'container' for their anxiety prevents fragmenting or significantly distressing subjective experiences. In particular, a group is a rich soup of projections emanating from all people present including leaders. A well-contained group enables the group-as-a-whole to accept and deal with the projections, much like a mother who accepts the raw projections from her infant, 'digests' or processes them, and reflects them back in a more acceptable form to the infant.

The second function is 'linking' which involves creating and maintaining the links that hold the internal 'structure' of the group together and create the potential for high quality interaction in the group. Linking can be likened to building what Foulkes referred to as the 'group matrix' and is described also by Kaës (1993) and Ashbach and Schermer (1987) particularly in relation to what they describe as the interactive (delta) level of the group. At an unconscious level, linking is built by the processes of identification and projective identification. If a group member identifies with another there will be an unconscious link between them. Projective identification places pairs of group members in unconscious subgroups where one member does the feeling on behalf of the other. This latter form of linking can get messy as briefly described in Chapter 7 as role fixation.

Third, affiliative attachment refers to the subjective experience of group participants that the group provides a place of safety and protection from danger. This appears to be a paradoxical issue because it is often acknowledged that simply being in a group increases anxiety levels and can quickly result in unconscious phantasies of persecution or attack. Nonetheless, the group also provides potential for the subjective experience of being a responsive 'other' and as such can elicit feelings of safety and protection for participants.

Linking and containment are necessary for all types of group, ranging in purpose from therapy, through development and education, to recreation. Paying attention to patterns of affiliative attachment can also enhance the effectiveness of all groups at an unconscious level. This chapter focuses on how addressing unconscious processes in groups can create the potential for enjoyment in recreation groups, effective learning in education and development groups, and significant change in therapy groups.

Earlier chapters emphasized unconscious processes. This chapter reintroduces a focus on rational or conscious processes and describes the need to hold concurrent attention on both conscious/rational processes and on the unconscious. At a rational level, the clearest needs are those of building both the outer 'shell' and the inner structure of groups. Eggs provide an interesting comparison.

Of groups and eggs

If you remove from a raw egg the shell and the thin membrane inside the shell, the white and the yolk will slip through your fingers, and form a sticky mess on your hands and on the surface beneath your hands. The yolk and the white will mix, and the whole mess will flow in a glutinous glob, following the whims of gravity. This egg is no longer contained, and in a limited way resembles a group that is uncontained. There are few predictable patterns in the structure of the group and the group is fragmented and all mixed up. The experience of being in an uncontained group is messy and often very disturbing. This disorder in the group can generate a distressing disorder in participants' experience of themselves and of others in the group.

A raw egg that is adequately contained by its shell retains its form, but it is entirely dependent on that container to avoid it becoming an uncontained mess. If the egg is carefully boiled while still in its shell, it will be 'processed' to the extent that the white and yolk develop a stable form that is independent of the outer shell. In comparison, a 'raw' group is usually very dependent on structure, form and effective leadership to hold it together until it has had enough 'process' for adequate internal links to be built.

In the cooked egg the molecules in the egg-white have linked with each other to form a resilient shape that follows the shape of the shell and is strong enough to remain intact after the shell has been removed. The yolk has solidified and also holds its own shape. Even when peeled, this egg will retain its shape and form. In other words, if the container is removed, the *links* inside the egg will enable it to retain its form. The comparison between eggs and groups should not be pursued with too much enthusiasm, but the key comparison remains valid that a group with excellent internal links will be less dependent on its external boundaries than a group that has poor internal links.

There are some very important differences between eggs and groups and so it is not helpful to push the simile too far. The most important of these differences is that groups are composed of intelligent creatures each of whom has his or her own will and initiative. The components that make up eggs are not active agents in the same way. Second, there is no clear parallel between the passive role taken by the egg shell and the active role of the leader in facilitating containment of a group. Third, the rigidity and permanence of the links between molecules in a cooked egg do not resemble the dynamic process of linking that occurs in the internal 'matrix' of a group (Foulkes and Anthony 1990). Finally, the egg is a physical item but groups have two key elements in addition to their physical existence. These are: *interaction* that determines in part the nature of the containment and linking, and an unspoken out-of-awareness (or *group climate*) element that exists in the minds of the participants and has a substantial influence on the subjective experience of being in the group. The simile of the cooked and uncooked egg fails completely when applied to the concept of affiliative attachment, but it does add interest when presenting a talk about groups. The audience becomes very engaged when a raw egg is broken and the contents dribble through the fingers of the presenter onto the surface below his or her hands.

In groups, each of the three elements (structural, interactive and group climate) is inextricably related to the other two, but it is helpful at times to discuss them separately to simplify the narrative. *Structural elements* refer mainly to the boundaries that create the container, *interactional elements* refer mainly to the quality of interaction that supports linking. *Elements relating to group climate* include both the subjective imaginings, impressions and fantasies of each group member and the overall 'feel' or 'ambience' of the group-as-a-whole. Linking, containment and affiliative attachment influence and are, in turn, influenced by each of these elements. Building an adequate container for the group involves addressing primarily the structural elements required for boundary building and the group climate elements that influence group members' feelings of comfort or anxiety. Linking involves mainly the interactional elements and affiliative attachment occurs primarily through processes related to group climate. These three elements are discussed more fully in Chapter 11 and so the next step in this chapter is to examine in more detail each of the three concepts of containment, linking and affiliative attachment.

Containment

At an unconscious level, the container helps group members manage the anxiety that results from being in the group, and at a more rational level, the container provides some of the structures that enable group members to locate themselves securely in the group. The group container provides tangible evidence to group members about what (and whom) is inside the group and what is outside the group. Without this clarity the group may be unable to achieve its task. This container is woven collectively by the group and the leader(s). Early in the life of the group the leader usually has to take a very active role in constructing the container. It is constructed through building a shared understanding that the group is *purposeful, bounded* and *safe*.

In particular, *purposeful* means that the purpose of the group and primary task for the group is shared and understood. In agreeing to a primary task, group members delegate their authority to the leader to assist the group to achieve that task. For example, the primary task of a group may be to 'use abseiling as a means of developing the trust of group members in their own courage and competence as well as building trust in relationships with others'. Whilst the purpose of a group may seem easy to identify and to agree upon, this is seldom the case. Instead, unconscious factors in groups and organizations all too often result in them acting in ways that seem to pursue a goal that is very different from the articulated primary task of the group. The concept of 'pseudo-tasks' is expanded on in chapter 11.

Even if the leader(s) are clear about the primary task of the group, the participants may well have different ideas. For instance, adventure therapy programmes often work with what is euphemistically called 'adjudicated youth' who have been sentenced in court for a misdemeanour and who are subsequently referred to a programme that uses adventure activities for personal and therapeutic change. Some of the group members in the wombat story fall into this category. In such cases, the group members often have different expectations and different primary tasks than do the leaders or the agencies that provide the funding for the programme. Referring to the wombat story, one wonders what Jack's intention was in joining the programme. Was it similar to the primary task that was stated by the leaders?

An example from the corporate arena: a kayaking cover-up

A client organization asked a provider of corporate adventure training to run a day of 'relaxation and fun and stress relief' for a small team. Gordon, the team leader, told Kylie, the adventure programme co-ordinator, that the team was due for a reward because they had been working under too much stress for too long. A day of kayaking, rock climbing and abseiling would be great. Gordon specifically asked that the group should not do too much 'navel gazing' on the day out. When questioned about the primary task for the day, Gordon said it was 'relaxation and gaining a feeling of being rewarded for an outstanding effort by having a time of quality interaction in a nice environment'.

Kylie asked Gordon about what the team members saw as the primary task for the day and Gordon assured her that they were all in agreement with him. Kylie asked to meet with the team but was told that they did not have time before the scheduled day out. She told her programme manager that she did not want to proceed without meeting the team because she was uneasy about what was really going on but she was told to proceed anyway.

On the morning of the programme, two team members were twenty minutes late, and after waiting for another ten minutes, two others still had not arrived and so the group transport vehicle left without them. Gordon had left a message to say that he had been called away at short notice to a meeting at Head Office and so would not be able to attend. Kylie was now convinced that Gordon's description of the primary task was not only false, but also was not the same primary task as was held by the group members.

Before starting the kayak instruction Kylie stated the primary task for the group as it had been presented to her. She asked group members to introduce themselves and to tell the group why they were attending. Group members were sullen and withdrawn. They talked in whispers amongst themselves and spoke to the group briefly and without feeling.

What was going on?

In fact, Gordon was extremely unpopular as a team leader and he was generally considered to be not only incompetent, but also a 'glory grabber'. His personal assistant (Brendon) was on the trip and it was generally considered by group members that Gordon wanted Brendon to eavesdrop on conversations during the day to give him an idea of who was undermining him. In the opinion of most group members, Gordon's real primary task was to find out who was undermining him so he could fire them. The group members' primary task then became to stay as safe as possible in a corporate environment that felt dangerous. Kylie had a difficult task on her hands because none of this could be voiced out loud in case Brendon told Gordon who had said what.

How does one work with this kind of situation?

Kylie was right in the first place. Do not get into situations like this if you can avoid it. But avoidance is not always possible. Once in the situation, Kylie described what she saw – a reserved, cautious group that, on the face of it, would have been expected to be excited and cheerful. She said that she did not know what was going on and she did not have a mandate to work with the organization's dynamic. Nonetheless, she wanted to gather opinions on what the group could do to have as successful a time as possible. The weather was fine and conditions were perfect for having a relaxing and enjoyable time.

After a period of careful facilitation, Kylie established with the group that there were undercurrents present that made it difficult to talk openly. She negotiated that they would carry out the planned activities in order to have as relaxing and enjoyable a day as possible, and that she would tell her programme manager that there were issues in the organization that might need addressing.

Bounded means that adequate boundaries are established so that:

- *Membership* boundaries are clear, that is, only people who legitimately belong to the group are present.

- There is a shared understanding of the *physical space(s)* (territory) for the group and an expectation that the group can conduct its business without being intruded on or disrupted. In adventure activities physical space has particular importance where there needs to be safety zones set up – such as during rock climbing or abseiling.

- There is a shared understanding of the way in which *time* limits will provide boundaries for the group. For example, groups need to know about start, break and stopping times, as well as the transition times at which a change in type of activity requires group members to change roles. Time boundaries are essential so that group members and group leaders have clear signals that indicate changes in roles.

- Group members understand the distribution of *roles and tasks* in the group. Here, all of the roles required to conduct the group are established and they are allocated to leaders and to group members.

Safety is created both through good-enough containment and through effective linking in the group. The elements of containment that build safety are:

- 'Confidentiality' or the expectation that participation in the group will not create damage in the world outside the group. I find it useful to talk about the principle of 'no jeopardy' in which group members agree not to disclose anything to people outside the group that may create jeopardy for group members.

- 'Psychological depth', which largely determines at what psychological level the group will operate. Psychotherapy is seen to be much 'deeper' than recreation or education. More detail can be found in Ringer and Gillis (1995), Ringer and Spanoghe (1997) and Vincent (1995).

- 'Responsiveness' or the expectation that the group and/or leader will respond effectively to communications of all kinds that are engaged in by group members (Bacal 1998).

Most groups have an unspoken understanding that the designated leader(s) of the group will take prime responsibility for establishing and maintaining all of the elements necessary for containment. However, during the maturing process for most groups, the building and maintaining of the holding environment becomes distributed between all persons in the group. Most groups do not talk about the need to build this container but when it is missing people talk about the negative impact of containment being missing or flawed. For example, a lack of clarity about the primary task of the group may lead to people complaining that they are confused and that the group feels pointless – 'What are we doing here; why bother?' For instance, a lack of clarity about whether the group is a recreational or a therapy group may result in some participants complaining about 'not wanting the Freudian crap imposed on us' (as has happened in my experience).

While containment holds the basic 'shape' of the group, the internal structure also needs to develop. Participants need some evidence that they will be safe to interact in the group without undue fear of being attacked, ridiculed, ignored or abandoned. In other words, they need some assurance that the quality of linking in the group will be adequate (Gordon 1994).

Linking

A group involves more than just making connections between a number of people who happen to be in one place at one time. In fact, groups do not always need to be physically together to constitute a group. One key characteristic of groups is the interconnection between members and their common connection with a leader and a task. At an unconscious level a group comes into existence when members adequately share a connection with a mental representation of the 'group' (Anzieu 1984). The existence of the unconscious element of the group occurs when there is a significant commonality in the sense or feel of this group-in-the-mind.

At the start of any group the leader can facilitate the development of six different kinds of link that directly assist in building an effective group. These six links are:

1. Leader with task

2. Group with task

3. Leader with individuals and vice versa

4. Leader with group (group-in-the-mind)

5. Individuals with group (group-in-the-mind)

6. Individuals with other individuals.

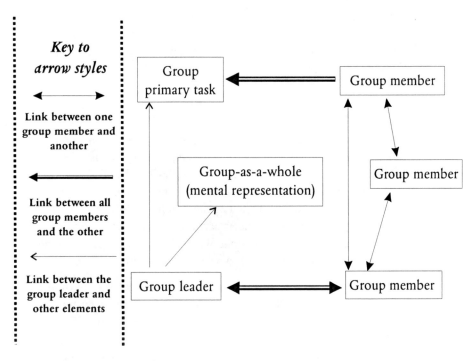

Figure 9.1 Linking between key elements in a group
Note 1: for simplicity, only three group members are shown.
Note 2: links between human beings are bi-directional but links between human beings and other ele-
ments are uni-directional.

These links are examined in more detail below.

1. Leader with task

The leader needs to demonstrate to the group that he or she has an understanding of the primary task of the group and also has some personal
affinity for and/or competence to work with that primary task. For
example, as a part of the introduction to an abseiling group for building
interpersonal trust and 'trust in self' for participants, the leader might say,
'Although I am experienced at abseiling and rock climbing, I still find it
exciting the way that holding a safety line for someone else is such a
powerful way of building a trusting relationship. I also really appreciate the
creativity that each person uses in managing his or her fear. Some do so by
tightening every muscle in their bodies and overriding the fear. Others do it
by talking to the instructors, and still others joke and laugh so as to push

the fear out of their awareness. I still feel the fear at the moment that I go over the edge, but I use my rational mind to reassure myself that the whole set-up is safe and that I've never had problems during the many abseils that I've done in the past'.

2. Group with task

The fundamental building block for a group is the existence of a shared task that requires interdependence between participants. Task clarity is also one of the boundaries mentioned above, so the leader's role includes assisting participants to connect themselves emotionally and subjectively to the task that is to be conducted by the group. The leader of the abseiling group could say, 'This group meets here today to use abseiling as a stimulus for personal growth. To do that we will need to work together on supporting others in the group to achieve what is best for them'.

During the life of a typical group there are numerous opportunities to remind the group of its primary task and simultaneously to facilitate linking between group members and the task of the group. Each time a person raises a topic that is peripheral to the primary task, the leader can make a statement such as, 'I can see that you're fascinated by [topic] and it seems from the response of some others in the group that they are too. I'm not sure though, how that helps this group make progress on [primary task statement]'. Such statements can easily be made in a way that seems discounting to the speaker, so they need to be carefully constructed.

3. Leader with individuals

The leader needs to build links actively between him or herself and each member of the group. Much of this is done non-verbally through being *attentive and responsive*. Being seen to link with the wishes and fears expressed by group members is an important component of building the links, but some early runs on the board can be achieved by introducing oneself in a way that also links your own life with the lives of the group participants. This is a fine art because the leader necessarily needs to remain differentiated from the group – not 'one of the boys or girls' – and simultaneously needs to be seen by group members as 'someone with whom we can relate'. Some of this linking occurs as a spin-off from the leader facilitating the building of the boundaries described above. If group members have already introduced themselves, a part of the leader's introduction to the abseiling group could be, 'Well, it seems as though some of you can't wait to get over that cliff, some of you aren't sure, and some of you are wondering why on earth you came today. I'm not going to push anyone past where they want to go, but I will try to work with you so you end the day satisfied with the choices you made. As I work with each of you, I'd like you to let me know how much you want to be nudged in the direction of the cliff and how much you just want me to be there in a quiet supportive sort of a way'.

4. Leader with group

Each participant in a group is simultaneously aware of two different realities. On one hand he or she is an individual with his or her own life, will and autonomy. On the other hand there is a single collective that has assembled to achieve a collective purpose, is gathered in a collective space and has some form of interdependence that involves all group members. To assist in the formation of a psychic reality that the group exists, the leader also needs to link with this collective 'group-in-the-mind'. An example, relating to the abseiling group mentioned above, could be, 'This is a mature group and so I'll keep my lectures about safety and responsible behaviour to a minimum'.

Regular reference to 'the group' helps to reinforce the shared unconscious expectation that the group-as-a-whole exists as some form of tangible entity. The leader's statement above about modifying her usual talk about safety in response to the level of maturity of the group signals clearly to group members that she has noticed a characteristic of the group-as-a-whole and is responding to that characteristic. This responsiveness to the group-as-a-whole helps to build links between the leader and the group.

There are numerous theories about the existence of the group-as-a-whole, each of which has its own merits and can help leaders be more responsive and attentive to both group-level concerns and individual concerns. A summary of a number of these group-as-a-whole models appeared in Chapter 7. One such model that I find particularly helpful is described in detail in Dorothy Stock Whitaker's recent update of the book *Using Groups to Help People* (Whitaker 2001). This is the 'focal conflict model' which develops the idea that at any moment in the life of any group there will be a 'central concern' that consciously and/or unconsciously influences the thinking, perception and behaviour of group members. The leader's ability to identify and respond to both the 'fear' based and the 'wish' based pole of the central concern will help the group to make emotional and practical progress.

5. Individuals with group

The leader's role includes assisting to facilitate the building of links between individuals and the group-as-a-whole. We could think of this as encouraging affiliative attachment between individuals and the fantasy or unconscious image-in-the-mind that each member holds of the group (Marrone 1998; Stapley 1996). Linking of individuals with the group-as-a-whole is one of the most powerful factors in group cohesion (Neri 1998), but is one that many leaders have difficulty in conceptualizing, let alone working with. The difficulties occur because: the link between individual and group occurs primarily at an unconscious level; it often defies description; and it can seldom be addressed overtly. Imagery, symbolism and drama provide some useful tools for working directly with the group image, but these techniques are often outside the comfort level of both participants and leaders.

Returning to the abseiling group described above, one statement that a leader could make during the day to help linking between each individual and the group is, 'Well, how are you finding this group? Let's pause for a few minutes and we'll make space for each of you to comment on how you're doing and if you want any changes to the way you interact with the group or the way the group interacts with you'. This acknowledges that each person has a relationship with the 'group' and interacts with the 'group'. The statement also provides a chance for the leader to get overt feedback about the extent to which participants experience their needs being met.

6. Individuals with other individuals

Imagine that there is a thread connecting every group member to every other group member. Even if each thread is not particularly strong, the end result is that every participant is held firmly as a member of the group and cannot easily be pulled away. These metaphoric threads are the relationships that each member has with each other member in the context of the group. The subjective experience of safety in a group depends in part on being able to look around the group and find at least one other face that is perceived as friendly or supportive. With this in mind, I usually conduct a deliberate linking exercise early in the group that enables participants to have brief one-on-one interaction to start the building of relationships. An example of this would be to ask the participants in the abseiling group described above to, 'Find at least one other person in this group whose reason for attending is similar to yours. You will need to hold one or two-minute conversations with most of the others in the group to find this or these persons'. This exercise also facilitates the linking of the individual with the task of the group.

Safety and attacks on linking

These six links form the basis for building a well-linked group, but they are not all that is required. The group also needs to build an understanding of the nature of the allowable interactions – or the norms of interaction. In other words, participants need to build a justifiable expectation that neither the quality nor the content of the interaction in the group will damage any member of the group – either during the group meeting or after it ends. Safety depends on the quality of interaction in the group including non-verbal cues of respect, trust and absence of intrusion (Hinshelwood 1994; Nitsun 1996).

The development of norms, expectations and group 'culture' is a broad topic that is well articulated in other sources (Agazarian 1997; Ashby and DeGraaf 1999; Johnson and Johnson 1991; Tyson 1998). A common element amongst most literature on the development of group culture and norms where safety and sound linking successfully emerges, is the central role of the leader in the facilitation of the group's progress.

Affiliative attachment

Affiliative attachment refers to the intuitive sense that grows within each group member that their group is attractive to them, meets their needs or provides a place for nurture, growth or safety. When affiliative attachment is strong, the person experiencing it will start to link a part of his or her personal or professional identity with being a member of the group. In other words, when there is strong affiliative attachment between a group member and the group, this member experiences an emotional 'pull' to be in the group. This affiliative attachment can occur with all kinds of group including work place teams, volunteer groups, therapy groups, classes in schools, community action groups and so on.

There is in human beings an innate 'drive' for affiliation not only with others on a one-to-one basis but also for affiliation with groups of others (Marrone 1998). Just as John Bowlby claimed that the need for safety, nurture and security were fundamental drives in the baby's life, it seems likely that the drive for affiliation with groups is a fundamental drive in the maturation of human beings, at least from childhood onwards. It is my understanding that human beings have the innate need for and capacity to relate to groups as well as the innate need for and capacity to relate to others on a one-to-one basis. We talk freely in common language about a group being good, bad, or helpful, and so on.

What can we call this sense of durable affiliation with the group-as-a-whole (Bowlby 1969)? My temptation is to call on attachment theory which was developed to describe the quality of one-to-one relationships, but attachment theory relates to early childhood and is not entirely applicable to describe group members' relationships with the group-as-a-whole. What I am trying to describe here is the unconscious truth in the experience of the group member that the group-as-a-whole is a 'significant other' in his or her life. Furthermore, that he or she has a durable affective/emotional relationship with the group-as-a-whole. This 'significant other' (the group) meets important psychological needs for the group member. These include the need for security, affiliation/belonging, and protection from the fear of being alone or isolated from others.

Attachment theory provides a convenient starting point for theory-building about the phenomenon of human affiliation with groups. Parallels between attachment theory and the theory about how people relate to groups are examined in Tables 9.1 and 9.2.

Table 9.1 Similarities between attachment theory and group theory

Psychoanalytic group theory	Attachment theory
There is an innate human 'drive' to affiliate to groups.	There is an innate human 'drive' to develop secure attachment with other human beings on a one-to-one basis.
The affiliation to a group occurs primarily at an unconscious level.	The attachment to others occurs primarily at an unconscious level.
Internal working models of oneself and the world have a strong influence on (and are in turn influenced by) the quality of affiliation with groups.	Internal working models of oneself and the world have a strong influence on (and are in turn influenced by) the quality of attachment to others.

Affiliation with groups has a significant affective component.	Attachment has a strong affective component.
Procedural memory is significant in the enactment of group behaviours.	Procedural memory is a significant factor in the enactment of patterns of attachment.

Table 9.2 Differences between attachment theory and group theory

Psychoanalytic group theory	Attachment theory
Groups do not become a significant part of people's worlds until they are at least at the verbal level of development.	Patterns of attachment begin to be internalized from the earliest days in an infant's life.
Group experiences – apart from those in the original family – are often of relatively short duration, although friendship groups in childhood and adolescence can be of long duration.	The relationships that lead to a person's building of patterns of attachment are often long term, lasting for years.

In summary, there is a difference between the theory base for attachment in one-to-one relationships and the theory base that is relevant to 'attachment' or affiliation with groups. Nonetheless, there is a normal human tendency to seek affiliation with groups and it is likely that the patterns of preference for affiliation with groups are built from early childhood. The processes by which affiliation with groups occurs are likely to be largely unconscious and are probably contained in the procedural memory system. The subjective experience of the connection between group member and group has elements of 'connectedness' and 'attachment' in terms of everyday language, and so to avoid confusion with the formal language of attachment theory I will call this phenomenon 'affiliative attachment to the group-as-a-whole' or for brevity, 'affiliative attachment'. The term is useful because the person who experiences affiliative attachment to a group is unconsciously involved in an impossibility. The unconscious phantasy of the group-as-a-whole does not differentiate between members and therefore includes the person who experiences the affiliative attachment to the group. On the other hand, the same person is experiencing him or herself as separate from the group-as-a-whole. This logical impossibility does not affect the unconscious mind and does not detract from the sense of affiliative attachment to the group.

I believe that some of the literature about groups makes it difficult to acknowledge a helpful form of affiliative attachment to groups. For instance it is often assumed that Bion's (1961) Basic Assumption Dependency signifies that the intuitive sense of being affiliated with or attached to a group is necessarily unhelpful and is a defence against feeling alone. Turquet's formulation of Basic Assumption One-ness (Lawrence *et al.* 1996) can easily lead to a similar conclusion. Fortunately, more recent writers such as Neri are clear that a level of intuitive attunement with a group is necessary in order for the group experience to be useful.

All group members develop a mental representation of their relationship with the group-as-a-whole. This mental representation can be likened to the internal working models or world models described in Chapter 2 in that the working model includes three main elements: mental representations of (a) the person (b) the group and (c) the relationship between them. This working model is influenced by long-term patterns such as the person's history of groups and the resulting unconscious sets of expectations about (a) themselves (b) groups in general and (c) their relationships with groups in the past. This durable pattern of expectations can be related to what Bion (1961) refers to as 'valencies'.

Equally, group members' mental representations of any particular group will be influenced by their subjective experience of the group and the social discourse that occurs about the group by those who are associated with it. Thus, group members' working models about a specific group will be modified forms of their working models about 'groups in general'. This subjective experience of affiliative attachment with the group is relatively often put into words by group members but is less simple to describe in psychological terms or in terms of group process. A group member will seldom use psychologically sophisticated language and will say something like, 'That's a great group. I love it. If I'm feeling down I just remind myself that we've got a group meeting coming up and I immediately feel better'. In psychological terms we could say that this group member has developed a durable mental representation of the group and of her connection to the group. The group is seen as an essential element of her affiliative system. That is, she sees an important part of her affiliative needs being met by the group (Marrone 1998).

It is also true that a group can be experienced by members as persecutory, particularly at an unconscious level (Anzieu 1984), and so the need for an unconscious phantasy of the group-as-a-whole as an accessible 'significant other' can be frustrated by the actual experience of the group at any time. The same frustration is true of a child's experience of a caregiver. It is in part the resolution of the child's frustration over failure to achieve the wish for constantly accessible significant others that leads to healthy emotional psychological development. Perhaps, then, a part of the benefit to group members of their participation in groups is their learning to deal with the frustration of the phantasy that the group-as-a-whole will be a fully accessible 'significant other'.

Whilst it is necessary to differentiate between attachment theory and the theory of affiliative attachment, as corroborated in conversations with Françoise Ringer (F. Ringer 2000), it is also very likely that patterns of attachment that occur in each group member will be activated again in the group. Participants with 'dismissing' patterns of attachment will, in the group, enact dismissing patterns which include avoidance of intimacy with others or accepting comfort from others, avoidance of feelings, and idealization of group leaders. Dismissing people tend to devalue feeling and emphasize thinking. Perhaps the avoidance of intimacy and dependency on others will be enacted not only in relation to individual group members but also in relation to the group-as-a-whole. This is an interesting question that deserves investigation. On the other hand, persons with preoccupied patterns of attachment are likely to be overwhelmed by affect, clingy, and emotionally needy. They are also likely to have poor cognitive capacity when they are immersed in their feeling states. They, too, may enact this pattern in relation to the group-as-a-whole, and not just in relation to individual members.

Building affiliative attachment in the group: the role of the leader

What is the essence of affiliative attachment? What enables a particular group member to build this particular type of connection with the group?

The intuitive sense of the group is the critical factor. Claudio Neri provides a useful image in the term 'genius loci':

> The main aspect of Genius Loci's function in the group is preserving its identity. The function of preserving, enlivening and re-enlivening identity of the group, is strictly tied up with maintaining the permeability of its

borders and the possibility of exchange between what is recognized as internal and what is, on the contrary, considered external to it. The Genius Loci allows a strong feeling of belonging to be maintained, without the need to resort to a contra-position between 'group' and 'non-group', between 'us' and 'outsiders' in order to achieve this goal. (Neri 2001, www.funzionegamma.edu)

This genius loci is not the leader and may not even be a person. It could even be seen to have a spiritual element to it. Affiliative attachment is a challenging idea for group leaders who insist on being useful because sometimes the most useful thing a leader can do is stay out of the way of interfering with the affiliative attachment that is building within the group. A leader may even experience conscious or unconscious jealousy if group members are developing attachment to an element of the group other than the leader. Leadership to facilitate affiliative attachment involves facilitating the growth in an environment where elements of that environment are attractive enough to group members for them to develop their own intuitive/emotional/spiritual bonds to those elements. The leader needs to ask of him or herself the question, 'What in this group at this time is attractive to, satisfying for and experienced as meeting the needs of group members?'

The problem with affiliative attachment as an idea is that it can be mistaken for unconscious defence mechanisms in groups. For example, Turquet's 'Basic Assumption One-ness' as described by Lawrence *et al.* (1996) describes the state of group mentality where the collective illusion exists that all members are a happy conflict-free unit. This 'one-ness' illusion (which is closely related to Anzieu's (1984) 'group illusion') defends against the anxiety of the existence of interpersonal conflict in the group. In contrast, my intention here is to describe a state of mind in participants that will vary widely from participant to participant and that, for most, will result in group members feeling a reality-based attraction towards their membership of and participation in the group.

Implications for leaders

The leader plays a key role in facilitating the building of links early in the group and in helping the group to deal with attacks on the linking. Also, the leader plays a vital role in building and maintaining the container for the group. This involves also applying judgement about the way in which the rigidity of the boundaries needs to be varied at any time depending on the level of anxiety in the group and depending on the strength of linking in the group. Both successful containment and successful linking arise from the development of a complex combination of rational structures, relationships and unconscious processes. Establishing these elements requires significant skill on the part of leaders. Some of the skills and attributes required to build containment are the same as those required to facilitate linking in the group, but for simplicity I have divided the requisite skills and attributes into two sets in the text below. These sets are:

1. Skills and attributes required in building containment

2. Skills and attributes required in facilitating and protecting linking.

1. Skills and attributes required in building containment

The effective leader is able to imagine the group before it starts and to apply his or her prior experience with other groups to plan a suitable introduction to the group. When the group begins he or she is attuned to anxiety in the group and demonstrates confidence in his or her ability to manage the forthcoming challenges. Early in the formation of the group he or she works with the group to surface and acknowledge the range of hopes and fears in the group. He or she does not become preoccupied with only the hopes or only the fears (Whitaker 1989, 2001).

The leader puts into language that is appropriate for the group the basic boundaries for the group (outlined above) and negotiates changes in response to group members' requests. He or she judges and matches the level of psychological depth at which he or she introduces him or herself and assists the group to understand the level at which the group will work. Early interaction with the group includes a high level of observation and assessment of the group's level of maturity and the information from this assessment is applied to match the group's needs (Neill 1997a).

The leader is also aware of his or her emotional response to the group (countertransference) and he or she manages her behaviour to use the countertransference as information rather than 'acting out' with the group to reduce his or her own anxiety. The group is not used to meet the leader's own social needs, but is focused on as a group of clients for whom he or she is available. The leader makes him or herself visible enough to the group so that members see him or her as a human being who is capable of warmth and empathy, but is not so present with his or her own narrative that he or she dominates the life of the group as it forms. Finally, he or she demonstrates to the group that he or she has a sense of passion and ownership for the group.

2. Skills and attributes required in facilitating and protecting linking

The fundamental competence for the effective leader in facilitating and protecting linking in groups is that of 'appropriate responsiveness'. This means he or she is responsive to events in the group in a way that facilitates the group in achieving its primary task and maintaining adequate quality of relationships. Responsiveness contrasts with reactiveness, where the leader acts in opposition to, or as if driven by events in the group. Underlying the ability to be appropriately responsive is the ability to keep track of the leader's own emotional state and to be able to periodically tune into the unconscious aspects of his or her own functioning. Deeper still, in support of this function, is the leader's confidence that in the process of exploring his or her own perceptions, he or she will find a 'good' person in him or herself. This confidence is achieved by building an acceptance of him or herself and his or her history through sustained self-reflection, resulting in an ability to reclaim the parts of his or her history and personality that have previously been too painful to acknowledge and integrate (Kottler and Forester-Miller 1998; Smith 1995).

The leader demonstrates responsiveness by being constantly empathic and attuned to the unconscious elements in the group and responding to them in a way that enables 'stuckness' to be resolved without showing him or her to be some sort of guru who is cleverer and more perceptive than group members. He or she builds linking between members by acting as 'consultant to relationships' in the group and intercepting attacks on group members in ways that minimize damage to the linking in the group (Hinshelwood 1994). He or she demonstrates by his or her actions an understanding of the basic unconscious processes that are involved in conflict – those of splitting and projection (Gordon 1994; Wells 1995). Interventions are timed with precision. Too much too soon is just as unhelpful as too little too late (Ashbach and Schermer 1987).

When an event occurs in a group that raises levels of anxiety past what is tolerable for most members, each person will retreat into their own emotional 'safe space' and severely limit their visibility to the group and their emotional investment in the group. This retreat seriously limits the quality of linking between members. The effective leader facilitates the management of anxiety in groups to avoid serious retreats. Defence mechanisms are recognized and addressed appropriately.

Anxiety can be raised through boundaries being broken, through inappropriate psychological depth being reached, through confusion about roles, through loss of confidence in the leader or the process, and through many other factors (Berg and Smith 1995). The leader needs to be able to manage his or her own anxiety as a prerequisite to being able to facilitate the management of anxiety in the group. Anxiety creates a powerful invitation to regression into child-like emotional and psychological states. Leaders who are relatively mature psychologically and emotionally are more likely than their 'immature' counterparts to be able to manage their own anxiety in a group situation.

A case study: a conservation group

Let us illustrate these ideas in more detail through an imaginary scene. First, we will listen in on an introductory talk for a volunteer group run under the umbrella of the 'Department of Conservation' (DoC) in New Zealand. DoC is a government-funded conservation organization. Samuel, a DoC field-based Conservation Officer, was responsible for erecting a one-kilometre long possum-proof fence across a peninsula. (In New Zealand the introduced Australian Bush-tailed Opossum – a tree-climbing marsupial introduced from Australia – destroys native vegetation.) Samuel had a volunteer group from a local polytechnic (a tertiary educational institution) to assist him. Samuel's drive and energy had succeeded in getting sponsorship from a local business, and the Department of Conservation was providing Samuel's time and the use of a vehicle. He had lived in the area all his life and he had grieved to see the damage being done to the flora and bird life on the peninsula as possums had invaded the area and multiplied to plague proportions. This project was Samuel's passion.

Volunteer students from the polytechnic outdoor education course gathered in the Department of Conservation vehicle shed on the first morning of the project. It was raining. The first job was to carry heavy posts and rolls of wire from the road end to the fence. Sam was in the shed when the first students arrived and he had arranged impromptu benches for them to sit on. He had hot water available for tea and coffee. He was a bit of a comic figure, with a heavy yellow raincoat streaming with rain, short stubby hairy legs with short gumboots (Wellington boots) with wires instead of laces, and a large beer gut visible even through the bulk of his raincoat. Samuel's approach is summarized in Table 9.3.

Table 9.3 An example of creating linking and containment in a conservation group

What Samuel said	What he was doing
'Well, thanks for coming along today, it's a real stinker, eh? I thought you'd like kayak lessons in a warm pool more than struggling through mud and rain with heavy loads.' (*Some laughter and comments like, 'You don't know our tutors' from the group.*)	Linking himself with the group and introducing the task or purpose of the group.
'I'm Sam Johnstone. I work for the Department of Conservation so I'm in charge of this job we are all about to start. How much do you know about the project? You must know a bit to want to come here, or did someone force you along?'	Linking himself with the group and beginning to link the group members with the task. Acknowledging potential resistance.
(*He answers some questions about the duration of the project, then cuts in…*) 'Right, it seems like a good idea to go over a bit of the background of the project before we go out there and get wet. We are going to fence off the Moturoa peninsula with a possum-proof fence. When we've done that, we will exterminate the possums on the peninsula and we'll also keep rat and cat numbers down.'	Linking himself with the purpose of the group and the group with the purpose.

'You know, when I was a kid I used to paddle a dinghy around the peninsula to fish on the other side, and in the mornings you could hardly hear yourself think with all the Bellbirds and other birds shouting away at each other. Now it's like a graveyard. I don't like going there any more because it seems like such a sad place with no life. So after we've done our bit, the Department of Conservation is going to reintroduce many of the bird species that used to live there.'	Linking himself with the purpose of the group and linking himself with the group by relating his history, sense of place, passion and interest in the project.
'But first we've got another job. Who knows what that is?' (*Students answer that re-planting needs to be carried out first for food sources.*)	Linking himself with the group by encouraging them to share their knowledge.
'Now, we can't stay inside all day gasbagging, but there are a few more things we need to talk about before we go out and get rained on. First, do you all know each other? Are you all in the same course?' (*Some students say 'no'.*)	Encouraging group members to link with each other.
'Well, I don't know your names yet either, so let's start simple. Just say your name and why you volunteered for this project. I mean, why would anybody in their right mind get wet, tired and dirty when you have the option of staying inside?' (*The students all say their names and what interested them in the project. Samuel asks some of them a question to clarify their interest. He then goes around the group repeating the students' names, and asking for help when he forgets.*)	Facilitating group members to link with each other and with the purpose of the group at the same time.

'Now, the business end. The whole project involves… (*he summarizes the work plan – see the text below this table.*) I am the architect, engineer, fencing skills instructor and driver on this project. For a start most of you will probably rely on me quite a bit for skills training and advice, but you will quite quickly become pretty good fencing contractors yourselves.'	Clarifying the overall project and describing the role relationships and the authority system.

Linking with participants by showing that they will gain skills by working with him. |
| 'Now, you need to listen very carefully to this next bit because it may save your life or at least your leg.' (*He does the basic safety talk on the use of tools and what to do if separated from the rest of the group.*)' | Starting the practical task of passing on essential safety information to the group. |
| 'OK, hop in the bus and let's go…' | Starting the task. |

After this early linking, the boundaries were established to achieve the level of containment that was necessary. Basic containment for this group involves achieving clarity on boundaries and relationships: task, time, territory and roles. In practice, the leader would pay close attention to how the group was responding and make sure that the talking was broken up with practical tasks to avoid a long and tedious talk session at the start.

TASK

A gathering of people becomes a group when all members share a common purpose. Just as the Department of Conservation would not be an effective organization if its members did not share a common purpose, a group needs to know what their purpose or 'primary task' is. A typical statement of a primary task includes both the expected outcome and some clues about how the outcome will be achieved. In the example above, Samuel described the primary task:

> **We are going to fence off the Moturoa peninsula with a possum-proof fence**. First we need to clear a walking track along the route (that has already been surveyed and marked with red tape), then we carry in the materials. In early spring, while the ground is still soft, we'll dig the post holes, dig the trench for burying the bottom of the netting and then place

the posts. Then as the ground hardens in early summer we'll hang the netting and bury the bottom of the netting. In January we'll thoroughly check the stability of the whole structure. Then we're done!

That was a fairly elaborate statement of the primary task[3], but the essential element is in bold print. The 'how' is the text that follows that statement.

TIME

Being clear about time boundaries enables participants to know when they're 'on task' and when they can relate in a purely social way. Time boundaries provide the marker points so that participants know what roles both participants and leaders are in at any given time. Volunteer groups need social time, but it can be difficult to balance work with play. Clarity about time makes it easier for all participants to manage this balance. Again, listening to Samuel:

> The whole job is likely to take about six months in all. Now that's a long time to sacrifice your spare time, so we'll make sure you have a bit of fun. Each work day we'll gather in the depot to catch the bus for the car park. The bus leaves at 7.30 am sharp. We'll work until 12.00 with a twenty minute break at around 10.00. Lunch is thirty minutes and we knock off at 3.30. From 3.30 to 5.00 we will have free time. I'll offer informal walks around the peninsula to talk about plants, birds, creepy-crawlies and life in the lake, but that is just for those of you who are interested. Others can swim, sleep or whatever, so long as you stay in groups of at least four people. The bus leaves at 5.00 pm sharp. It's a long walk if you miss it.

Here, the overall time commitment is stated and the time boundaries within each work day are specified. This will be fine-tuned as the project unfolds, but clarity up-front reduces ambiguity and conflict later on.

TERRITORY

In talking about territory, the purpose is to establish clarity about the function of and restraints on the physical spaces that participants will be entering or will be excluded from. Samuel tells these participants about the territory involved in the conservation project:

> We won't be spending much time at this depot, but I'll point out the parts that matter. The toilets are over there behind you. They are locked and you need to get the key from me and return it to me. We've had vandalism problems, not only with the toilets, but also with the workshop, so it's locked too. For your own protection you should only go into the workshop

with a Department of Conservation staff member. Otherwise we can accuse you of ripping off our gear (*he smiles*). Seriously, you have to be pretty careful not to cause bad blood – partly because some of our permanent staff think that volunteers do work that permanent staff should be doing.

Out at the car park you can't get back into the bus after we've left it because it has to be locked to stop the thieves who cruise around the car parks ripping things off. You can go anywhere on the peninsula itself except Puketata. There's an old burial ground on the slopes of Puketata and there's no way we're going to mess with that.

The territory statements enable participants to move with confidence so they are more likely to act with initiative and enthusiasm. Not knowing what is 'off bounds' creates anxiety and reduces a group's effectiveness.

ROLES

Finally, each group member needs to know what their legitimate role is in the group and what responsibilities and authority are held by themselves and other group members. Samuel clarifies this:

I'm the one in charge of this big adventure. I put my neck on the line for the project and I really want it to work. If it doesn't you might see me in the queue to collect my unemployment benefit next year (*he smiles*). Also I am responsible for your safety and welfare. I have a contract with your poly-technic to organize this project and I need to report each month on how it is going. I don't like throwing my weight around, but in accepting this job you also accept that in case of any disagreements I do have the authority to tell you what to do. Otherwise I couldn't handle the safety requirements properly. Your tutor, Julie Jones, is responsible for your written reports to the polytechnic and for dealing with problems with attendance and other stuff that relates to you being officially at the polytechnic. Finally, we will be organizing you into what we call 'self-managed work teams' which means that each will appoint its own management system for keeping on-task and not messing around. I will visit each team at least twice each day for technical advice, for a safety check …

Here we leave Samuel and his team as Samuel has been effective in covering the essential elements of linking and containment for his group.

Conclusion

In addition to having to deal with the activities involved in their groups, leaders face the challenge of building a climate for group members that supports the group in achieving its task – whether that be recreation, education, development or therapy. Successful groups are bounded, purposeful and safe. Key components of such groups are the level of containment, the degree to which effective links have been developed in the group and the extent to which group members experience affiliative attachment to the group. Having the subjective experience of being contained and having adequate links in the group results in a positive experience. This is contributed by a diminishing of anxiety, an implicit hopefulness about the future, a perception of being in relationship with other human beings, a feeling of being loved or cared for, a sense of being worthy and often an expansion of awareness from self to others and the world. Affiliative attachment to a group reinforces self-worth and commitment to contribute in an effective way to the group. Effective leaders can play an important part in constructing the conditions for such experiences to take place.

Notes

1. This chapter is an edited version of an article that I wrote for the *Australian Journal of Outdoor Education 4* (1), 5–11. Thank you to Dr Tonia Gray for kindly giving me permission to reprint the article.

2. This is a slightly different use of the word 'containment' than was used by Wilfred Bion (1961).

3. Note that whilst the task we consider here is a physical task this is not always the case. The task of the group could also be to develop a sense of enthusiasm for conservation, to get to know others in the community who share a common interest in the environment and so on (i.e. the physical activities may be a means to an end).

CHAPTER 10

Enhancing group effectiveness through creating and maintaining a 'reflective space'[1]

Introduction

In this chapter I develop the view that groups, whether for education, therapy, decision making or organizational development will benefit when the leader focuses on building in the group a climate of attentive reflectiveness. This reflectiveness provides participants with an unconsciously held 'internal companion' with whom conversations can be held at a 'thought level'. The conscious or preconscious thoughts contribute to participants' ability to participate in the effective functioning of decision making, learning, developmental or therapeutic groups. In short, the existence of a reflective space in the group facilitates the group's effective functioning and therefore the likelihood that group members will achieve the outcomes or processes desired by the group. When the leader successfully facilitates secure containment and effective linking, groups are likely to support the development of reflective spaces. Leaders who themselves have a robust capacity for sustaining their own reflectiveness are likely to be able to facilitate reflectiveness effectively in their groups. This personal reflectiveness can be built through personal psychotherapy, group experiences and professional supervision (DeLucia-Waack 1999), although relatively few adventure therapy programmes currently include such things as professional supervision for their staff in their programme implementation.

I do my best thinking in conversations with other people, but sometimes these conversations occur when no one else is present. As a result, I find it hard to have such conversations out loud because people keep looking at me in surprise seeking to find the person with whom I am talking. That is because the other party to my conversations is someone in my mind, rather than what we might call a 'real' person. However, I do not think I am alone –

in two ways that is. First, when I am having these rich conversations with an imaginary[2] person I am operating in a benign kind of phantasy that there is an attentive friend there with me. Second, I am not alone because I think that many people do a lot of their thinking in imaginary conversations with other people – even if not at a conscious level. Whilst thinking may seem to be a solitary activity, perhaps it actually requires more than one real or imaginary person to create a place for thinking to occur? (For a thorough exploration of this concept the reader should consult Wilfred Bion's works on thinking including Bion 1962). Perhaps, too, emotions can only be raised to awareness in the context of a real or an unconscious (phantasy) relationship (Segal 1985).

Phantasy:

a kind of imagining of something that remains outside our awareness (unconscious) and in a generalized form. We might feel hopeful because of a background sense that there is someone bigger, wiser and stronger 'out there' who will prevent harm from befalling us. This is a phantasy.

Fantasy:

a consciously held imagining that has a tangible shape or form. For example, we might have a fantasy of inheriting a country estate with a Rolls Royce and servants to look after us. For further information see Segal (1985).

Might it be that to move from pre-cognition to cognition, and to move affect into consciousness, requires the presence in-the-mind of an 'other'? That is, thinking in its broadest sense, and hence learning, may only occur in the context of a real or imagined relationship. The relationship with the 'other' in these real or imaginary conversations creates a 'reflective space' in which the thinking occurs. The idea that a reflective space is created in a one-to-one conversation with an imaginary other can be extended to the idea that groups develop reflective spaces in their midst and that these reflective spaces support effective learning and human change processes. Learning occurs best in groups when group members experience two components:

- a psychological/emotional space in the group that will accept their ideas as a contribution to the collective thinking
- a corresponding 'container' for their anxiety (McCollom and Gillette 1995).

For group members the equivalent to the solitary thinker's 'imaginary other' is the 'group-in-the-mind'. In other words, the group-in-the-mind takes the place of the other person in conversations in which ideas are conceived and developed (Karterud 1998; Pines 1998).

Creating a reflective space

The reflective space for the group participant is created by the idea in the mind that the group is receptive to his or her ideas and feelings, that there is a psychic space for his or her ideas and feelings. This reflective space supports not only talking about ideas and feelings, but also supports the participant actually *having* these ideas and *experiencing* the feelings. The internalized picture of a receptive group contrasts with the idea-in-the-mind that the group will attack or reject the participant's thoughts or feelings. Generally speaking too, the phantasy in the mind of the group member of being in an 'attacking' group not only prevents the voicing of ideas, but also seriously inhibits the thinking of ideas and the experiencing of emotions. In an attempt to achieve simplicity, I have termed the imaginary space in which thinking and experiencing successfully occurs as the 'reflective space'.

The remainder of the chapter names and expands on a number of the characteristics of the reflective space and examines the way in which existence of an image in the mind of group members of a reflective space promotes the initiation, development and voicing of ideas and emotions. Some attention is also paid to how the mental representation on the part of group members of a receptive 'container' for their thoughts and feelings provides a sound environment for learning and change.

The characteristics of reflective space[3] in groups

Nine key characteristics of group reflective space are shown in Table 10.1.

Table 10.1 Nine key characteristics of group reflective space

1. Group reflective space is a mental construction and has no physical form
2. Each group member's internal emotional, cognitive and intellectual state contributes to the nature of the reflective space
3. Different group members have varying degrees of ability to contribute to and support the reflective space
4. The reflective space is simultaneously an individual and a collective phenomenon
5. Group reflective space evolves over time and changes as the group develops
6. The existence of group reflective space is reinforced when group members and group leaders act as if it exists
7. Group reflective space is vulnerable to attack and can be destroyed or damaged
8. Linking and containment of the group and attachment to the group are major factors in the creation of a reflective space (see also Chapter 9)
9. Reflective space is demonstrated by associative chains of thinking and feeling (Neri 1998)

Taking each of these nine points in turn enables a fuller picture to emerge.

Group reflective space is a mental construction and has no physical form

From the very first time the group becomes real in the mind of each group member, he or she develops a mental picture of what the group will be like. Receiving an email to say that there will be a meeting of a project group in the work place creates a group-in-the-mind. Reading a flyer and deciding to attend a personal growth group creates a different group-in-the-mind. The group-in-the-mind may seem hostile, friendly or have other characteristics. Once the group starts to meet, each participant modifies this initial internal representation of the group to match their actual experience of the group. Curiously enough, the mental representation is not purely based on 'reality'. A key characteristic of group life is the presence of mental representations at both fantasy and at phantasy level. These phantasy/fantasy level phenomena go by many names such as 'group illusion' (Anzieu 1984) and 'Genius Loci' (Neri 1988).

A part of the mental representation of the reflective space will include visual imagining and remembering as well as other sensory imagining and remembering such as smells and sounds. The pre-group imagining will be replaced mostly by remembering once the group space, smells and sounds have been experienced. But the nature of the reflective space that is created in response to sensory data about the group will depend on the level of anxiety that is evoked by those images, sounds, and so on. Low to medium levels of anxiety are likely to result in an intuitive sense of there being a functional reflective space.

Each participant, then, carries with them his or her own particular, durable but dynamic, representation of the quality of the reflective space that exists in the group. Some group participants will have had numerous prior group experiences. The mental representation of the quality of the reflective space that they hold at any given time will be an amalgam of their long-term working models and the overlay of their experience of the particular group of which they are currently members. Similarly, the mental representation of each participant's place in and contribution to the reflective space will depend to a great degree on the quality of their mental and emotional func-tioning.

Each group member's internal emotional, cognitive and intellectual state contributes to the nature of the reflective space

Each participant carries with him or herself internal working models of the world and their place in it (see in particular Chapter 2). These internal working models affect the way each participant experiences the group and him or herself in the context of the group. Similarly, different people have different levels of psychological maturity and therefore different ways of par-ticipating in a group reflective space. We could consider each participant's durable internal reflective capacity as either contributing to or detracting from the group reflective space.

People with a low trust of others will find it more difficult to experience the group as providing a safe, receptive reflective space than will those who are secure in themselves and implicitly trusting of others. Often therapy groups work with people whose internal working models are already quite dysfunctional for them and so many participants will already approach the therapeutic group with a great deal of mistrust. In the work place, the group participants' overall mental models about the level of trust, generosity and safety in the organization will influence their expectations about the nature of specific groups that are convened under the umbrella of that organization (Smith 1997).

Similarly, the immediate emotional state of participants at the start of each group session will influence their perception of the group. For instance, a participant will be nervous and unsettled if he or she is suffering from shock because of a near miss with another car on the way to the group. In that case the group itself may not provide for him or her the level of safety and containment – at that particular moment – that is necessary to provide an adequate reflective space. Conversely, even a noisy group with some elements of aggression may still be experienced as providing an adequate reflective space for a person who is robust and at peace with the world when the group session starts. Each person experiences the group differently and this experience depends to a great extent on projective processes such as projection, transference and identification, as previously referred to. What emerges then, in the life of the group is an interactive 'matrix' where each individual's reflective capacity influences the collective reflective capacity and vice versa.

Different group members have varying degrees of ability to contribute to and support the reflective space

Each individual in the group has a different personality, different working models and a different capacity to tolerate anxiety, uncertainty and the 'not-knowing' (Bion 1961) that is an integral part of participation in any group. The uncertainty and 'not-knowing' exist for two reasons:

- first, because each participant is aware that any other person can generate unexpected events at any time

- second, because the complexity of any group exceeds the capacity of any person to comprehend fully what is occurring at all levels at all times.

The reflective space is supported by a tolerance for and space for not-knowing, inquiry and reflection. Consequently, exploration is stifled when participants or the leader jump in with hard and fast answers (Neri 1998). When there appears to be only one answer to any question, no further space exists for curiosity or inquiry, with a consequent loss of the reflective space. Therefore, any person who consistently makes definitive statements about what is true in the group will potentially close down the reflective space. In particular, leaders who respond to the group's implicit request to tell them what is going on, will reduce the room in the group for open reflection and inquiry. Thus, leaders who provide too much information or interpretation too soon will reduce the reflective space in the group (Anzieu 1984; Neri 1998). Furthermore, a leader's compliance with the request to keep providing answers will support the evolution of what Bion (1961) described as a pervasive phantasy that the leader is all-knowing and all-powerful. The group that acts as if this unhelpful phantasy is true is said to be immersed in Basic Assumption Dependency (Bion 1961).

This suggests that individual participants who are very insecure in themselves will not usually be able to tolerate the fear of 'death of knowledge' that occurs at a phantasy level when inquiry and exploration dominate group process rather than the answers being provided by the leader. 'Not-knowing' creates a void that can be experienced as terrifying to the person whose own internal coherence is shaky – as is the case with people who are 'borderline' or 'narcissistic' in the sense in which these terms are used in the field of self-psychology.[4] One client in psychotherapy expressed a fear that if she told her story in full to the therapist, she would cease to exist because she would be emptied out (Meares 1992). This client demonstrated a very frail (borderline) sense of self and if the same person was in a group she would probably work hard to ensure that people around her demonstrated a confidence that the world was known and predictable. A second type of person who does not fit well in a reflective space is one who has 'narcissistic' tendencies, that is, their emotional survival depends on constant reassurance that they are competent, knowledgeable, likeable, and so on. Narcissistic or borderline people may fill the (otherwise) reflective space with words that are intended to demonstrate without doubt to the group that they are knowledgeable, competent and likeable. Failure to create room for narcissistic or borderline group members can result in their attacking the group or the leader (Schermer and Pines 1994; Yalom 1985). This attack, in turn, reduces the reflective space in the group. Cline (1993) has written an excellent chapter on the issues involved in working with narcissistic and borderline patients in adventure therapy programmes.

The reflective space is simultaneously an individual and a collective phenomenon

Both verbal and non-verbal contributions of each member to the group help to shape the overall group experience and each group participant's internal experience is influenced by the sum of actions and interactions of members in the group. The life of the group unfolds as an emerging tapestry, woven simultaneously as a series of individual experiences and as a collective experience. The reflective space, as an integral part of the group experience, also emerges in both the multiple threads of individual experience of all group members and in the collective fabric of the group. A significant change to any one thread will change the nature of the collective. Conversely, a significant change to the existence of or context for the group-as-a-whole will change the subjective experience for each group member. The concept of the group matrix helps here:

> The group matrix can be regarded as the operational basis of all mental processes in the group in the same way as the individual's 'mind' is the operational basis of all mental processes in the individual. Its lines of force may be conceived as passing right through the individual members and may therefore be called a transpersonal network, comparable to magnetic field. The individual is thought of as a nodal point in this network. (Foulkes and Anthony 1990)

This concept can be challenging to Western thinkers who have been raised with strong cultural assumptions that there is a clear differentiation between individual and group experience. Emerging views indicate that the Western distinction between group and individual is in part an illusion (Pines 1998).

Group reflective space evolves over time and changes as the group develops

Participants' mental representations early in the group will be mainly the result of their durable working models about groups. These gradually evolving working models are taken from group to group throughout life. As any particular group evolves, participants' experience of the current group will come to the foreground and start to dominate their mental representations of that particular group.

The first time group members are together they have no lived experience of being able to work together, to support each others' thinking and to trust each others' goodwill. As the group develops, the group-in-the-mind that each person initially brought with them is gradually modified. As a result, the nature of the reflective space changes as the experience and expectations of each group member changes. Models of group development tend to agree on the principle that adequately conducted 'healthy' groups deal effectively with their developmental crises and so become progressively more able to carry out the task for which they meet (McCollom 1995b). Among other things, effective leadership that deals with crises in the group can contribute to the growth in the group of a generous reflective space.

So, the group-in-the-mind for each participant gradually evolves. A part of this mental representation is the degree of confidence that the member has that his or her contributions will fall on fertile ground. To what extent will other group members and the leader be responsive to his or her thoughts, feelings and ideas? A further part will change in response to the way in which the group and leader act as if the reflective space is real and present.

The existence of group reflective space is reinforced when group members and group leaders act as if it exists

The way in which group members experience the group is built through the evolution of exchanges between the various perceptions of each group member (both phantasy and fantasy) and the observable ('real') events in the group. Primarily, though, what counts is the existence in the minds of group members of a pervasive belief or intuitive sense that there is an accepting space in the group for their thoughts, feelings and expressions. So a paradox is that participants' and leaders' collective belief that the reflective space exists is in part what creates the reflective space: a self-fulfilling prophecy. The contrary also occurs. If the group is swept by a contagious shadow of doubt about the existence of the group reflective space then the reflective space is reduced purely by the collective doubt in its continued existence. Therefore, when leaders and participants act as if the reflective space exists, this can assist others in the group to build and retain a belief that the reflective space is present in that moment for them too. Particularly for leaders, the existence of strong destructive invitations to projective identification can make it very difficult to maintain the reflective space through continued belief in its existence.

Group reflective space is vulnerable to attack and can be destroyed or damaged

The complex interweaving of phantasy, fantasy, and reality as the group-in-the-mind is constructed means that even one powerful negating event can create a crisis of confidence with participants and leaders. 'Attacks on the reflective space' (Hinshelwood 1994) can occur quickly, with devastating effects. Most major sources of anxiety in a group will severely reduce the quiet confidence that supports reflection. Similarly, anything that breaks the containment of the group will threaten its coherence. Changes to times, places, programme events or leaders can do this. A reduction in the linking between key elements in the group also reduces reflective capacity in groups. For example, aggressive verbal or physical events, sudden departure of members, complete emotional collapse of a member and many other events can threaten the existence of this essential linking and so can threaten the existence of the reflective space (see also Chapter 9).

There is another interesting twist in working with reflective space: the existence of a powerful reflective space in itself may be enough to stimulate attempts to destroy it. This is because a high level of reflectivity in a group can lead to deep levels of self-analysis and exploration, accompanied by minimal physical activity in the group. The quiet nature of the group favours verbalization rather than action. If uncomfortable psychological material emerges this can lead to impulsive activity in the group because action can be used as a means of avoiding anxiety. This acting out then diminishes the reflective space (Bateman and Holmes 1995).

Even in action-oriented groups such as in adventure therapy programmes there are many potential threats to reflective space. Participants may be anxious about physical activities, physical accidents can occur, task-oriented and directive leadership can lead participants to experience a sense of being emotionally abandoned. Participants easily feel alone and uncontained and this loss of either linking or containment reduces the reflective space. There is no easy solution for recovering from the shattering of a group's capacity to reflect, but effective leadership from a person who has a strong capacity to hold his or her own reflectivity is immensely helpful.

Linking and containment of the group and attachment to the group are major factors in the creation of a reflective space

Linking (see Chapter 9) refers to the existence of links at both conscious and unconscious levels. These links involve each group member, the group-as-a-whole, the leader, and the primary task of the group. Adequate containment refers to group members having the conscious and unconscious sense of being firmly held in the group and its task, and yet not immobilized or held rigidly by their participation in the group. Key aspects of the containment of a group are achieved through good 'boundary' conditions. These boundaries include clarity about the primary task the group sets out to achieve, the time limits for group life, the physical space that the group will utilize and the roles taken respectively by group members and leaders (Ringer and O'Brien 1997). Containment arises also from the quality of responsiveness (Bascal 1998) of the leader and his or her ability to facilitate conscious and unconscious communication between group members. The leader has a vital role in facilitating both linking and containment, and to do so requires a sound level of skills and a degree of emotional and psychological maturity (Ashbach and Schermer 1987).

A related characteristic of groups that achieve the development of a successful reflective space is that participants experience a sense of 'affiliative attachment' to the collective, to the representation of the group that exists in their minds (Marrone 1998; Stapley 1996). This sense of attachment enables them to retain an internal phantasy that the group is intact, even at the time that they are experiencing difficulty in the group. The idea of affiliative attachment to the group was developed in the previous chapter.

Reflective space is demonstrated by associative chains of thinking and feeling

The presence of a reflective space is demonstrated by the spontaneous flow of ideas expressed by group members which often appears as the emergence of a chain of associated thoughts that collectively move the group towards achieving its task (Neri 1998). Because the reflective space is not a tangible object we are left with the challenge of knowing when it is present. There exist a number of indicators that the reflective space is operational in a group. One of these indicators is that the leader him or herself experiences an attentive alertness that welcomes input from the group, but this alone is not adequate evidence. Such attentive alertness could also be the leader joining what is described by Bion (1961) as Basic Assumption pairing, where –

beneath his or her awareness – he or she is awaiting the birth of some miraculous idea. A second indicator of the presence of the reflective space is that the group conversation is likely to be relatively free-wheeling so that not every idea expressed is deliberately linked with the one before it (Anzieu 1984). In such situations an individual's thinking and verbalization can enter 'primary process' or 'free association' which is a state where one unconscious association flows relatively freely to the next (Neri 1998). The presence of a reflective space in groups enables one person's speech or action to trigger associations for others who speak freely of that association. In this case, without any intervention on the part of the leader, we experience an 'associative chain' (Neri 1998). This consists of a seemingly haphazard but deceptively progressive pattern of interaction where group participants stimulate each other in a flow of ideas that in general moves the group towards its purpose. This process lies on the boundary between conscious and unconscious and the pace of the group may vary rapidly from times of intense, excited and even confused talking, to relatively long periods of silence where most of the associations are occurring inside the heads of participants. Only with experience can group leaders tell when an intensely active group is also reflective or when an active group is avoiding reflection. Similarly, it can be difficult to discern between a silent reflective group and a group that is paralyzed by survival anxiety (Nitsun 1996) or the collective phantasy of being devoured or destroyed by the group (Anzieu 1984).

An illustration of damage to the reflective space

I attended a five-day Gestalt therapy group that was advertized for professionals who wanted to enhance their ability to work with therapeutic groups. In fact, the group was simply a Gestalt psychotherapy event where we all sequentially received attention from the therapist and did our own therapeutic 'work'. By Day 4 the group had formed an intense mood of self-reflection. The group felt well contained and most group members appeared quite strongly attached to the mental representation of a safe group. The leader/therapist was relatively gentle in his approach, he worked on the expectation that a reflective space existed and as a result of all of this some very significant personal issues had been worked through by participants.

Group members had developed confidence in the group boundaries, and had built a network of strong empathic links between members. When the group started on the morning of Day 4, I looked around the group of people sitting in various positions of recline on the cushions on the floor and noticed that two people were missing. One of them arrived fifteen minutes late, opened the door (which was directly behind where I was sitting) and moved slowly and quietly around the perimeter of the group to the place that she had taken the day before. Nobody spoke of the other missing member and the therapist began working with a person in the group.

I was completely immersed in this participant's story (probably identifying strongly with him) when the door behind me opened abruptly, hard shoes clattered across the floor and the latecomer rushed noisily, breathing heavily, directly across the centre of the group space to plonk herself down in her place. I was shocked. My heart raced and I felt anger, verging on rage, rise in my belly. It seemed to me that the reflective space that we had built had been ripped apart. I looked around the room and saw most people looking at the floor. No longer was there any overt focus in the group. Each person had retreated into their inner worlds to recover from the shock and to regain a sense of composure. The therapist did not comment at all. He paused his work, looked at the intruder – who was still noisily scrabbling around in her bag – and then continued where he had left off with the participant who had been working when the interruption occurred. I recall feeling as though a part of me had been ripped open and left to bleed. I had completely lost my empathy for the intruder and to this day still find it difficult to wonder what her needs might have been.

What I now understand is that the individual psychological 'skin' that in everyday life we hold close to us had been gradually loosened during the three days of intensive group work. Each participant had opened their 'skin' to include the group-as-a-whole, and in doing so had made themselves vulnerable to experiencing intrusion on the group space as an intrusion on their personal space (Anzieu 1984). Before the intrusion, while the group was functioning well, the personal reflective space that we normally hold close to ourselves had, for most of us, been extended to include the whole group. This collectivizing of the psychic skin also seems to accompany the existence of a group reflective space. The noisy latecomer had transgressed the very tender and vulnerable group space and so had created an event that many of us experienced as an attack on our internal psychic space. No longer did we have a lived experience of a hard boundary around each of us that was distinct from the psychic boundary around the group. So, the latecomer had walked across tender parts of our psychic intestines. I want to emphasize that this group had reached high levels of boundedness, linking, a significant subjective experience of the existence of a reflective space, and a strong attachment to the group. At this stage in the group's development we were relatively often experiencing the free floating associative chain of thinking and feeling.

The leader's lack of acknowledgement of the intrusion left us with no avenue to re-build the space. The container had been broken into, some of the linking had been broken and as a result the group felt stuck and lifeless for the remainder of that session. At the tea break there was intense angry talk about the intrusion and almost all group members shunned the offender. No doubt we were projecting our own intrusiveness and lack of consideration onto her in that it was much easier for myself and other group members to see inconsiderate and intrusive characteristics in another person (the intruder) than to acknowledge those characteristics in ourselves.

After the tea break the group slowly re-gained most of its sense of intimacy and reflectivity. I believe that the tea break had enabled most of us to begin to process the sense of trauma that had occurred in the group that morning. The leader's failure to deal with the transgression soon after it happened resulted in an arrest of the group's ability to achieve its task, and in Bion's (1961) terms had led to a collective 'flight' through each of us psycho- logically tuning out from being engaged with the group. Similarly, no one group member acted in a way to assist the healing. Any one of us could have named our feelings and helped to re-form a reflective space in which we would 'digest' our feelings of hurt and intrusion.

Reflective space: implications for group leaders

A reflective space in a group creates the potential for each group member to develop his or her own internal reflective space. A key component of this personal internal space is the presence of a phantasy of an 'other' with whom conversations can be held without fear of shaming or over-exposure. Therefore, a part of the task of the group leader is to assist the group-as-a-whole to develop the collective reflective space and also to help each person internalize that space, using the phantasy figure of the group-as-a-whole as each person's internal partner in conversation. A particular challenge emerges from the fact that very little of each participant's building of the reflective space occurs consciously.

Most of the growth of a group reflective space is experienced by partici- pants as an intuitive and emotional experience that is not accompanied by an intellectual understanding of the process. Therefore, often the leader alone carries the conceptual knowledge of what is happening and can only appeal to group members for assistance in creating the reflective space by indirect means.

Early in the formation of the group the creation of clear boundaries – and in particular those of task, time, territory and role – helps to provide the group with a container in which the reflective space can be nurtured (Berg and Smith 1995). However, even this can be done in a way that creates a sense of rigidity and therefore reduces the reflective space. A common experience of first-time participants in 'group relations' conferences is that perceived rigidity in the way that task, time, territory and role boundaries are implemented by conference staff creates excessive levels of anxiety. This anxiety is often experienced as reducing the quality of the reflective space. So even early in groups it can be useful to enlist the help of phantasy-level phenomena to build a sense of group coherence and reflectiveness (Neri 1998) rather than enforcing structural limits such as rigid time boundaries to the extent that they contradict even basic social norms.

As the group develops, building of links between the many parts of the group system – members, leader, group purpose, and group-as-a-whole – develops a resilient interconnectedness in the group. Provided that the nature of these connections is primarily benevolent, this complex matrix forms the basis at a phantasy level of the reflective space. This reflective space is at the same time 'taken inside' (introjected) by group members and nurtured by them. Once the reflective space has begun to form, it is accompanied by a growth of participant attachment to the group and a sense that 'the group is working' grows as thinking and feeling in and between group members takes the form of associative chains. Nonetheless, the reflective space sometimes needs to be protected by the leader's actions and interventions. Attacks to linking and containment need to be deflected and any resultant damage to the reflective space needs to be acknowledged and healed.

Further development of the reflective space is facilitated by optimal responsiveness on the part of the group leader (Bacal 1998). Over-enthusiastic facilitation or interpretation on the part of the leader intrudes on participants' own contributions to building a group-as-a-whole reflective space (Neri 1998). Filling the emerging space with the leader's own knowledge or enthusiasm builds dependence on the leader and diminishes the collective phantasy of a multi-faceted group with rich and diverse components. However, the leader's active support of the reflective space is seen as a cue that it 'really' exists. In some groups, participants themselves can start to contribute to the leadership actions so that the group space is protected from intrusions and attacks by other group members or by those outside the group. That is, with groups where most members have reasonable levels of psychological maturity, group members themselves can take a significant role in building and maintaining the reflective space in the group.

Conversely, therapy programmes sometimes work with participants whose pre-existing capacity for reflective feeling and thought is damaged and groups in such programmes are likely to already be high risk environments where attacks on the reflective space can often occur. Healing of participants occurs in part through their successfully expanding their psychic boundaries and 'taking in' (introjecting) the lived experience of a group reflective space. Gradually, this experience can lead to participants' building in themselves a more durable personal capacity for thinking, feeling and reflecting on their own place in the world. For these reasons, the ability of therapy group leaders to facilitate the growth and maintenance of group reflective space is vital.

In all of the complex choreography that is involved in calling forth the reflective space in a group, one key characteristic stands out for leaders. That is the intrinsic capacity to hold inside oneself a durable reflective space that stands up to the inevitable challenges that occur in the life of most groups. Particularly early in the life of the group, the myriad of non-verbal and mostly unconscious cues that emanate from the group leader provides the essential backdrop to the more deliberate actions that are being carried out to create containment and linking. The management of countertransference onto the group and onto individual participants is the most significant competence for group leaders. If there is resulting congruence between the leader's actions and his or her unconscious communication about the value and safety of reflection, then group members will willingly join in the building of a collective space as much as their personal make-up allows. In contrast, a group leader who lacks a personal sense of safety in a group will issue (unconscious) non-verbal signals that constantly warn participants that there is not a safe place for openness and collective reflection. In such cases, the group will fail to build the collective reflective space that supports the kind of powerful learning that we usually seek in our groups (Maxwell 1996).

A more subtle implication for group leaders is that the leader should not strive solely for the kind of reflective space in a group that resembles the glassy surface of a pool in calm weather. In contrast, the purpose of creating what I call a reflective space is to *enable thoughts to be thought and feelings to be felt.*

This environment is often not quiet, but nonetheless has a feeling of openness about it, even if it appears noisy and active to the observer.

The leader's own reflective capacity

If it is true that having a robust internally held reflective capacity is a major contributor to our ability to facilitate the growth of reflective capacity in groups, then how do we build and nurture this in ourselves?

The basic process that enables leaders to build their reflective capacity is that of internalization. What is internalized is a durable expectation that there are other people or other groups in the world that can provide the leader with a space in which to reflect. This provides a kind of portable internally held reflective space for the leader. I said at the start of this chapter that I often have good conversations with imaginary others. These phantasy figures have come to life in my mind as a sort of generalized memory of the numerous occasions during which I have been with others and experienced a high quality reflective space. Any experience that we have of working with any other person or group when there are high degrees of reflectiveness will contribute to building our own internal reflective space. The building of such a phantasy space begins at birth and is associated with having experiences of secure attachment to caregivers (Marrone 1998). Later in life, positive relationships with significant others and positive experiences in groups strengthen the internalized reflective capacity. As adults, we have at least four major opportunities to build or maintain our reflective capacity. Personal or group psychotherapy is one; professional supervision is another; successful intimate friendships provide yet further internalized secure connection with our reflectiveness; and successfully operating in groups where we assist to facilitate reflectivity is another potential contributor to internalized reflective capacity.

Unfortunately, with the exception of therapeutic organizations that are informed by psychodynamic or humanistic principles, most environments in which we work do not value reflection. Most work places in Australia and New Zealand are driven by 'outcomes' that ignore quality of life and the emotional health and mental health of employees. A particular challenge that I have faced in building my own capacity for reflectiveness and my capacity to facilitate reflective spaces in groups has been the relatively low value that I believe has been placed on responsible self-reflection in the culture of adventure-based learning organizations where action tends to be valued more than thinking, feeling or reflection. Similarly, most corporations do not acknowledge the central role of reflective thinking and collaborative learning. It is difficult to fly in the face of the dominant culture, but my own experience is that having personal psychotherapy, professional clinical supervision, and a disciplined focus on my own process-in-relation-to-others has been very worthwhile.

Reflective spaces in organizations: a central issue

Whilst there seems to be an indisputable argument for reflective spaces in therapeutic and educational work, advocating for reflective spaces in corporate work is more challenging. The corporate world has largely managed to perpetuate the myth that reflective, emotional and relational matters are either 'fringe' or at best peripheral to 'core business'. The cost is exceptionally high levels of splitting, projection, projective identification and consequent scapegoating in organizations.

Nonetheless, there is a strong theoretical basis of support for the development of reflective group process in organizations. For instance, Hutton (1997, p.67) is unequivocal about 'the centrality of reflective thinking as an activity of management'.

One of the problems that I face in writing a book of this nature is the translation of ideas into action that will make sense in a rationalistic corporate environment. One exciting inroad into the psyche of an organization was achieved by working in collaboration with a talented team of employees in an oil and gas engineering consulting company in Western Australia. After two years of consulting within the organization during which time we gradually built a tolerance for psychodynamic thinking, we were able to introduce an experiential learning programme for consulting engineers that was based on the principle of reflective space, although it was couched in slightly different language. The main participants were engineers who were carrying out work for a large subsidiary of Shell Oil. The main issue was how to work in collaboration with the client, thinking together to create optimum solutions to engineering problems. The conceptual schema for the programme is presented in Figure 10.1.

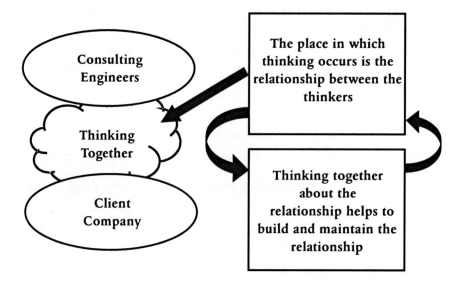

Figure 10.1 Thinking together between clients and consultants

The part of the figure labelled 'thinking together' represents the reflective space not just in one-to-one relationships but also in teams, project groups and meetings. Whilst many other concepts were involved in a total of four days of experiential workshop, the idea of a thinking space was one of the three most significant contributions to making changes in the effectiveness of the organization.

For group leaders who work with organizations, including private corporations and government departments, one of the most difficult challenges we face is to maintain our own belief in the importance of and the need for developing and maintaining reflective spaces in our work with client organizations.

Conclusion

Group leaders who have a robust capacity to remain reflective and curious, even in the midst of difficult events in the groups that they are leading, are likely to be able to facilitate in their groups the development and maintenance of a reflective space. The context of adventure therapy is a difficult one in which to nurture reflective spaces in groups. Many participants are referred because they do not have good reflective capacities themselves; adventure activities can be more glamorous and captivating than reflection; and adventure therapists are themselves likely to be the kind of people who are attracted more to action than to reflection. Nonetheless group reflective space is a vital part of the therapeutic system and, when present, can be a powerful positive therapeutic force.

The existence of a good reflective space results in a climate that supports open and curious reflection, thinking and experiencing on the part of participants. The reflective space supports internal processes of cognition and processing of affect that enable participants to derive learning from their participation in the group. Leaders can, through their own personal efforts, build their own internal reflective capacity. The skills that are required to build containment and linking in groups assist leaders to facilitate reflectiveness in groups. Other skills enable leaders to protect groups against attacks on the reflective space. The focus on reflectivity in groups may provide some practitioners with a previously under-utilized addition to their effectiveness.

For further reading on the reflective space see Neri's (1998, pp.80–111) eloquent description of 'group thought' which has some clear parallels with the idea of group reflective space. That section of his book will provide the more interested reader with further ideas that relate to the group reflective space.

Notes

1.   At the same time that this book goes to print two different versions of this chapter are being published elsewhere. Thanks to Dr Susan Long, editor of *Socio-Analysis*, and Dr Kaye Richards, editor of the Second International Adventure Therapy Conference for their support for the simultaneous publication of these two versions.

2.   I use the term 'imaginary' here to mean both creations in my mind of people (or groups) who do not exist in any real physical form, and memories of people (or groups) whom I do know or have known.

3.   Conventional thinking about groups and individuals creates a difficulty in describing the 'reflective space' or 'group reflective space'. In my view the reflective space that I describe is simultaneously 'group' and 'individual' and so depending on which aspect I wish to emphasize at any one time I will use both terms 'group reflective space' and 'reflective space'.

4.   For the purposes of this book 'borderline' participants demonstrate a pervasive absence of a coherent self and therefore look for 'self' in others. 'Narcissistic' participants depend on others for validation of their sense of self because their internal sense of self is so flimsy.

CHAPTER 11

Six perspectives on facilitation and group leadership competencies

Integrating the rational with the non-rational

This chapter provides a framework for looking at how groups function. The framework consists of six 'windows' or perspectives through which the group leader can view the functioning of the group. What is viewed from each perspective ranges from rational and logical issues such as 'group task' through the more emotional and relationship-based topics and then on to the perspectives that rely largely on an awareness of unconscious functioning. The chapter re-visits and summarizes some of the material covered earlier in the book, and in particular focuses on the rationale for looking 'beneath the surface' of groups and work place teams. This rationale may provide for the reader an easily communicated raison d'être that can be used in his or her own work place to influence others to look more closely at group and work place dynamics. The fundamental framework for the six windows was derived from a paper (Ringer and Robinson 1996) that applied similar criteria to examining the culture of organizations and so the principles articulated in this chapter have a wider application than just experiential groups.

Introduction

'You can't measure the skills involved in facilitation, they are all "soft" skills' is a common cry in fields such as adventure education or corporate development training. Most practitioners in these areas are skilled in educational processes or in conducting adventure activities or are skilled as deliverers of work place development training. In the fields of development training and adventure education there is a strong push for group leaders and facilitators to have 'demonstrable skills'. Therefore practitioner competence can be assessed using rationally derived and relatively empirical means such as those required by the national training authorities that exist in Australia, New Zealand and England. This means that group work leaders and facilitators can attend standardized courses and obtain standardized qualifications on the assumption that the course and the assessment process are subject to quality controls that guarantee certain 'learning outcomes'. My view is that systems of this nature that try to standardize human learning in areas where unconscious processes are significant achieve two things. First, they do achieve some level of consistency in the quality of education, training and competence of practitioners, but this consistency is so minimal as to be almost useless. Second, they create the illusion that issues of competence have been adequately dealt with. Having created this illusion, it is important not to look too closely at the actual competence of practitioners and this close look is forbidden by saying that it would be 'too subjective'. As you will see later in this chapter, I believe that creating and defending this illusion is highly unprofessional.

Competency-based training and assessment schemes for group leaders appear to be built on two fundamental premises that are so deeply held that they seldom surface and are even less often articulated. These premises are that:

1. Empirical, sensory-based evidence is the only data that are valid in assessing the ability of people to carry out tasks, functions or roles. By inference, subjective data such as feelings, intuition, and impressions are invalid – though some assessment schemes acknowledge the importance of values.

2. A measure of competence can only be valid if that measure can be replicated reliably by different people. In other words, a measure of competence is valid only if it is 'objective' in the sense that a wide range of different people with different personalities and outlooks would give a similar rating to the same event.

Both of these criteria are useful in some settings, particularly in fields of endeavour where practical tasks are conducted. The two above assumptions enable tasks to be broken down into flow charts or 'algorithms' that can be applied by anyone who has the competencies to complete each step in the algorithm. However, some tension arises when the two above principles are compared to the principles that can be shown to underpin a more psychodynamic approach to the leadership of groups and teams. The most significant of these principles are that:

1.   Participants' patterns of mental representations are the most significant aspects of a group. These are an amalgam of thinking, intuition, emotions and expectations, and include two main elements. One is the overall representation that participants have of the group, and the other is the participants' mental representation of their own place in the group. These internally held constructs range from fully conscious to completely unconscious. A shorthand for this complex array of mental and emotional expectations is the 'internal working model' which is explained in Chapter 2.

2.   These mental representations depend in part on the personal patterns or 'valencies' (Bion 1961) of each individual and at the same time have characteristics that are common across the group-as-a-whole.

3.   The commonalities in mental representations across the group result from symbolic communication between group members, in both verbal and non-verbal forms.

4.   The group leader is an integral part of the conscious and unconscious field of symbolic communication and therefore he or she personally experiences patterns of affect that are present in the group psyche as his or her own. Thus, the group leader's subjective experience is the most accurate 'measure' of what is happening in the group at any given time.

5.   Even in identical situations, every different group leader would have different feelings, thoughts and intuition. Therefore there is an essentially subjective element to what each leader perceives to be going on in the group at any given time. As a consequence of this subjectivity, the vital information that is provided by the group leader's own subjective experience is flawed by the possibility that a particular group leader could be incorrectly reading the group at any given time.

6.   The loss of validity of information that is available to the group leader through paying attention to his or her own feelings and intuition can be partly counteracted by refining the perceptive

ability of the group leader. The ability of the group leader to make accurate meaning of his or her perception of events in the group depends heavily on the degree to which he or she is aware of his or her own implicit patterns of perceiving and making meaning from life events (working models). This ability is sometimes summarized as 'self-awareness'.

These principles underlying psychodynamic group work are simply not compatible with 'objective' measures of performance. Instead, the measurement of competency depends both on having clearly articulated criteria and on the quality of the person who is doing the measuring. In this frame, objectivity is impossible. It is no wonder that Priest and Gass (1997) in their comprehensive book on leadership in adventure programming describe the tendency for adventure-based practitioners either to relegate group work leadership skills to the realm of 'alchemy' or to seek the 'touchstone' that will magically enable excellence in group facilitation. Similarly, the business world that requires everything to be measured and related to bottom-line profit and shareholder value leaves no room for the psychodynamic principles outlined above. It takes a courageous manager to make room for the more subjective approaches to be applied in the work place.

The two worlds collide because the principles underpinning one appear to discount the principles underpinning the other. All too often such clashes in ideology are 'solved' by drawing lines in the sand of professional theory and practice. These lines of demarcation enable each 'camp' to look with metaphoric binoculars at the other camp and to laugh at the ridiculous antics of the other. Some such divisions even turn into warfare where each camp seeks to destroy the other. It is my view that in the field of adventure education and outdoor leadership there has long been an implicit and therefore invisible discounting of aspects of group leadership that do not fit into algorithmic schemes. My experience in business is that there is hardly even a battle there. Psychodynamic approaches are so marginalized that they are almost invisible and can be ignored.

Two main defences seem to be in place. One is that psychodynamic approaches are said to belong to other fields such as social work and group therapy and therefore not to the field of experiential learning or business. This defence is helped along by the fact that a lot of the psychodynamic and psychoanalytic literature is written in jargon that is simply not accessible to those 'outside' the field. It took me years of persistent effort to learn enough to be able to understand even some psychoanalytic publications. The second defence is that, within the broad fields of business and experiential learning, it is said that only management psychologists or adventure therapists need to be able to apply such principles to their facilitation of groups and teams. Different people use different means to keep away the discomfort aroused by psychodynamic approaches. Some people keep challenges out of the literature in their area of practice. At the moment business and experiential learning literature is dominated by step-by-step descriptions of 'how to' conduct various aspects of facilitation or meeting procedures. Critiques of these are rarely published. Even in the last few years, a reviewer for a leading American experiential education journal rejected a submitted article because it 'did not reflect current views'. The unquestioned assumption that 'current views' are correct is a part of the system of over-rationalized thinking that is challenged by approaches that look at deeper issues such as unconscious processes.

The current political and economic climate in most of the western world supports the marginalization, trivialization and fragmentation of complex fields of endeavour such as group facilitation and leadership. In this vein, the title of this chapter was a deliberate play on the word 'facile'. If the meaning of the word – as derived from the French 'facile' (easy) – signifies the state of being easy, then 'facilitation' translates into the term 'making easy'. However, the meaning of 'facile' in English has migrated to something akin to 'trivial'. Bending a few grammatical rules enables us to see 'facile-itation' as trivialization. Is not the activity of 'making easy' a group so simple as to warrant trivialization? Should we not simply chunk facilitation into a number of algorithms, and derive from each algorithm the requisite competencies? Then we could divide these competencies into a few manageable portions, describe empirical evidence required for each, and then set about developing an objective, 'portable' training and certification scheme? This makes sound economic sense. Training and certification could then be licensed to certified operators (with franchise fees) and run to prescribed standards in any setting. Uniformity would be guaranteed across states and even between countries, greater accessibility could be achieved for the training and costs could be minimized. Unfortunately, the introduction of the principles that underpin effective leadership of groups and teams, as articulated above, makes such simplistic schemes virtually impossible.

The seemingly impossible tension between the 'algorithmic' competency schemes and the above 'emergent' schemes can be partly resolved by acknowledging that each has its place, depending on the level of complexity of the competency that is being developed and assessed. The algorithmic approach to groups has its place in building foundation and intermediate competencies. Rules and principles are essential for starting out on the journey of group work leadership. In the field of outdoor leadership, excellent examples of these basic and intermediate competencies can be found in Priest and Gass (1997). The business literature abounds with descriptions of how to achieve significant results by following a number of prescribed steps and these too may be useful as a starting point but will rarely hold up for long periods in complex or conflicted situations. One problem in the business literature is the sheer volume of available literature. There is no shortage of excellent psychodynamic literature that provides excellent insights into the unconscious workings of individuals, teams and organizations. The problem is finding it in the avalanche of quick-fix publications. Some examples of excellent publications are: Kets-de-Vries 1991; Obholzer and Roberts 1994; and Stapley 1996.

There remains a shortfall in the published literature in the field of adventure education and in experiential learning that both deals with more psychodynamic aspects of group facilitation and that is written in language comprehensible to the average practitioner (with some notable exceptions, such as Hovelynck 1999 and 2000). Accordingly, the remainder of this chapter emphasizes the psychodynamic/subjectivist end of the spectrum in an attempt to start filling this gap. It seems most important to emphasize that for most group facilitators, leaders or conductors it is useful firstly to have a strong foundation of practical facilitation and leadership skills before exploring in depth psychodynamic approaches. Once facilitators have a sound grasp of active listening, assertiveness, models of group development and tools for facilitation they will be in a stronger position to focus on building their capacity to work directly on unconscious, intuitive and systemic aspects of groups. Concurrent focus is fine, but the emergent aspects of groups tend only to make sense fully once the more pragmatic aspects are understood. It should be added that group leaders need themselves to have had extensive experience of being a participant in experiential learning groups because this lived experience is an essential building block in the development of group leaders' own capacity to understand unconscious processes in groups.

Competencies for group leaders

A paper written and presented in 1994 introduced an outline of competencies for adventure leaders whose application ranged from recreational to therapeutic (Ringer 1994). This was followed by a plea to the field to make a place for passion and aliveness in outdoor leadership (Ringer 1995). The same plea could just have easily been made to people in business.

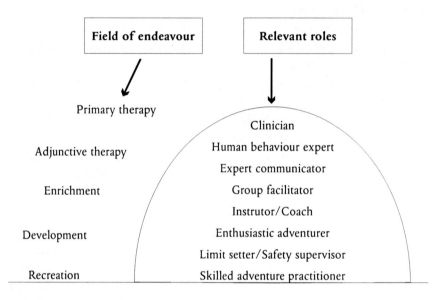

Figure 11.1 Competencies for outdoor leaders
Source: Ringer (1994)

The eight layers of competence shown in Figure 11.1 range from the practical, rational competencies of adventure skills, through to the non-rational competencies involved in demonstrating passion and aliveness – that is the leaders' emotional connection with and enthusiasm for their work as evidenced in the role of the 'enthusiastic adventurer'. Further up the diagram towards the top are the competencies involved in being able to deal with human interaction and human dysfunction. The implicit assumption when this model was written was that each of the roles toward the bottom of the igloo were pre-requisites for the roles that appeared above them. So, recreational leaders needed to have well-developed roles of limit setter and safety supervisor. Leaders of developmental activities needed these two roles in addition to the role[1] of enthusiastic adventurer, and so on. Whilst this was originally intended only as an approximation, the scheme is clearly unhelpful because it reinforces the view that group work competencies and interpersonal competencies are only required by leaders who work in the fields of human change – that is in the areas of enrichment and therapy. Similarly, many texts on facilitation in the corporate sector make the assumption that because the overt work that is done does not involve psychotherapy, the leaders or facilitators have no need to understand group dynamics or only need very limited understanding. This is an unhelpful assumption.

An examination of Priest and Gass's (1997) model of competence shows a limited acknowledgement of the need for experiential educators to have high levels of competence in dealing with the emergent aspects of groups. Their text provides excellent algorithmic methods that form the backbone for processes that can be carried out by inexperienced group leaders, along with an extensive underpinning theory for those techniques. However, unconscious and emergent aspects of groups are not described. Given the small amount written in adventure education about unconscious processes in groups, there seems adequate justification for looking again at competencies required by group work leaders in that field as well as in business settings. Therefore, the exploration that constitutes the remainder of this chapter is intended to provide an extension to current thinking about the role of and requisite competencies of leaders of experiential groups in many different settings. Whilst most of the remainder of this text refers to experiential education settings, the same principles apply to groups and teams in corporate situations.

Six perspectives on group leadership competencies

In the following sections, six perspectives are taken on effective group functioning, and for each perspective some thinking is offered about the competencies required by leaders. It is acknowledged that leadership competency is only one of many factors that leads to successful groups. In the interests of brevity, other factors are not considered in this chapter.

The six perspectives chosen are:

1. The *task and activity* perspective, where the focus is on the group's success in identifying and pursuing its primary task and the group's success in carrying out the activities that enable it to achieve its task.

2.   The *structural perspective*, where the focus is on the existence and awareness amongst group members of the roles, authority and boundaries that are required to enable the group to function well.

3.   The *relational perspective*, where the focus is on the quality of interaction and linking between key elements of the group, including members, leaders and the environment in which the group is working.

4.   The *perspective of efficacy-in-the-role*, where the focus is on how effectively each participant in the group deals with the activities, roles and structures that group membership demands of them in their particular role in the group.

5.   The *internal management* perspective, where the focus is on how well each participant manages his or her own (conscious and unconscious) inner emotional and imaginative world in order to gain benefit from the group and in order to support others.

6.   The *group climate perspective*, where the focus is almost entirely on unconscious processes involving the group-as-a-whole and the way in which these unconscious elements support or detract from the group's functioning.

This chapter focuses primarily on the competence of the leader to assist in facilitating the group to enhance the level of functioning as viewed from all six perspectives, even though participants will also have a place in supporting the group's actions towards achieving its goal. Neither the group alone nor the leader alone has it in their power to ensure effective group functioning: the group and leader are all a part of an interdependent system. Nonetheless, in this chapter, relatively little attention is paid to participant contributions. Instead, the focus is on how the leader should respond to participants' input. Some suggestions about leadership competence are made under each of the six headings below.

Task and activity

The primary task of the group establishes the reason for its existence. This primary task, when agreed amongst participants, facilitator and any other agent/agency that has a say over group resources, gives participants the authority to support or to challenge the leader in his or her facilitation of the group. Accordingly, the ability to establish with the group its primary task is a core competency. Whilst each group will have a different primary task, there are patterns in the nature of the primary task that have been well documented.

Group leaders will be better able to assist their groups to establish the specific task for the group if they (the leaders) have understanding of one or more systems of categorization of group primary task/purpose. One form of categorization for experiential learning groups was originated by and later modified by a number of different authors. This classification system outlines four levels of category for group primary task, as shown in Table 11.1.

Table 11.1 Goals for adventure experiences

	Recreation	Education/ Training	Development	Psychotherapy
Primary goal (Primary task)	Fun, laughter, challenge, excitement, initiative, and so on.	Change in sense of identity or self-concept.	Learning associated with a *generic* theme such as co-operation, communication and trust.	Learning about interpersonal processes that will be applied with participants' *significant others.*
Distinguishing features	May be therapeutic, but focus is on enjoyment.	Often associated with learning for an occupation, vocation or course of study; often used with work teams.	Associated with the desire to improve behaviour in important relationships.	Often (but not always) applied to remedy personal dysfunction. Usually preceded by assessment of clients.

Source: Ringer and Gillis (1995)

In Table 11.1, adventure experiences are classified into categories of recreation, education/training, development and psychotherapy. The progression from recreation to psychotherapy implies decreasing focus on fun as a goal and increasing focus on the intention to improve the psychological functioning of group members.

Another form of classification originated by members of the Association for Specialists in Group Work (ASGW) divides groups into four categories:

1. Task/work groups: task forces, committees, community organizations, discussion groups, study circles, and learning groups that serve to accomplish identified work goals.

2. Guidance/psychoeducational groups: educational groups that teach group participants knowledge and skills for coping adaptively with potential and/or immediate environmental challenges, developmental transitions, and life crises.

3. Counselling/interpersonal problem solving: groups that offer interpersonal support and an environment for problem solving in which common career, educational, personal, social and developmental concerns can be addressed.

4. Psychotherapy/personality reconstruction: groups that address in-depth psychological disturbance through reconstruction of major dimensions of group participants' personalities. (ASGW 1992, cited by Waldo and Bauman 1998)

Both of the above classification systems for the primary task of groups provide a conceptual framework from which practitioners can establish with their groups the goal for each group in their care. The conceptual framework is used by the facilitator as a guiding principle while he or she negotiates with the group to establish the specific primary task for the group. For example, the primary task for a work place team might be to 'improve the quality of interaction in this team so as to improve productivity and satisfaction of team members'. This primary task would fit into the 'developmental' category of Ringer and Gillis and into the guidance/psychoeducational category of the ASGW classification.

A further competency required by group leaders is the ability to take into account the potential conflicts that arise between the goals of group members and other stakeholders who are not present in the group. This competency requires the group leader to be able to perceive and act on the unspoken and often unconscious aspects of organizational culture. In the case of work groups, managers and other branches or divisions of the corporation may have wishes that are different from the wishes of group members and many of these wishes may be communicated in subtle ways rather than directly. Similarly, a facilitator who works under the administrative umbrella of a therapeutic organization needs to be able to adapt his or her style to match the expectations of the host organization. Even further challenges arise from the tendency for all groups to create unconscious collusion and so to act 'as if' the group exists to conduct a primary task other than the one to which the group has previously consciously agreed. The group leader is inevitably involved in this unconscious collusion. To notice one's own collusion, to catch oneself and to be able to act in ways that re-focus the group on the actual primary task requires a high level of competence on the part of the leader.

It is all very well to have arrived at a clear agreed purpose for the group, but the next challenge is to conduct activities that facilitate the group to make progress toward achieving their primary task. The skills required to conduct the required activities vary widely depending on the category of primary task and consequent psychological level at which the group is to operate. For example, a facilitator in a business setting may use structured activities such as brainstorming or focus group process but the 'director' of a psychodrama group with families will need the many competencies derived from the fields of family therapy and psychodrama. Whilst the group leader needs to have learned the competencies relevant to his or her field of specialization, there will be many times when the complexity and speed of events in the group are so confusing that it may be difficult to select the appropriate technique for a given time. Also, the emotional impact on the leader of some events creates a temporary disabling of that person's ability to function. Instead, the challenge of managing intense feelings takes over. Accordingly, the ability of leaders to manage their own internal emotional/psychological worlds becomes a core competency. This is addressed later in this chapter under the heading 'Internal management'.

Structural

Competencies at the structural level are those involved in establishing adequate structure in the group and around the group. Primarily, structure is provided by boundaries and roles. Critical boundaries are those of time and territory. As described elsewhere, time boundaries are the marker points in time that enable a group to know when it starts, when it breaks for meals and so on, and when it ends. Time boundaries are also essential for marking when participants and leaders change their activities and roles. Territory boundaries are real physical constraints on where the group can conduct its activities, as well as agreed physical zones within the group space that determine what roles participants will take when in each zone. A good example is the psychodrama stage, where entering the stage area requires participants to shift from current reality to the reality that is being enacted in the psychodrama. In outdoor activities safety requirements have a great deal of influence on the territories used by groups and the nature of activities and roles that are allowable in each zone.

Formal roles provide a second form of structure for groups. Clarity about roles enables the group to work towards its primary task. Lack of clarity may result in a group acting as if its primary task is to achieve role clarity – rather than the primary task for which the group was formed. Key roles are those of facilitator, analyst, leader, director or conductor. Each of these roles implies a leadership function where group members are being led. Co-leadership involves negotiation between co-leaders to achieve clarity about who is enacting the leadership role at any moment in time. Confusion, ambivalence or conflict about roles between co-leaders will quickly lead to difficulty and anxiety in the functioning of the group.

Group members also have formal roles that they enact in the group, though this is sometimes not well understood by group leaders. The role of 'learner' is just as distinct as the role of 'leader'. The formal roles of participants vary from time to time in some groups where participants take different parts in the group. Small group discussions where participants often report back to the whole group after the discussion are an example of when group members take different roles from those in the larger group. Less obvious is the role differentiation that occurs when specific techniques such as psychodrama are used in group work. In such cases, group members need to be informed about role expectations and sometimes coached to learn how to take on their formal roles as participants.

Roles that are not consciously acknowledged and role relationships that are not specifically identified as being a part of the formal structure of the group will emerge through the interaction as 'informal roles'. These informal roles form a part of the focus through the relational perspective – described in the next section. Additional leadership effectiveness can be gained from having an awareness of the different formal roles that a leader can take and by having the ability to move from role to role, depending on the needs of the group at the time (Wells 1995). Other times that roles need to be clarified in groups are when people enter the group in roles other than leader or participant. For example, observer, volunteer, recorder and researcher roles need to be identified and explained to participants. These roles carry an implication of observation or non-authoritative interaction with the group and, as such, they attract transference that is often tinged with suspicion that comes from a lack of interaction with the group. This lack of interaction can evoke phantasies that the observer is hostile or malicious. Therefore, it can be useful to clarify with the group the kind of behaviours that are expected from the relevant role.

An essential part of the structure of a group is the appropriate utilization of authority. This includes the personal authority of the designated leader. This personal authority is derived from the leader's appropriate confidence in his or her ability to act in the relevant leadership role. Personal authority results from having the ability to manage one's own internal world of feelings and phantasies so that one is not overwhelmed or seduced by feelings or phantasies. In a later section of this chapter we re-visit this idea in the area of 'internal management'. Authority is also often delegated by the organization that provides the professional mandate to run the group and which also often provides the resources. Examples are schools, therapeutic organizations and consulting organizations. However, the most significant authority in a group is its own authority to work towards its primary task. In well-facilitated groups, this authority is usually delegated 'upwards' by the group to the leader. This is why it is so important for the group to reach agreement on its primary task. The primary task provides the authority for the group to act.

There are numerous forms of 'contract' that are used to reinforce the structure of groups. These include verbal agreements between leaders and groups, written contracts between groups and umbrella organizations, indemnity contracts, health release forms, and so on. A significant competency is to know what types of agreement or contract are appropriate for any group at any particular time in its development. Even the advertising flyer for a group forms a significant part of the structure of a group. Another useful competency is that required to interact effectively with the group so as to arrive at a suitable contract or agreement.

Relational

The relational perspective makes visible the quality of interaction between key elements in a group. These key elements include group members, the leader and the mental representation of the group-as-a-whole. This quality of interaction becomes visible as patterns of interaction during the life of the group. In brief, the relational perspective makes visible the 'linking' that is described in Chapter 9. The main elements that are considered from the relational perspective on groups are people and the informal roles that they enact, but some other elements such as the group primary task and the organizational context are also relevant here. The competence that is most relevant here is the leader's capacity to work with the group to build and maintain the links that enable the group to function. Sociometry, the study of relationships, is a useful area of competence in working effectively with relationships between people. Other links are important though, including links between:

1.   Each of the group members and the primary task

2.   The group leader and the primary task

3.   Each of the group members and others

4.   Each of the group members and the leader and vice versa

5.   Group members and the group-as-a-whole

6.   The leader with the group-as-a-whole.

These links are described in detail in Chapter 9 and so only a brief revision is given here. The links between group members and the primary task, and between the group leader and the primary task are the essential foundations for any type of group, regardless of whether it is a task, educational, developmental or psychotherapeutic group. Task clarity provides the fundamental mandate for the group to exist. Therefore, developing these links is an essential competency for group work leaders. However, the way in which the relationships between group members are managed varies from one type of group to another, depending on the group purpose. In task and educational groups sound relationships enable the group to focus on its practical or learning task and so provide the foundation for an effective group. In developmental/counselling and psychotherapy groups, strained relationships in the group may provide the grist for the therapeutic mill. In this case, the single-minded determination of the group leader to 'fix' the relationships in the group will work against the effectiveness of the group in achieving its primary task – that of learning from the relationship difficulties.

Similarly, the nature of the relationship between the leader and the group provides essential information about the group itself, and so a lack of comfort in this relationship can sometimes enhance the functioning of the group, for a time anyway. This topic is covered extensively in group work literature under the term 'countertransference' (see, for example, Ashbach and Schermer 1987; Schermer and Pines 1994). Also, the different forms and qualities of the relationships between the leader and the group-as-a-whole and between participants and the group-as-a-whole provide essential information about the functioning of the group. These relationships operate primarily at an unconscious level. Given their unconscious nature, they are dealt with later in the section on group climate.

All groups evolve an internal structure and so any roles and consequent role relationships that are not included in the formal structure will emerge as informal roles. If, for instance, the formal group leader consistently fails to negotiate and act on time boundaries, one or more of the group participants will begin to take on the role of timekeeper. Other informal roles emerge in the group, not because they fill a deficit in the formal structure, but because of unconscious patterns of communication that inevitably occur in groups. That is, group members bring to the group their internal working models of themselves and their place in the world and these unconscious expectations are communicated in subtle ways to other group members. Gradually, group members shape each other's behaviour through repeated acts of communication and different members adopt clearer patterns of behaviour that can become more restricted in their range as the life of the group evolves. Role differentiation is one measure of the maturity of a group, and the emergence of helpful roles in a group can add to its effectiveness. However, role differentiation through projective identification involving negativity can lead to serious problems such as scapegoating (Schermer and Pines 1994; Wells 1995).

Finally, on the topic of the relational perspective, there are other aspects of linking between elements of a group that exist at unconscious levels. Links occur at spiritual, emotional, sexual and intuitive levels as well as the more rational/cognitive levels (Neri 1998). The leader and individuals in the group form a complex dynamic interdependent human system that functions in ways that often run counter to rationality. A key competency is that of managing the complexity of linking, much of which occurs beyond immediate awareness. Having an understanding of the factors described in the section on group climate (described later in this chapter) enhances this competency.

Efficacy

'Efficacy' in this case is used to mean the general capacity to act in a role. It is made up of competence and the degree to which practitioners fit with the professional role in which they find themselves. A person can be competent in some contexts but not in others. Efficacy implies having the ability to act and finding the setting in which this ability is mobilized. Each group member needs to be competent to perform the role that he or she has in the group. There are two main types of role. The first is the formal role – the one(s) agreed to in establishing the purpose and formal structure of the group. For example, a psychotherapy group consists of leader(s) and participants. The participants agree to adopt the role of client, and usually the conditions of that role are specified in setting up the group. These conditions include such things as the level of participation, the nature of participation, expectations about disclosure, and so on. Examples of the main formal roles in different types of group are: 'team member' for corporate groups; 'learner' for educational groups; 'client' for counselling groups; 'patient' for psychoanalysis groups. Just as people in organizations have job descriptions, members of groups have the equivalent role descriptions. The 'full value contract' (Schoel et al. 1988) for adventure education groups provides the essence of the role description, whereas for psychoanalytic groups Anzieu's (1984) 'rules of diagnostic groups' provide role descriptions for participants and leaders where expectations of each role are specified.

The second aspect of role that participants enact is that of the informal role, as mentioned earlier in the section about relational aspects of group functioning. Leadership effectiveness can be enhanced by considering that group members will, through such unconscious processes as projective identification, allocate roles amongst themselves whether or not the leader facilitates the allocation of formal roles. As described in Chapter 7, over time group members develop an unconscious agreement about who will take which informal roles in the group. These informal roles are a part of what is often generically described as 'group norms' (Johnson and Johnson 1991; Tyson 1998). The presence of informal roles is made visible when a person acts in an 'uncharacteristic' way and attracts from other group members comments such as, 'Wow, I didn't expect you to come up with that!' The meta-communication there is that the person has acted outside his or her informal role in the group.

Whilst the major focus in group leadership is on the competency of the group leader, it is also important to focus on the competence of group members to enact their roles in the group. Thus an important competency for leaders is that of supporting and coaching group members in the development of 'group membership' competence – in order for them to take useful active parts in the group. Also, group leaders need to have the judgement that enables them to effectively screen out potential group members whose personal competence is not up to the standard required for the group in question. Occasionally, leaders will need to remove a member because the member does not have the capacity to take part in the group, even with coaching. Perhaps one of the most difficult tasks ever undertaken by a leader is to work simultaneously with an unsuitable group member and with the group so as to remove the group member. The group member in question is likely to feel extremely threatened, and the remaining group members will have a heightened sensitivity to the risk that they too will be asked to leave. Very high levels of competency in group leadership are required to deal with this thorny issue.

To summarize from the perspective of participant efficacy, leaders need to be competent at supporting the competence of participants to be effective group members. The relevant leadership competencies include coaching and supporting participants in adopting and enacting appropriate roles, setting and enforcing limits, and empowering participants to make the most of the developmental space that is created by the group itself.

Internal management

Group leaders have the simultaneous tasks of keeping track of and adequately managing their own internal worlds, and facilitating group members to adequately manage their internal worlds. I sometimes think that at almost any time in any group, if we stopped to ask group members what they were doing, most might say, 'I'm working on managing my internal world so that I can participate effectively in this group'. In reality many people do not have the self-awareness (or self-absorption!) to know that they are actively managing their emotional state, but perhaps if they did have that awareness we might get the response that I imagine. In other words, an essential competency for group leaders is that of facilitating group members in the process of managing their internal emotional worlds. This is the case for all kinds of groups, not just for therapy groups. I derive this view from the observation that many people seem to be competent to do many things in life, but once they reach a certain point of emotional or psychological stress, they lose their competency. So in order for group participants to retain the competencies that they already have in participating in the functioning of the group, we need to assist them in managing their internal worlds so as to retain access to those competencies. A case in point was when I was involved with a large consulting engineering organization and a major competency that was identified was for the consulting engineers to adequately manage their internal emotional worlds when their clients behaved in a bullying fashion. Engineers who were skilled at design work and who were quite skilled communicators lost their ability to function when they had their 'buttons pushed' by domineering clients. A person facilitating a meeting between the consulting firm and a client group would need to be able to support all participants in managing their internal worlds in order for the group to achieve its purpose.

A second aspect of group members' internal functioning that calls for specific leadership competencies is that of projection and projective identification. Leaders need to be able to identify when group members are losing their effectiveness through projective processes and need to be able to intervene in helpful ways. As described earlier, projection involves the unconscious disowning of aspects of self that create excessive anxiety or threaten the person's ideal view of him or herself. Not only is this aspect of self disowned, but it is also perceived by the person doing the disowning to be a characteristic of another person. At times the disowned aspects of self can be projected onto an inanimate object, the environment or an organization. In other words the 'badness' (or sometimes 'goodness') is projected onto the other person or object. Rather than face the disturbance of having to acknowledge that this person him or herself has a characteristic that he or she perceives to be undesirable, he or she 'finds' it in someone else or something else. Projection is not entirely an imaginary process; it is triggered by 'real' characteristics in the other person. In groups there are plenty of other people who can be identified by one group member as having undesirable characteristics. For example, a group member (Sam) who constantly smiles, quickly finds another group member (Sally) to be aggressive and rude. What Sam does not realize is that his idealized picture of himself is that of an amiable person who is tolerant of others and nice to everyone. So he is (unconsciously) terrified of the presence in other people of intolerance and aggression because he cannot tolerate the possibility that he can be intolerant and aggressive himself. As soon as another person in the group shows intolerance and aggression, Sam jumps to point this out, thereby completely avoiding having to face his own intolerance.

Any member of a group will adopt roles that are initially based on his or her own preconception of him or herself. Then as the group progresses these initial roles will be modified or added to by projective processes. In particular, new roles or modifications to existing roles will occur through internalizing projections from all other members of the group. The internalization of others' projections is the early stage of projective identification. For some people, the idea that their behaviour in groups is not entirely of their own independent making is intolerable. When I am in a group and experiencing intense feelings it is almost always very difficult for me to believe at a level of lived experience that what I feel as so entirely my own feelings are in part 'not mine' because they occur through having others' feelings projected onto/into me. Often it is only after a group has ended and when I am reflecting on my role with my professional supervisor that I will understand retrospectively how much of what I had felt was originating in other people.

So although it can be difficult to acknowledge at an experiential level, leaders too, are active participants in the complex matrix of projective processes that occur in groups and therefore they are influenced at unconscious levels by the unspoken undercurrents in the group. These unconscious influences are most often experienced by the leader as feelings and intuition. There are two main issues relating to group work leadership competency that arise from this fact. First, the level of emotion sometimes experienced by group leaders can 'knock out' their ability to apply the competence that they have. Flooded with emotion, the leader becomes temporarily immobilized or partly disabled. It is not surprising, then, that group leaders need to be highly effective at managing their internal worlds so that they retain their competencies as group leaders. Second, the leader needs to find ways to discern between the emotion and intuition that is primarily derived from his or her own internal functioning, and what has been picked up by a combination of projective processes and pragmatic observation from the group.

As mentioned earlier, in order for a facilitator to be able to choose an intervention, he or she needs to have some idea about what is happening and what needs to change. Awareness of what is happening in the group is derived directly from the group leader's awareness of his or her own emotional/intuitive state because that provides information about what is occurring at an unconscious level in the group. In other words, the group leader's own emotional state is inextricably linked with the emotional 'field' that exists in the group. The group leader's own emotions are the thermometer or perhaps litmus paper that reads the nature of the patterns of unconscious interaction in the group.

You might object, 'But my emotions are affected by my own pathology, neuroses, and other unresolved stuff that I've got going on. Surely my own emotions are a very unreliable way of sensing what is going on in the group, purely because of this?'

The subject of psychological maturity is too large to do justice to here,

---

PSYCHOLOGICAL MATURITY

The core aspects of psychological maturity for group leaders are:

1. Ability to reflect on and take responsibility for one's own assumptions, actions and views, rather than disown them and project them onto others.

2. Degree of tolerance of involvement with the other individuals or with groups, and appropriateness of involvement with others. Low tolerance of engagement leads to hostile or distant relationships, and inappropriate closeness leads to invasion or overpowering of others.

3. Congruence between feelings and actions/speech and with reality. Disconnection between feelings and thinking creates a sense of being untrustworthy. Disconnection between observed reality and one's own description of the world is disconcerting to others (Ashbach and Schermer 1987).

4. Ability to tolerate complexity, ambiguity, contradiction and 'not-knowing' (Bion 1961; Senge 1992). Also the ability to separate self from one's ideas. Ideas contribute to the sense of self and so when core ideas are challenged by experience the sense of self can be threatened unless it is very secure (Meares 1992).

This is far from an exhaustive list, but it provides a useful first base to begin making sense of the capabilities that are required of group leaders in order for them to be able to develop adequate containment of their groups and for them to be able to facilitate and maintain adequate linking in the groups that they lead (Neill 1997b). Further ideas about psychological maturity can be found in psychodynamic literature (Ashbach and Schermer 1987; Tyson and Tyson 1990).

---

but because of the importance of this subject to group leaders, a summary of key points is included in a text box.

The difficulty in managing reality in groups is that there is not a single objective truth about what is going on in any group. Whilst leaders, group members and even whole groups can be caught in unhelpful phantasies, the observations, intuition and feelings of participants and leaders alike are what defines the 'truth' about what is going on. Leaders need to develop high levels of personal functioning to enable them to determine when it is likely that they are entering an unhelpful phantasy about the group. This is achieved at an individual level by the group leader knowing about and understanding his or her own idiosyncratic responses to others' behaviour and his or her own habitual patterns of projection. Means of catching oneself entering a 'group illusion' (Anzien 1984) are best gained through being a participant in such events, and through having a thorough understanding of unconscious processes in the group-as-a-whole, as discussed in the next section on 'group climate'.

Now I will digress briefly to give an example of how my internal functioning can get me into trouble with groups, and in particular with some male participants. Specifically I have a long personal history of difficult relationships with men in authority. When I have an arrogant pushy man as a participant in my group it is very likely that I will get angry. I then have the difficult task of deciding to what extent my anger arises from my unconscious perception of anger of other group members and to what extent my anger comes from my own exaggerated dislike of men in authority. This ability to differentiate is still not yet quite as good as I would like, but it keeps improving with practice, professional supervision, the ability to question the usefulness of my first impulses to act and the ability to search for the origin of my feelings.

The simplest means of exploring one's patterns of perceiving and reacting to life events is to unearth one's 'internal working models' as described in Chapter 2. Because internal working models are so central to the functioning of group leaders I will summarize them here before discussing their application to this section. Internal working models are personal, individualized 'maps' of the way in which each person expects significant aspects of the world to interact with him or herself. Each aspect of the world is the subject of one or more working models. 'The term "working model" can be used to denote all the representations about the world and ourselves in it that we build in the course of experience, including people, places, ideas, cultural patterns, social structures and so on' (Marrone 1998, p.72). For instance, each person has a working model that includes expectations of how families should work; '...there are specialized forms of working model which can be defined as a set of conscious and unconscious notions about oneself as a person and the other as a significant figure in one's life' (Marrone 1998, p.72). These specialized working models provide for ourselves a durable set of expectations about how other people will relate to us.

Included in our internal working models is a set of expectations about how people should behave in relation to others – including ourselves. When another person behaves in a way that is significantly different from that determined by our internal working models, we feel shock or anxiety. Each person's internal working models prescribe different behaviours and so the shock and anxiety is experienced differently in response to similar events by different people. The greater the extent of our awareness of our own internal working models, the greater the extent to which we can be aware that other people will react differently than we do. It may be an over-simplification, but we could say that the main emotional challenge for group members and group leaders is managing the emotional impact that occurs when we see others in the group behaving in ways that contradict or contravene our own internal working models. The most significant development of our internal working models occurs in our families of origin, which is why it can be so useful for group leaders to spent some of their time in professional training exploring the ways in which they functioned in their original families and so the patterns of internal working models that they developed.

Understanding unconscious processes in human interaction, and more specifically in groups, is a further factor in helping group leaders to manage their own internal worlds in ways that assist the group to achieve its purpose. These unconscious processes are described more fully in the earlier chapters of this book.

By now it will be obvious that there is no clean line that differentiates the unconscious functioning of any one person in the group – whether leader or participant – from the unconscious functioning of any other person. This potentially confusing insight can create difficulties for leaders who are seeking to influence the group, because they are faced with the challenge of influencing a system from the inside rather than being an external agent who influences the group from the outside. To support the competencies of the leader, new theoretical models are required that promote an understanding of the connection between group leader's feelings and the unconscious patterns in groups. The competencies derived from understanding the group-as-a-whole are outlined below under the heading 'Group climate'.

Group climate

The perspective on group leadership competencies that is described under this heading is primarily a symbolic one. At this level rationality and logic are no longer prevalent means of understanding groups. Here we focus on the process of making meaning and building mental representations of the group. In fact, this chapter largely refers to the *unconscious thematic* level of group-as-a-whole functioning that was described in Chapter 7.

The key leadership competency is that of being able to perceive events and to intervene in the group at symbolic levels. The leader needs to understand his or her place as one that is strongly influenced, beyond his or her awareness, by the powerful unconscious processes that are operating in the group. Leaders who cling to the illusion that they are 'in control' of events in the group are not able to operate from this perspective. Rather, leaders who view the group-as-a-whole and watch for patterns of perception, interaction and influence are able to assist the group to work through its unconsciously expressed blocks to progress. Here, theoretical models which describe the group-as-a-whole provide the conceptual maps for the leader. Such models as Agazarian's functional subgrouping, Whitaker and Lieberman's focal conflict model, Neri's genius loci, Foulkes' group matrix, Bion's basic assumptions and Anzieu's group phantasy are all useful at different times in different settings.

Leaders who are able to work with unconscious processes in groups will recognize that all other elements of the group both influence and are influenced by the unconscious life of the group. The task established for the group affects some aspects of the climate. For instance, a psychotherapy group will have a different feel from an educational group that is made up of the same members. The formal structure for a group has a major impact on its climate. In particular, groups with low levels of structure tend to be more fragmented, anxious, and regressed than groups with moderate levels of structure. The relational aspects of the group are an important contributor to the climate of the group. A group with strong links between members will develop a sense of robustness that is not present in a group where links are fragile or even hostile. Conversely, when the group climate contains suppressed hostility, links between members and the sense of containment in the group will feel weak. A sense of fragility or fearfulness will also emerge in groups where a number of individuals, or the leader, do not have the basic competencies to carry out their roles. Finally, groups where members are not capable of managing their inner emotional and psychological worlds will not feel robust and will not retain their sense of purpose because the insecure participants will project their unmanageable feelings onto other group members. Other defences used by insecure group members are to attack the group leader or idealize him or her with a resulting over-reliance on the leader. Competent group leaders will recognize this plethora of pitfalls and will be able to respond effectively in ways that facilitate the group working effectively towards its goal.

As mentioned earlier, a further influence on group climate is that of the umbrella organization or 'host' organization for the group. The assumptions and conditions that underlie an organization's structure will also influence any group that is held under the auspices of that organization. 'Truths' about human nature and about human change processes are automatically conveyed to group participants purely through their involvement in the umbrella organization. Sometimes these influences are relatively subtle. For instance, I led a workshop for an organization that was suffering from a crisis in its leadership at the very top level. The people I was working with were not directly involved in this leadership crisis. Nonetheless, group members turned up late, the room we had booked was not available at the last minute, a staff meeting was called part way during the workshop. All in all, the chaos and ambivalence in the organization's leadership had a direct influence on our workshop. Until I raised the question, none of the group members considered that there was a link between the chaos in the organization's leadership and the chaos in our workshop. It all happened at an unconscious level.

Conclusion

Leadership of groups is one of the most complex tasks that human beings can undertake. As a result, the competencies required to be an effective group leader are many and diverse. They range from practical skills in managing tasks, boundaries and roles, through to the potentially elusive 'arts' of working with intuitive and unconscious processes. Such an array of competencies is potentially overwhelming, and can create a great deal of anxiety for those seeking excellence in group leadership. The task already faced by leaders in educational, therapeutic and corporate fields is complex enough without adding more requirements. Already these people need to have competencies and qualifications in their own professions, as well as in interpersonal communication. Adding to this the above competencies for group work leadership can be almost intolerable. Therefore, the temptation facing many of us is to simplify the group work competencies to make them seem more manageable. In support of this wish for simplicity, we can call in the tenets of rationalism thereby dismissing aspects of group work that call for understanding of unconscious processes. My call is to tolerate the anxiety arising from the awareness that group work leadership is such a complex task. An appropriate response is to include in our personal development plans ways of improving the competencies that enable us to grapple effectively with unconscious processes.

Group and team leaders not only need to have learned the knowledge, skills and competencies for group work leadership, but also to have developed the personal capacity to manage themselves during challenging times in groups so that they retain access to the essential knowledge, skill and competence. This second factor involves managing one's own internal world so as to retain connection with self in the midst of the complexity of group life.

Returning to the six 'windows' described in this chapter, some core competencies (skills, knowledge and abilities) become visible:

1. The task and activity perspective: a core competency is to help groups to identify and move towards their primary task.

2. The structural perspective: a core competency is to develop role clarity in groups and work constructively with role confusion when it arises.

3. The relational perspective: a core competency is to work strategically with the relationships in the group and to ensure the means of working with relationships assists the group to work towards its primary task.

4. The efficacy-in-the-role perspective: a core competency is to coach group members to support their competencies as effective group members.

5. The internal management perspective: core competencies are to

    • manage leader's own internal world in a way that ensures that he or she retains access to accurate perception and skills even in the midst of emotionally challenging events (that is, ability to manage feelings, anxiety, defensiveness, and so on)

- develop robust self-awareness, in a way that provides useful data about what is occurring in the group.

6. The group climate perspective: core competencies are to

- intervene in the group in a way that balances the conscious and unconscious demands, and that balances the individual needs with the needs of the group-as-a-whole

- facilitate the growth of the emotional 'container' for the group and to facilitate the development of links between key elements in the group.

The reader will, it is hoped, identify more or different key competencies through his or her own application of the six windows on group functioning. What is intended in the list above is not artificially to over-simplify the competencies required to lead groups, but to sharpen the focus and prioritize where to start looking. The competencies outlined and advocated in this chapter need to be supported by the overall view that groups and their leaders are complex interdependent human systems, where all aspects of group life are inextricably woven together. A second aspect of the supporting mind-set is the awareness that human beings, both in groups and as individuals, work by a system of logic that is not exclusively rational and therefore that the creation of meaning in human systems – involving unconscious processes – is of paramount importance.

Note: whilst this chapter focuses specifically on experiential learning groups, most of the principles outlined here are directly applicable to social groups, work groups, political groups and groups that form for a myriad of other reasons. The framework above can be applied much more widely than is implied in this chapter.

Notes

1. For an excellent description of role in the sense that I use it here, see Williams (1989).

CHAPTER 12

Leaders as artists

Unconscious processes in groups[1]

Introduction

The previous chapter could well be taken as the final chapter in the story of groups in therapeutic, educational and corporate settings, but if that was the case I would have sold the reader short. There is an implication in the structured nature of the last chapter that one can systematically or sequentially focus on six levels of functioning in a group and that each level ranging from quite rational to entirely a-rational, has an integrity in itself. Nothing could be further from the truth. The parallel that comes to mind is the nonsensical notion that one could replace the subjective experience of viewing a piece of art with an analytic description of the work of art using six different levels of analysis.

In this chapter my hope is to reintroduce strongly the irreducible complexity of group life by making a comparison between elements of group life and elements of art. The chapter begins with a revision of the key elements of unconscious processes and then moves to the comparison between groups and art. The purpose of the chapter, then, is to provide some kind of integration of many of the ideas that have been presented earlier and to stimulate thinking about the nature of unconscious processes in groups. I also raise a few ideas and questions about the leaders' role in working with unconscious processes.

A brief review of unconscious processes

Given that the theme of this chapter relates to unconscious processes, we start with some discussion about the differences between conscious and unconscious processes. In brief:

- Conscious processes follow a logical rational sequence where logical reasoning determines what is connected to what. For example, in conscious processes the number 'one' is followed by the number 'two'. In contrast, unconscious processes are apparently illogical and occur by association. In unconscious processes 'one' may be followed by 'it's cold today', depending on whose unconscious process we are keeping track of and at what time we ask. The link between 'one' and 'it's cold today' may never be revealed – not even to the person who made that unconscious link.

- Conscious time is different from unconscious time. Time in conscious awareness follows the clock and the calendar, but in unconscious processes time follows very different rules. A good illustration is in dreams where one can dream of being an adult but in the same setting as where one actually existed as a child. This logical impossibility fits comfortably in the unconscious world of dreams, but is nonsense in the rational world of conscious process.

- A popular view of the unconscious is that of a kind of mental hide-out where all sorts of shameful or unpleasant aspects of the personality are hidden. My view is that whilst some unpalatable aspects of our mental functioning are kept hidden in the unconscious, there is also present in the unconscious a host of other material such as the source of our many flashes of intuition. In contrast, the conscious mind may be rather more simple – somewhat like a set of small moving windows that enables us to become momentarily aware of what is going on in the outside world and in our inside worlds.

- The 'language' of the unconscious is mainly that of symbols, whereas the 'language' of the conscious mind is mainly words, phrases and what we conventionally call 'language'. The shorthand phrase that is used for unconscious process is 'primary process' whereas 'secondary process' is the term used for the more logical rational mode of conscious mental functioning.

Whilst there are other aspects of unconscious functioning that would deserve attention in a longer chapter, it is now time to turn to art for some inspiration.

Logic is not art and art is not logic

Art evokes different responses in different people. What differentiates art from not-art is that art is derived from, and in turn evokes, 'primary process' as distinct from its logical, sequential, and rational counterpart – secondary process (Bateson 1972)[2]. The pre-existing internal world of the viewer interacts with the symbolism of the work of art to create a unique experience for each viewer. Because visual art is a language form that uses symbolism as a medium, the quality of communication created by art is fundamentally different from the quality of communication achieved by the rational use of spoken or written prose. Thus, any attempt to 'translate' a piece of visual art into conventional language must in part fail because the medium of language is not capable of capturing or communicating the quality of experience that is achieved by viewing a piece of visual art. So the truism that 'a picture tells a thousand words' is both true and false. It is true because any one person's attempt to describe the full detail of a picture would take at least a thousand words. It is false in two ways because, first, it is not possible to convey in words the quality of the communication implicit in the picture and, second, each person who described the picture would use a different 'thousand words'. As we will explore later, the experience of the viewer of art and the participant in a group share the above characteristics.

Art, then, is a symbolic system where each viewer may interpret the symbolism differently. I was struck by the importance of symbolism in art when I was shown what was claimed to be a piece of art that consisted of a series of small boxes that were arranged in a set sequence. In each box was an arrangement of miniature human figures that were very easily recognizable as priests, saints, and so on. Miniature furniture and models of rooms, doorways and stairways completed the detail in each scene. A friend of the artist explained to me the meaning of the contents of each box and was proud that the artist had been so able to produce an unambiguous depiction of the original scene. There was no intention on the part of the artist that there should be more than one way of interpreting the piece of art. I discussed my disappointment with this 'work of art' with the group of friends whom I was with at the time. We agreed this specific work of art did not meet our under-standing of 'true' art. Our main reasoning was that instead of symbolism there was 'literalism' that was intended to evoke exactly the same response in each viewer. The possibility for each viewer to interpret the work of art through primary process was replaced by the secondary process that was implicit in the 'literalism' of the art. Art is a form of communication that uses 'signs' (in a semiotic sense) to evoke a response in the viewer. The particular response for each viewer is what is 'signified' for that viewer by each of the sign systems in the piece of art. As such, art depends for its effect on the existence of culturally embedded ways of communicating, but simulta-neously is intended to provide stimulus for each viewer to have a unique experience. Exactly the same can be said of groups.

Parallels between groups and art: a summary

Three parallels between the art/artist and group/leader systems are apparent. First, there are similarities between groups and pieces of visual art; second, there are parallels between the function of group leaders and that of artists; and third, the experience of a participant in a group can be compared with the experience of the viewer of a piece of visual art. As was emphasized above, an overriding similarity between groups and art is that both rely to a great extent on unconscious processes for their effect. This theme of uncon-scious processes has been an essential thread throughout the book and will remain in place for the remainder of this chapter. With this in mind, the three parallel systems are examined in more detail below.

Parallels between groups and pieces of visual art

Here we take a look at some ways of comparing a work of visual art – a painting – with a group. The following comparisons range from those involving largely rational and conscious processes through to those largely involving non-rational and unconcious processes.

Primary process/Prevalence of unconscious processes

The experience of looking at an excellent piece of art is a powerful one with a strong feelings-based component. It is not unusual for someone to say 'wow, that really hit me in the guts' or 'that tears at the heart strings'. In other words, the visual image in the work of art evokes feelings with no input from the conscious mind. It is true that often the conscious mind can find an explanation for why a work of art is powerful, but the reasoning comes after the feeling. So, the main form of communication involved in viewing visual arts occurs at an unconscious level. The same is true for groups. Most of the communication in any group occurs at an unconscious level. This is not a popular opinion for people in corporate settings who insist on rationality as the only legitimate form of functioning. Nonetheless, most people who are honest with themselves would admit that the experience of being in a group is one where their emotions can quickly and easily become a roller-coaster ride regardless of how much they try to maintain a particular feeling state. Primary process, then, is a prevalent form of functioning in groups.

Framing/Containment

A painting has a frame. The frame communicates to the viewer that what is inside the frame is art. It distinguishes between the piece of art and the rest of the world. Some forms of art deliberately play with this boundary, for instance paintings that are extended from the canvas onto the frame. Similarly, every group has some form of 'container' or frame (Miller and Rice 1990). This is constructed in collaboration between the leader and group members. The main elements of the container are clarity of task, time boundaries, physical boundaries, and the roles of leaders and participants (see also Chapter 9). The group container provides a place into which group members can project unwanted or unacceptable psychic material. In effective groups, the quality of reflective space enables the raw and unprocessed projections to be processed and re-introjected by the participant(s). See Chapter 10 for more detail.

Linking between elements

A piece of art is a unit in that each element in the piece relates to other elements. The artist may deliberately seek to disturb the viewer by including in one piece of art elements that do not normally go together. A square red block in the midst of a realist landscape disturbs the viewer because of the juxtaposition of elements that are normally considered incompatible.

Similarly, a group that is functioning well is likely to be well linked. The main elements of any group are: (1) the leader(s) (2) each participant (3) the task or purpose of the group (4) elements of the unconscious mental 'image' that are shared between group members. Linking in a group provides durability and elasticity so that when, during difficult times in the group, relationships feel difficult, the total linked system retains the integrity of the group rather than the group fragmenting. See Chapter 9 for more detail.

Personal responses

A piece of art will evoke quite different responses in each viewer. The same signifier (element in the work of art) will evoke different 'signified' for each viewer depending on the viewer's previously encoded internal working models relating to the symbolism used in the work of art. Similarly, in a group, each person's history, working models and idiosyncrasies will be activated by the presence of others in the group. For instance, Jack, sitting opposite me, may evoke for me an unconscious recall of my obsessively clean uncle, whilst Jack may remind Susan (who is sitting next to me) of her warm and loving father.

Differently coded communication

Visual art utilizes visual symbols as a form of communication. Only rarely do we see written words in works of visual art because visual symbolism is a fundamentally different type from verbal symbolism. The two types even utlize different parts of the brain. In visual art, information is encoded in a way that does not involve verbal language; instead the language is visual. Just as verbal language has to be learned, so do (at least some of the) elements of visual language. For instance, a westerner who looks at New Zealand Maori carvings or tukutuku (woven panels) will simply not *see* the same things as would a person who was raised in the culture where the symbolism originated and therefore is embedded. Western English-speaking societies use verbal language mainly to express the rational elements of thought and human experience. As such, verbal language is well suited to encode secondary process (facts and reason) but only in poetry, in 'Freudian slips' or in free association does it communicate primary process. In fact, people who constantly use verbal language to communicate primary process are formally classified as suffering from mental illness.

Similarly, in the group experience information is *coded* in a different way when it occurs as one person's lived experience than when it appears as written or spoken language. I believe that many group experiences are encoded in procedural memory and in visual/perceptual memory, thus escaping verbal encoding. In any case, whether in a group or not, it is not possible for any human being to communicate accurately his or her full lived experience to any other human being using written or spoken language. In particular, the kind of primary process experience that people achieve in groups is difficult to 'encode' in conventional language, which operates mainly in secondary process.

Parallels between the experience of looking at visual art and taking part in a group

Four points of comparison are offered here. Groups and art both evoke *unconcious processes* in leaders, artists, viewers and participants; they create a point of *emotional attachment* – groups for the participant and art for the viewer; groups and art both *draw out* or evoke previously inaccessible unconscious material for the viewer or for the group participant; and, finally, people *identify* with both groups and art where the word 'identify' is used in its psychodynamic sense. These four parallels are examined next.

Both groups and art evoke a response that is both unconscious and conscious.

As we look at a piece of art that was created at another time in another place, we have both conscious and unconscious responses. (There is a difference, though, between art and group in relation to timing. Whatever was going on in the artist's conscious and unconscious mind when he or she was creating the piece, the result appears in front of us as a static, finished work of art. This is different from leading groups because the group leader remains an active part of the group throughout the time that he or she is co-creating the 'art' that is the group process.) As I said earlier, the viewer's response to seeing a piece of art has an immediate emotional element that emerges directly from the unconscious component of the viewer's experience. The thinking about why a particular response occurred is likely to largely involve the conscious mind.

Similarly, every action taken by a group leader or group member, whether emerging from deliberation or intuition, will evoke a response from others in the group that includes unconscious and rational elements. Whilst we describe conscious processes as being different from unconscious processes, one evokes the other – they are always interrelated. In my view, the unconscious elements are likely to evoke immediate responses – unless strong defences are in place – whereas the conscious elements are more likely to surface in conversations about the participant's experience.

Identification

A painting enables the viewer to identify with elements of the work, or with the whole work of art. That is, a part of the viewer's psyche is unconsciously 'located' by the viewer in the painting. At some level, the viewer experiences that the work of art represents a part of his or her own world. For example, when I see paintings of the sea or of rainforest I have an unconscious phantasy[3] that I am in the scene because I spent my youth in New Zealand living by the sea in a location where all the forests were rainforests. With abstract paintings the identification is less obvious but it is still possible to identify with a swirl of colours and shapes. The identification with an abstract painting is likely to be less clear but can be equally strong. For example, dark, confused swirls may provide a place for one's own fears and confusion, whilst light, elegant brushstrokes may provide a place for one's hopes to rest. Each viewer will identify in different ways with different visual symbols, just as one's dream symbols cannot be interpreted accurately by anyone other than the dreamer.

Similarly, a group is a place where the participants all see elements of themselves located in the group. They identify with the group by achieving a sense of belonging. The statement 'this is my group' is also a statement 'a part of me rests in this group' (Pines 1998). Participants will identify with other participants, the leader, or the unconscious phantasy of the group that is the 'group-in-the-mind'. This identification achieves two things. First, it enables the participant to experience the group as a part of himself or herself and, second, it enables the participant to make personal changes because when the group evolves or develops, the participant then experiences him or herself as evolving or developing.

Drawing out

A painting draws the viewer out of him or herself and makes part of the viewer available for reflection, discussion and potentially for development. Before my eyes rest on a work of art most of the aspects of my personality are relatively undifferentiated in my mind and are outside my awareness. As soon as a piece of art makes its first impression on me, one or more specific aspects of myself are raised to the surface and in a curious way interact with the work of art. For instance, when I see a fourteenth-century religious fresco where devils kill, maim and torture humans, my sociological side and my puritan side are both activated. I feel both relief and curiosity that fourteeenth-century artists acknowledged the dark side of human spirituality and simultaneously I feel revulsion at seeing such gruesome pictures. I think, too, that another aspect of my personality is activated and that is the fascination with death. That part is more difficult to admit to.

Similarly, a group draws out aspects of the participant for interaction with him or herself and with the group. As the group evolves, group members find aspects of themselves being evoked. Mostly at an unconscious level they make decisions about how much of each aspect they will allow to come to the attention of themselves and the group. An effective group creates a kind of attraction to group members that draws out into the group the kind of material that will help each group member to benefit from the group and the group to benefit from what the participant brings. It is as though there is a kind of magic stone in the centre of the group that creates a field of attraction for aspects of participants' personalities that are otherwise pushed down, avoided or simply not noticed. This is not to say that material that is useful for group and individual progress is always *overtly* helpful. Sometimes groups and individuals achieve good progress by working with very challenging and 'unpalatable' material.

Affiliative attachment

Art evokes elements of emotional attachment[4] in the viewer. Sometimes the attachment is positive, in which case with repeated exposure and familiarity, the piece of art becomes a part of our internal comfort zone. Many people, myself included, have one or more pieces of art in their essential personal belongings. Our homes are not complete without them and therefore we are not complete until they appear on the walls of our homes (or offices). On the other hand, sometimes the attachment is negative, in which case we seek to avoid contact with the piece of art or any memory of it.

Similarly, group members develop elements of attachment to groups that they attend or belong to. It is my claim that most successful groups evoke positive attachments for group members. In such cases the group is experienced as being a place that the person could return to for nurture, safety and emotional protection – or at least for psychological growth if not for nurture. It is my view that a sustained experience of being in safe nurturing groups leads participants to internalize that safe 'psychic space' and so to become more healthily functioning human beings. The implication here is that one way in which people can improve their functioning in the world is to have sustained experience of groups where the group provides an 'object' of attachment and therefore that the participant integrates the 'group-in-the-mind' into his or her personality structure.

A parallel between the function of the artist and the function of the group leader

Here, only one comparison is made between the function of the artist and the function of the group leader. That is, both excellent group leadership and excellent art may *appear simple* to the group member or viewer, but may nevertheless be the result of the practitioner applying a very thorough knowledge and high levels of skill in his or her field of endeavour.

Powerful art is often apparently simple. Powerful group work will also often appear to the participant to be simple. I will refer to the combination of simplicity and excellence in both group work leadership and in art as 'elegance'.

To achieve elegant art requires the artist to have such high levels of skill that the rational elements of the work of art are done automatically so that the artist has access to his or her primary process and the hand moves in response to some apparently ephemeral force, rather than in response to conscious thoughts about which line should go where. This level of functioning is described by Dreyfus and Dreyfus as 'mastery' in their analysis of how people develop competence in their work (Dreyfus 1999; Dreyfus and Dreyfus 1987).

To achieve elegant group work leadership requires the leader to have enough experience in dealing with the more rational and conscious aspects of group work leadership so as to have ready access to his or her feelings and intuition (Ringer 2000). Reaching elegance in group work leadership requires high levels of ability to reflect on one's own practice and persistent curiosity about oneself, groups and the way that the world works. As stated earlier, peer groups, professional supervision and one's own therapy are of great assistance in the journey toward achieving elegance in group work leadership.

I think that it is possible to achieve moments of elegance in group work leadership, though I am the first to admit that I have not yet seen anyone who can sustain what I would describe as elegance for the whole duration of a workshop. I think that it is important to strive for elegance but not punish ourselves when we fail to reach it.

What are the practical implications for group leaders of the comparison between artists and group leaders?

Whilst it is an interesting intellectual exercise to compare group leaders and artists, for practitioners there remains the important question of how one might improve one's group leadership or facilitation through having achieved an understanding of this comparison. Whilst numerous implications could be drawn from the above material, I will follow only two paths. The first is the view that everything that happens in a group is relevant and needs to be taken into account by the group leader. The second is that the leader is an integral part of the conscious and unconscious system of the group and can benefit from acting on this realization.

Everything is relevant

I think that everything everyone in the group does, says, does not do and does not say affects the unconscious life of the group. So, it can be useful to think of your own actions and inactions as a form of communication. Even if you think that you are only doing something very practical such as shutting a door to keep out noise from an adjoining passageway, this might have an effect on the unconscious life of the group. For instance, if the group feels safe, your shutting the door may be experienced as increasing the level of containment – like providing a clear frame for a work of art. However, if any group members feel coerced to be there or feel unsafe in the group they may experience your shutting the door as an imprisonment.

Other examples of common activities might help to illustrate the idea that everything that happens in a group can affect the unconscious life of the group. The example above was about shutting a door and related to the containment of the group. The others that follow will relate to other aspects of art and of groups described above. These are:

1. linking
2. identification
3. drawing out
4. attachment.

1. *In relation to linking:* activities that involve group participants saying their names, introducing themselves, and saying something about themselves can increase the unconscious phantasy that the group is an interdependent matrix, and therefore an entity in itself rather than a disparate collection of different individuals.

2. *In relation to identification:* encouraging participants to talk about emotional aspects of their experience can assist participants to build unconscious identifications with each other. Each participant links with the similarities in other participants as those similarities become apparent. At a deeper level participants identify with the phantasy of the 'Group-in-the-mind' or an equivalent (Anzieu 1984; Neri 1998).

3. *In relation to the 'drawing out' aspect of groups:* sociometric exercises (Hale 1985) such as continuums can help to draw out aspects of participants' experience of themselves. For instance, in a group of managers who have been told – in some cases against their will – to attend a training programme, the leader could ask them to stand in a position in the room by saying something like:

> 'I understand that many of you may have other things to do right now that may seem more important to you than attending this programme. I'm keen to understand more fully the range of enthusiasm that is present in the room so that we can work together to meet your needs as much as is possible. If being a part of this programme right now is your first preference as to how you'd like to be spending your time, stand here (*indicating one end of the room*). If being a part of this programme right now is very low on your set of priorities, stand here (*indicating the other end of the room*). Depending on your preference, you may wish to stand anywhere in between. When you have chosen your place to stand, talk to the person next to you about why you chose to stand where you did.'

This exercise can, in the right circumstances, assist group members to make an emotional connection with, talk about and integrate their relative willingness to be present in the group. At an unconscious level, this starts to draw out aspects of the participants' emotional experience and bring it into the group.

4. *In relation to the group becoming an attachment 'figure' for participants:* particularly as the group matures, each participant develops a

complex unconscious phantasy about the group and about his or her place in and connection with the group. This 'group-in-the-mind' becomes something in the mind of the participant that is similar to a significant person (Marrone 1998). If the group-in-the-mind is benign and nurturing, then the participant creates an emotional attachment to the group (Stapley 1996). For each participant this involves a dynamic between the group and the participant, but the nature of the group-in-the-mind for participants can be influenced by the actions of the leader. An example is when one group member launches a verbal attack on another. The group leader can name the fact that this may have been experienced by the recipient as an attack and work with both attacker and recipient on their experience of the interaction while retaining an attitude of dispassionate warmth. If this occurs then all group participants are likely to increase the 'safe and nurturing' aspects of their group-in-the-mind. Therefore, participants are more likely to develop a positive emotional attachment to the group. However, I want to be clear that developing a positive emotional attachment is not the main task of most groups and so the task of the group should be balanced with the attempt to foster an appropriately safe and nurturing group climate.

So, to summarize this last part: everything in a group that is said and done, and everything in a group that is not said and is not done can all be considered as a form of communication that may influence aspects of the conscious and unconscious life of the group.

The leader is a part of the system

A second aspect of group leadership that seems to belong in this discussion is that *the leader's own experience of him or herself in the context of the group is one of the most important indicators of what is happening in the unconscious life of the group* (Maxwell 1996). One can think of the unconscious life of a group as being a field where the sense that every group member is a discrete, separate entity is diminished as compared to when people are functioning outside group meetings (Foulkes and Anthony 1990). Thus, the leader's own emotional experience is firmly connected to the evolving emotional 'field' that is present at all times in the group. But just as the group affects the subjective experience of all who are present, any one person can also strongly influence the unconscious life of a group quickly and easily (Ashbach and Schermer 1987). In other words there is a continual unconscious exchange occurring between all individuals in the group and the group-as-a-whole. For an example of how easily one member can influence the group 'field' recall what happens when a person starts to cry in a group. Usually the whole group becomes still, attentive and focused on the person who is crying. This shift from whatever was going on before the person began to cry is not just a rational decision of each group member. It also involves a shift in the group unconscious. Every group member is involved in this shift, including the group leader.

A person crying is a fairly obvious and recognizable signal, but there are many other more subtle aspects of group unconscious that can be picked up by the leader and experienced as his or her own personal emotional issues when they may also be important aspects of the unconscious or affective life of the group. I think that modern western society teaches us (incorrectly) that our emotions are solely our own and are not connected to the people around us. Because of this, when a leader is connected to the emotional field of a group it can be difficult for him or her to acknowledge that his or her feelings are not solely his or her 'own' but are a mixture of personal tendencies and a response to what is unspoken in the group.

For instance, I was facilitating a series of six half-day workshops that were spaced one week apart. The participants were human resources, finance, and information technology staff of an organization and the primary task of the workshops was to improve participants' ability to function as internal consultants. At the start of the third workshop the venue was changed. As I walked into the room I was struck by a strong feeling of sadness. I could not identify any events that morning that would have evoked sadness so I wondered if there was something present in the group that I was picking up outside my rational functioning – that is at an unconscious level. The workshop started with a short period of reflection on participants' experience of the previous week in the role of internal consultants and I mentioned that I had experienced some sadness on entering the room. It soon became clear that many of the group members were extremely sad but had not felt it appropriate to mention their emotions because they could not see how that would fit with the planned workshop programme. The issue was that there was a major organizational re-structure occurring and in the process they were losing their manager who was both well liked and seen to be very effective. The workshop participants were expected to help facilitate the organizational change for others but had no means of dealing with their own grief and loss.

My decision to mention the sense of sadness proved to be very important because we were able to integrate the workshop participants' own experience of change with planned workshop content about managing change in organizations. If I had not talked about noticing my own sadness workshop participants and myself alike could easily have spent half a day in the workshop missing each other emotionally and therefore acting incongruently. This would have diminished the effectiveness of the workshop.

Conclusion

My thesis in this chapter is that working effectively with unconscious processes in groups increases the likelihood that a group will achieve its goals. Furthermore, I propose that denial of the importance of unconscious processes can unwittingly lead to a reduction in group effectiveness.

I have outlined some thoughts about the correspondence between (artistic) painters and group leaders in experiential settings. I have suggested that both effective painters and effective group leaders work with unconscious processes in addition to working with conscious processes. The artist's task is a little different from that of the group leader and so there are differences in how they work with unconscious processes. The artist's task is to work with symbolism so as to evoke a response in the viewer that leaves the viewer changed – in a different state from the one she or he was in before looking at the work of art. Symbolism is one of the aspects of the unconscious and so art is a language form that directly addresses the unconscious.

On the other hand, groups need to have a rationale, purpose and structure that can be expressed in terms of logic and rationality and so it is easy to consider that the main level of functioning for groups belongs in the domain of the conscious mind. My claim is that whilst rationality plays an essential part in groups, unconscious processes also inevitably occur in all groups whether or not we wish for this. For every aspect of a group that occurs within the consciousness of group leaders and group members there are associated processes that occur in the unconscious of the group. Nonetheless, both artists and group leaders share the same developmental task. Elegant practice is achieved by leaders gaining a substantial knowledge and skill base, and then integrating this into their functioning so that when they practise, the knowledge and skill are not directly visible, but the result of the

knowledge and skill can be experienced by the viewer or the group participant as elegance and simplicity.

This chapter – and indeed this book – has outlined a frame for inquiry,
observation and thinking rather than providing a set of tools on how to lead
groups. There are, however, some questions that guide the application of
these ideas in practice. They are intended to be useful either while the group
is running or later for reflection on recent experience as leader of a group. The
most powerful questions that leaders can ask themselves as the group
progresses are:

- Given what I'm feeling (or experiencing) right now, how might
  this inform me about what is going on in the group?

- How might this action/statement/inaction/silence, and so on be
  communicating something more than is immediately apparent?

Specific questions that explore aspects of containment, linking, identification, drawing out, and attachment include:

- What is the quality of containment for this group?

- What kind of linking is there between the elements in this
  group?

- To what extent are members of this group currently identifying
  with elements of the group?

- How successful is this group in providing a place that draws out
  aspects of participants' inner worlds?

- What kind of 'object for identification' is this group for various
  members?

Our choice, then, is not whether or not to 'allow' unconscious processes to
occur in groups because they will occur anyway. The choice becomes
whether or not we deliberately work with unconscious processes in our
groups. Given that both conscious and unconscious processes occur in all
groups, how do we as leaders adequately equip ourselves to work in an
integrated way with both conscious and unconscious processes in our
groups?

Notes

1.   An earlier version of this paper was first presented as a keynote talk at the Adven-
        ture-Based Experiential Learning conference in Pretoria in September 2000.

2.   I recommend the chapter in this (Bateson's) work entitled 'Style, grace and information in primitive art', pp.128–152. Whilst he does not refer specifically to groups, the concepts that he explores are very much applicable to groups.

3.   'Phantasy' is used here to denote a form of imagining that remains outside the subject's awareness at the time that it occurs. 'Fantasy' is used to mean an imagining that occurs within the subject's awareness.

4.   My use of the word 'attachment' refers to the term 'affiliative attachment' that was described more fully in Chapter 9. This is different from the way in which Bowlby used it.

References

Agazarian, Y. M. (1997) *Systems-centered Therapy for Groups.* New York: Guilford Press.

Anzieu, D. (1984) *The Group and the Unconscious* (translated by B. Kilborne) London: Routledge and Kegan Paul.

Applegate, J. S. and Bonovitz, J. M. (1995) *The Facilitating Partnership: A Winnicottian Approach for Social Workers and Other Helping Professionals.* Northvale, NJ: Jason Aronson.

Argyris, C. (1993) *Knowledge for Action: A Guide to Overcoming Barriers to Organisational Change.* San Francisco: Jossey-Bass.

ASGW (1992) 'Association for Specialists in Group Work: professional standards for the training of group workers.' *Journal for Specialists in Group Work 17* (1), 12–19.

Ashbach, C. and Schermer, V. L. (1987) *Object Relations, the Self and the Group.* London: Routledge.

Ashby, J. and DeGraaf, D. (1999) 'Re-examining group development in adventure therapy groups.' *Journal of Experiential Education 21* (3), 162–167.

Bacal, H. A. (1998) 'Notes on optimal responsiveness in the group process.' In N. H. Harwood and M. Pines (eds) *Self Experiences in Group: Intersubjective and Self Psychological Pathways to Human Understanding.* pp.175–180. London: Jessica Kingsley Publishers.

Bain, A. (1999) 'On socio-analysis.' *Socio-Analysis 1,* 1–17.

Bandler, R. and Grinder, J. (1975) *The Structure of Magic.* Palo Alto, CA: Science and Behavior Books.

Barrett-Lennard, G. T. (1975) 'Process, effects and structure in intensive groups: a theoretical-descriptive analysis.' In C. L. Cooper (ed) *Theories of Group Processes.* London: John Wiley and Sons.

Barthes, R. (1993) *Mythologies.* London: Vintage.

Bate, S. P. (1994) *Strategies for Cultural Change.* Oxford: Butterworth/Heinemann.

Bateman, A. and Holmes, J. (1995) *Introduction to Psychoanalysis: Contemporary Theory and Practice.* London: Routledge.

Bateson, G. (1972) *Steps to an Ecology of Mind.* New York: Ballantine.

Bateson, G. (1988) *Mind and Nature.* New York: Bantam.

Berg, D. N. and Smith, K. K. (1995) 'Paradox and groups.' In J. Gillette and M. McCollom (eds) *Groups in Context: A New Perspective on Group Dynamics.* pp.107–132. Lanham, Maryland: University Press of America.

Bion, W. R. (1961) *Experiences in Groups.* London: Tavistock/Routledge.

Bion, W. R. (1962) 'A theory of thinking.' *International Journal of Psycho-Analysis 43,* 306–310.

Bion, W. R. (1970) *Attention and Interpretation.* London: Karnac Books.

Blatner, A. B. A. (1988) *Foundations of Psychodrama: History, Theory and Practice* (3rd ed). New York: Springer.

Bolton, R. (1986) *People Skills: How to Assert Yourself, Listen to Others and Resolve Conflicts.* New York: Touchstone: Simon and Schuster.

Bowlby, J. (1969) (1991a edition) *Attachment and Loss Volume 1: Attachment.* London: Penguin.

Bowlby, J. (1973) (1991b edition) *Attachment and Loss Volume 2: Separation, Anxiety and Anger.* London: Penguin.

Bowlby, J. (1980) (1991c edition) *Attachment and Loss Volume 3: Loss, Sadness and Depression.* London: Penguin.

Boyd, R. D. (ed) (1991) *Personal Transformation in Small Groups: A Jungian Perspective.* London: Routledge.

Bradford, L. P., Gibb, K. D. and Benne, J. R. (eds) (1964) *T-Group Theory and Laboratory Method: Innovation in Re-education.* New York: Wiley.

Briggs, S. (2000) 'Patterns of early development in socially vulnerable circumstances.' Lecture to the Association for Psychodynamic Psychotherapy of Western Australia. Perth.

Brown, D. (2001) 'A contribution to the understanding of the social conscious.' *Group Analysis 34*, 29–38.

Brown, R. (2000) *Group Processes.* Malden, MA: Blackwell Publishers.

Cameron-Bandler, L. (1985) *Solutions: Enhancing Love, Sex, and Relationships.* Moab, Utah: Real People Press.

Cassidy, J. and Shaver, P.R. (eds) (1999) *Handbook of Attachment: Theory, Research and Clinical Applications.* New York: Guilford Press.

Cartwright, D. and Zander, A. (eds) (1970) *Group Dynamics: Research and Theory.* London: Tavistock Publications.

Cecchin, G. (1987) 'Hypothesizing, circularity, and neutrality revisited: an invitation to curiosity.' *Family process 26*, 40–413.

Chattopadhyay, G. P. and Malhotra, A. (1991) 'Hierarchy and modern organisation: a paradox leading to human wastage.' *The Indian Journal of Social Work LII*, 4, 562–584.

Clarke, H. (1998) 'Means and aims in adventure education.' In T. Lehtonen (ed) *Adventure for Life: Perspectives on Issues in Experimental Education.* pp.59–77. Jyvaaskylaa: Atena Kustannus Ltd.

Cline, F. (1993) 'Apples and onions.' In M. A. Gass (ed) *Adventure Therapy: Therapeutic Applications of Adventure Programming in Mental Health Settings.* pp.147–151. Dubuque, Iowa: Kendall Hunt.

Cobley, P. and Jansz, L. (1999) *Introducing semiotics.* Cambridge: Icon Books.

Colman, A. D. (1995) *Up from Scapegoating: Awakening Consciousness in Groups.* Wilmette, IL: Chiron Publications.

Crittenden, P. (1998) *Patterns of Attachment in Adulthood: A Dynamic-maturational Approach to Analyzing the Adult Attachment Interview.* Chapter 3, pp.3–6. Unpublished.

Crittenden, P. M. (1995) 'Attachment and psychopathology.' In S. Goldberg, R. Muir and J. Kerr (eds) *Attachment Theory: Social, Developmental, and Clinical Perspectives*. pp.367–406. Hillsdale, NJ: The Analytic Press.

Dalal, F. (1998) *Taking the Group Seriously: Towards a Post-Foulkesian Group Analytic Theory*. London: Jessica Kingsley Publishers.

Damasio, A. R. (2000a (1994)) *Descartes' Error: Emotion, Reason and the Human Brain*. New York: Quill.

Damasio, A. R. (2000b) *The Feeling of What Happens: Body, Emotion and the Making of Consciousness*. London: Vintage.

DeLucia-Waack, J. L. (1999) 'What makes an effective group leader?' *Journal for Specialists in Group Work 24*, 2, 131–132.

Dewey, J. (1938 (1963)) *Experience and Education*. New York: Collier Books.

Dreyfus, H. (1999, 4–8 June) 'How Neuro-Science Supports Merleau-Ponty's Account of Learning.' Paper presented at the Network for Non-scholastic Learning Conference, Jutland, Denmark.

Dreyfus, H. L. and Dreyfus, S. E. (1987) *Mind Over Machine: The Power of Human Intuition and Expertise in the Era of the Computer*. New York: The Free Press.

Edelson, M. and Berg, D. N. (1999) *Rediscovering Groups: A Psychoanalyst's Journey Beyond Individual Psychology*. London: Jessica Kingsley Publishers.

Epstein, S. (1991) 'Cognitive-experiential self theory: an integrative theory of personality.' In R. E. Curtis (ed) *The Relational Self: Theoretical Convergences in Psychoanalysis and Social Psychology*. pp.111–137. New York: Guilford Press.

Ettin, M.F. (1999) *Foundations and Applications of Group Psychotherapy*. London: Jessica Kingsley Publishers.

Ferrucci, P. (1986) *What We May Be: The Visions and Techniques of Psychosynthesis*. Wellingtonborough, Northamptonshire: Turnstone Press.

Fonagy, P. (1999) *Psyche Matters*. Www.psywww.chematters.com/papers/fonagy.htm

Foulkes, S. H. (1990) *My Philosophy in Psychotherapy: Selected Papers*. London: Karnac.

Foulkes, S. H. and Anthony, E. J. (1990) *Group Psychotherapy: The Psychoanalytic Approach*. London: Karnac.

Freeman, M. (1993) *Rewriting the Self: History, Memory, Narrative*. London: Routledge.

Gillis, H. L., Gass, M. A., Bandoroff, S., Rudolph, S., Clapp, C. and Nadler, R. (1991) 'Family Adventure Survey: Results and Discussion.' Paper presented at the 19th AEE Conference, Boulder.

Gillis, H. L. and Ringer, T. M. (1999) 'Adventure as therapy.' In J. C. Miles and S. Priest (eds) *Adventure Programming*. pp.29–37. State College, PA: Venture Publishing.

Gordon, J. (1994) 'Bion's post "Experiences in Groups" thinking on groups: a clinical example of -K.' In V. L. Schermer and M. Pines (eds) *Ring of Fire; Primitive Affects and Object Relations in Group Psychotherapy*. pp.107–127. London: Routledge.

Gosling, R. (1968) 'What is transference?' In J. D. Sutherland (ed) *The Psychoanalytic Approach*. pp.1–10. London: Bailliere, Tindall and Cassell Ltd.

Greenaway, R. (1993) *Playback: A Guide to Reviewing Activities*. Windsor: Duke of Edinbugh's Award Scheme.

Guetzkow, H. (1953) 'Differentiation of roles in task-oriented groups.' In D. Cartwright and A. Zandler (eds) *Group Dynamics: Research and Theory*. pp.513–526. London: Tavistock Publications.

Hale, A. (1985) *Conducting Clinical Sociometric Explorations: A Manual for Psychodramatists and Sociometrists*. Virginia: Royal Publishing Co.

Halton, W. (1994) 'Some unconscious aspects of organisational life: contributions from psychoanalysis.' In A. Obholzer and V.Z. Roberts (eds) *The Unconscious at Work: Individual and Organisational Stress in the Human Services*. pp.11–18. London: Routledge.

Hampden-Turner, C. (1982) *Maps of the Mind: Charts and Concepts of the Mind and its Labyinths*. New York: Collier Books.

Handley, R. (1993) 'Mirrors and mountaintops: cauldrons of tension: enhancement skills for wilderness programs.' In *Fifth National Conference on Children With Emotional and Behavioural Problems*. South Coast Wilderness Enhanced Program, Western Australia.

Hartley, P. (1997) *Group Communication*. London: Routledge.

Harwood, H. H. (1998) 'Advances in group psychotherapy and self psychology: an intersubjective approach.' In N. H. Harwood and M. Pines (eds) *Self Experiences in Group: Intersubjective and Self Psychological Pathways to Human Understanding*. pp.30–46. London: Jessica Kingsley Publishers.

Harwood, I. N. H. and Pines, M. (eds) (1998) *Self Experiences in Group: Intersubjective and Self Psychological Pathways to Human Understanding*. London: Jessica Kingsley Publishers.

Haskell, J. (2001) *Funzione Gamma* 7. http://www.funzionegamma.edu

Hinshelwood, R. D. (1987) *What Happens in Groups: Psychoanalysis, the Individual and the Community*. London: Free Association Books.

Hinshelwood, R. D. (1994) 'Attacks on the reflective space: containing primitive emotional states.' In V. L. Schermer and M. Pines (eds) *Ring of Fire; Primitive Affects and Object Relations in Group Psychotherapy*. pp.86–106. London: Routledge.

Hinshelwood, R. D. (1999) 'How Foulksian was Bion?' *Group Analysis 32*, 469–488.

Hinshelwood, R., Robinson, S. and Zarate, O. (1997) *Melanie Klein for Beginners*. Cambridge: Icon.

Hinton, P. R. (1993) *The Psychology of Interpersonal Perception*. London: Routledge.

Holland, R. (1977) *Self and Social Context*. London: MacMillan Press.

Hopper, E. (2001) 'The social unconscious: theoretical considerations.' *Group Analysis 34*, 9–27.

Hovelynck, J. (1999a) 'Facilitating the development of generative metaphors: re-emphasizing participants' guiding images.' *Australian Journal of Outdoor Education 4*, 1, 12–24.

Hovelynck, J. (1999b) *Experiential Education: A Project of Competence Development for Teachers and Tutors in the Peruvian Bachillerato Program*. Lima: British Council and the Peruvian Ministry of Education.

Hovelynck, J. (2000) 'Recognising and exploring action-theories: a refection-in-action approach to facilitating experiential learning.' *Journal of Adventure Education and Outdoor Learning 1* (1), 7–20.

Hutton, J. (1997) 'Re-imagining the organisation of an institution.' In E. Smith (ed) *Integrity and Change.* pp.66–82. London: Routledge.

Janis, I. L. (1982) *Groupthink* (2nd ed). Boston: Houghton Mifflin.

Johnson, D. W. and Johnson, F. P. (1991) *Joining Together: Group Theory and Group Skills.* Englewood Cliffs: Prentice-Hall inc.

Jung, C. G. (1968) *Man and his Symbols.* New York: Dell.

Kaës, R. (1993) *Le Groupe et le Subjet du Groupe.* Paris: Dunod.

Karterud, S. W. (1998) 'The group self, empathy, intersubjectivity, and hermeneutics.' In N. H. Harwood and M. Pines (eds) *Self Experiences in Group: Intersubjective and Self Psychological Pathways to Human Understanding.* pp.83–98. London: Jessica Kingsley Publishers.

Kast, V. (1992) *The Dynamics of Symbols: Fundamentals of Jungian Psychotherapy.* New York: Fromm International.

Kets-de-Vries, M. F. R. (ed) (1991) *Organizations on the Couch: Clinical Perspectives on Organizational Behaviour and Change.* San Francisco: Jossey-Bass.

Kimball, R. O. and Bacon, S, B. (1993) 'The wilderness challenge model.' In M.A. Gass (ed) *Adventure Therapy: Therapeutic Applications of Adventure Programming in Mental Health Settings.* pp.11–42. Dubuque, Iowa: Kendall Hunt.

Kipper, D. A. (1986) *Psychotherapy through Clinical Role Playing.* New York: Brunner/Mazel.

Klein, M. (1975) *Envy and Gratitude and Other Works 1946–1963.* London: Vintage.

Kolb, D. A. (1984) *Experience as the Source of Learning and Development.* Englewood Cliffs, New Jersey: Prentice Hall, Inc.

König, K. and Linder, W. V. (1994) *Psychoanalytic Group Therapy.* Northvale, NJ: Jason Aronson Inc.

Kottler, J. A. and Forester-Miller, H. (1998) 'Personal and social change in the lives of group leaders.' *The Journal for Specialists in Group Work 23,* 338–349.

Kuspit, D. (2000) 'Freud and the visual arts.' *Journal of Applied Psychoanalytic 2* (1), 25–39.

Laing, R. D. (1971) *Self and Others.* Harmondsworth: Pelican.

Larned, A. (1996) 'The client/clinical relationship: what is important? Comparing the therapeutic relationship in adventure-based therapy and traditional psychotherapy.' Unpublished Master of Social Work, Smith College, Massachusetts.

Lawrence, W. G., Bain, A. and Gould, L. (1996) 'The fifth basic assumption.' *Free Associations 6,* 28–55.

Leader, D. and Groves, J. (1995) *Lacan for Beginners.* Cambridge: Icon Books.

Lehtonen, T. (1998) 'Respectful attitude in experiential pedagogic work.' In T. Lehtonen (ed) *Adventure for Life: Perspectives on Issues in Experiential Education.* pp.95–105. Jyvaaskylaa: Atena Kustannus Ltd.

Lewis, B. and Pucelik, F. (1993) *Magic of NLP Demistified; A Pragmatic Guide to Communication and Change.* Portland, OR: Metamorphous Press.

Luckner, J. L. and Nadler, R. S. (1997) *Processing the Experience: Strategies to Enhance and Generalize Learning.* Dubuque: Kendall/Hunt.

Mahoney, M. J. (1991) *Human Change Processes: The Scientific Foundations of Psychotherapy.* USA: Basic Books.

Main, M. (1995) 'Recent studies in attachment.' In S. Goldberg, R. Muir and J. Kerr (eds) *Attachment Theory: Social, Developmental, and Clinical Perspectives.* pp.407–474. Hilsdale, NJ: The Analytic Press.

Marrone, M. (1998) *Attachment and Interaction.* London: Jessica Kingsley Publishers.

Maxwell, P. (1996) 'Psychoanalytic psychotherapy: a blank screen?' *Psychotherapy in Australia 2,* 4, 42–46.

McCollom, M. (1995a) 'Reevaluating group development: a critique of the familiar models.' In J. Gillette and M. McCollom (eds) *Groups in Context: A New Perspective on Group Dynamics.* pp.1–12. Lanham, Maryland: University Press of America.

McCollom, M. (1995b) 'Group formation: boundaries, leadership, and culture.' In J. Gillette and M. McCollom (eds) *Groups in Context: A New Perspective on Group Dynamics.* pp.34–48. Lanham, Maryland: University Press of America.

McCollom, M., and Gillette, J. (1995) *Groups in Context: A New Perspective on Group Dynamics.* Lanham, Maryland: University Press of America

McDougall, J. (1993) From the Silence of the Soma to the Worlds of the Psyche [video tape]. Melbourne: NSW Institute of Psychotherapy.

McPhee, P. J. and Gass, M. A. (1993) 'A group development model for adventure therapy programs.' In M. A. Gass (ed) *Adventure Therapy: Therapeutic Applications of Adventure Programming in Mental Health Settings.* Dubuque; Iowa: Kendall Hunt.

Meares, R. (1992) *The Metaphor of Play: on Self, the Secret and the Borderline Experience.* Maryborough, Victoria, Australia: Hill of Content.

Miller, E. J. and Rice, A., K. (1990) 'Task and sentient systems and their boundary controls.' In E. Trist and H. Murray (eds) *The Social Engagement of Social Science: Volume 1: the Socio-psychological Perspective.* pp.259–271. London: Free Association Books.

Moreno, J. L. (1953) *Who Shall Survive?* New York: Beacon House.

Neill, J. (1997a) *Instructor Effectiveness: Learning About Assumptions.* Canberra: National Outdoor Education & Leadership Services.

Neill, J. (1997b) *Instructor Effectiveness: Managing Experiential Tension.* Canberra: National Outdoor Education & Leadership Services.

Neill, J. (1997c) *Instructor Effectiveness: Pitfalls and Competencies.* Canberra: National Outdoor Education & Leadership Services.

Neri, C. (1998) *Group.* London: Jessica Kingsley Publishers.

Neri, C. (2001) 'Genius Loci: the spirit of a place, the spirit of a group.' *Funzione Gamma 7.* http://www.funzionegamma.edu

Neville, B. (1989) *Educating Psyche: Emotion, Imagination and the Unconscious in Learning.* Victoria, Australia: Collins Dove.

Nitsun, M. (1996) *The Anti-group: Destructive Forces in the Group and their Creative Potential.* London: Routledge.

Nuetzel (2000) 'Psychoanalysis and dramatic art.' *Journal of Applied Psychoanalytic 2* (1), 41–63.

Obholzer, A. and Roberts, V. Z. (eds) (1994) *The Unconscious at Work: Individual and Organizational Stress in the Human Services.* London: Routledge.

Parkes, C. M. (1975) 'What becomes of redundant world models? A contribution to the study of adaption to change.' *British Journal of Medical Psychology 48,* 131–137.

Pigott, C. (1990) *Introduction á la psychanalyse groupale.* Paris: Apsygée Editions.

Pines, M. (1998) 'The self as a group: the group as self.' In N. H. Harwood and M. Pines (eds) *Self Experiences in Group: Intersubjective and Self Psychological Pathways to Human Understanding.* pp.24–29. London: Jessica Kingsley Publishers.

Pinker, S. (1995) *The Language Instinct: How the Mind Creates Language.* New York: Harper Perennial.

Power, M. and Brewin, C. R. (eds) (1997) *The Transformation of Meaning in Psychological Therapies: Integrating Theory and Practice.* Chichester: John Wiley and Sons.

Priest, S. and Gass, M. (1997) *Effective Leadership in Adventure Programming.* Champaign, IL: Human Kinetics.

Raiola, E. D. (1992) 'Building Relationships: Communication Skills for Transformational Leadership.' Paper presented at the Celebrating our Tradition, Charting our Future: Proceedings of the 1992 Association for Experiential Education Twentieth International Conference, Banff, Canada.

Rhonke, K. (1988) *The Bottomless Bag.* Beverly, Massachusetts: Rhonke.

Ringer, F. (2000) 'Early attachment and eating disorders: a comparative study between anorexia nervosa and bulimia nervosa.' Unpublished PhD Study. Department of Psychology, Edith Cowan University, Perth.

Ringer, T. M. (1994) 'Leadership Competencies for Outdoor Adventure: From Recreation to Therapy.' Paper presented at Enabling troubled youth: Adventure-based interventions with young people in trouble and at risk. Basecamp: Ambleside, UK.

Ringer, T. M. (1995) 'Passion and aliveness in outdoor leadership: leadership competencies from recreation to therapy.' *Australian Journal of Outdoor Education 1,* 2, 3–15.

Ringer, T. M. (1996a) 'Critical analysis of obtaining desired outcomes from voluntary programmes.' *Science for Conservation 28.*

Ringer, T. M. (1996b) 'The self-reflective practicioner: examining the taken for granted in our work.' In *Insight: Newsletter of the Therapeutic Adventure Professional Group of the Association for Experiential Education 4.*

Ringer, T. M. (1998) 'Achieving the Celebration of Cultural Difference: The Impossible Task?' Paper presented at the Joint Congress of the European Institute for Adventure Education and Experiential Learning, Edinburgh.

Ringer, T. M. (1999) 'Groups in adventure therapy: contributions from psychodynamic approaches.' *Insight: Newsletter of the Therapeutic Adventure Professional Group of the Association for Experiential Education.* In print.

Ringer, T. M. (2000) 'The facile-itation of facilitation? Searching for competencies in group-work leadership.' *Scisco Conscientia 2*, 1, 1–19.

Ringer, T. M. and Gillis, H. L. (1995) 'Managing psychological depth in adventure/challenge groups.' *Journal of Experiential Education 18*, 1, 41–51.

Ringer, T. M. and Gillis, H. L. (1997) ' There is nothing so practical as a good theory: how theories of human change are applied in adventure therapy.' In T. Gray and B. Haylar (eds) *Catalysts for Change: 10th National Outdoor Education Conference.* pp.263–269. Collaroy Beach, New South Wales: The Outdoor Professionals.

Ringer, T. M. and O'Brien, M. (1997) *Building Relationships with Participants in Department of Conservation Programmes: Effective Management of Experiential Groups in the Outdoors.* Wellington: Department of Conservation.

Ringer, T. M. and Robinson, P. (1996) 'Focus and strategic action in management: using a systemic model of organisational culture to inform managerial actions.' *Work Study 45*, 6, 5–16.

Ringer, T. M. and Spanoghe, F. M. (1997) 'Can't he see me crying inside?: Managing psychological risk in adventure programming.' *Zip Lines, Summer* (32), pp.41–45.

Sandler, J., Dare, C. and Holder, A. (1973) *The Patient and the Analyst: The Basis of the Psychoanalytic Process.* London: Karnac.

Schacter, L. D. (1996) *Searching for Memory: The Brain, the Mind and the Past.* New York: Basic Books.

Schermer, V. L. and Pines, M. (eds) (1994) *Ring of Fire; Primitive Affects and Object Relations in Group Psychotherapy.* London: Routledge.

Schoel, J., Prouty, R. and Radcliffe, P. (1988) *Islands of Healing: A Guide to Adventure Based Counselling.* Hamilton, MA: Project Adventure.

Schon, D. A. (1995) *The Reflective Practitioner: How Professionals Think in Action.* Aldershot: Ashgate Publishing.

Segal, H. (1988) *Introduction to the Work of Melanie Klein.* London: Karnac Books.

Segal, J. (1985) *Phantasy in Everyday Life: A Psychoanalytical Approach to Understanding Ourselves.* Harmondsworth: Pelican.

Senge, P. M. (1992) *The Fifth Discipline: The Art and Practice of the Learning Organisation.* Sydney: Random House.

Smith, E. (ed) (1997) *Integrity and Change: Mental Health in the Market Place.* London: Routledge.

Smith, K. K. (1995) 'On using the self as instrument: lessons from a facilitator's experience.' In J. Gillette and M. McCollom (eds) *Groups in Context: A New Perspective on Group Dynamics.* pp.276–294. Lanham, Maryland: University Press of America.

Stapley, L. F. (1996) *The Personality of the Organisation: A Psychodynamic Explanation of Culture and Change.* London: Free Association Books.

Stokes, J. (1994) 'The unconscious at work in groups and teams: contributions from the work of Wilfred Bion.' In A. Obholzer and V. Z. Roberts (eds) *The Unconscious at Work: Individual and Organisational Stress in the Human Services.* pp.19–27. London: Routledge.

Trist, E. and Murray, H. (eds) (1990) *The Social Engagement of Social Science: Volume 1: The Socio-psychological Perspective.* London: Free Association Books.

Tyson, P. and Tyson, R. L. (1990) *Psychoanalytic Theories of Development: An Integration.* New Haven: Yale University Press.

Tyson, T. (1998) *Working with Groups.* Melbourne: Macmillan Education.

Valera, F. J., Thompson, E. and Rosch, E. (1992) *The Embodied Mind: Cognitive Science and Human Experience.* Cambridge, MA: The MIT Press.

Vincent, S. (1995) 'Emotional safety in adventure therapy programs: can it be defined?' *Journal of experiential education 18*, 76–81.

Waldo, M. and Bauman, S. (1998) 'Regrouping the categorization of group work: a goals and process (GAP) matrix for group work.' *Journal for Specialists in Group Work 23*, 2, 164–176.

Warren, K. (ed) (1996) *Women's Voices in Experiential Education.* Dubuque, Iowa: Kendall/Hunt.

Warren, K., Sakofs, M. and Hunt Jr., J. S. (eds) (1995) *The Theory of Experiential Education.* (Third edition) Dubuque, Iowa: Kendall/Hunt.

Watzlawick, P. (1978) *The Language of Change: Elements of Therapeutic Communication.* New York: Basic Books.

Watzlawick, P., Weakland, J. and Fisch, R. (1974) *Change: Principles of Problem Formation and Problem Resolution.* New York: Norton and Co.

Wells, L. J. (1995) 'The group as a whole: a systemic socioanalytic perspective on interpersonal and group relations.' In J. Gillette and M. McCollom (eds) *Groups in Context: A New Perspective on Group Dynamics.* pp.49–85. Lanham, Maryland: University Press of America.

Whitaker, D. S. (1989) *Using Groups to Help People.* London: Tavistock/Routledge.

Whitaker, D. S. (2001) *Using Groups to Help People.* London: Brunner-Routledge.

Whitaker, D. S. and Lieberman, M. A. (1964) *Psychotherapy through the Group Process.* Chicago: Aldine Publishing.

Williams, A. (1989) *The Passionate Technique: Strategic Psychodrama with Individuals, Families, and Groups.* London: Tavistock/Routledge.

Williams, A. (1991) *Forbidden Agendas: Strategic Action in Groups.* London: Tavistock/Routledge.

Yalom, I. D. (1985) *The Theory and Practice of Group Psychotherapy.* (Third edition) USA: Basic Books.

Zdenek, M. (1985) *The Right Brain Experience: An Intimate Programme to Free the Powers of your Imagination.* London: Corgi Books.

Author's web address

www.martinringer.com

Author Index

Subject Index

CPSIA information can be obtained at www.ICGtesting.com
Printed in the USA
BVOW01s2244300114

343457BV00004B/92/A